14-9

Status and Identity in West Africa

African Systems of Thought

General Editors
Charles S. Bird
Ivan Karp

Contributing Editors
James W. Fernandez
Luc de Heusch
John Middleton
Roy Willis

Status and Identity in West Africa

Nyamakalaw of Mande

EDITED BY DAVID C. CONRAD

AND BARBARA E. FRANK

INDIANA UNIVERSITY PRESS

Bloomington and Indianapolis

The paper used in this publication meets the minimum requirements of American
National Standard for Information Sciences—Permanence of Paper for Printed
Library Materials, ANSI Z39.48-1984.

Manufactured in the United States of America

Library of Congress Cataloging-in-Publication Data
Status and identity in West Africa : Nyamakalaw of Mande / edited by David C. Conrad and Barbara E. Frank.
    p.   cm.—(African systems of thought)
Includes index.
ISBN 0-253-31409-7 (cloth : acid-free paper)
ISBN 0-253-20929-3 (pbk. : acid-free paper)
1. Mandingo (African people)—Industries. 2. Mandingo (African people)—Kinship.
3. Mandingo (African people)—Social life and customs. 4. Artisans—Africa, West.
5. Social classes—Africa, West. 6. Social structure—Africa, West. 7. Endogamy and
exogamy—Africa, West. 8. Africa, West—Social life and custom.
I. Conrad, David C. II. Frank, Barbara E. III. Series.
        DT474.6.M36S73   1995
305.5'0966—dc20   94-20215

1 2 3 4 5 00 99 98 97 96 95

CONTENTS

Part Three: The Power of Agency and Identity

ACKNOWLEDGMENTS

The genesis of this volume was a double panel organized by the editors for the 1987 African Studies Association meeting in Chicago. The interest this panel generated convinced us that the effort to bring this material together in published form would be worthwhile. As the volume took shape, we relied heavily on family, friends, and colleagues. We appreciated the patience and cooperation of our contributors throughout the process, including those whose papers we were ultimately unable to include. In addition, we would especially like to thank Mary Jo Arnoldi, Kate Ezra, Kathryn Green, Barbara Hoffman, Adria LaViolette, and Thomas Martin for their advice and assistance at various stages along the way.

We would also like to acknowledge the support of the University of Tulsa during the early stages of the process, as well as the State Universities of New York at Oswego and Stony Brook, and various staff members at our respective institutions, especially Terry Berquist and Mary Bennett. We would not have been able to complete the project without the continuing encouragement, sharp criticism, and support of Ivan Karp as general editor of the series. We would also like to thank the staff at Indiana University Press for their efforts in seeing the volume through to publication.

Finally, we hope this volume will serve as a tribute to the Mande peoples, with whom we have had the honor to become acquainted as colleagues, researchers, guests, and friends. Their insight and generosity have enriched our work and our lives. With this volume we hope to share some of this richness with a wider audience.

A NOTE ON ORTHOGRAPHY
AND TERMINOLOGY

It is standard practice for authors to provide a note to readers concerning the particular orthography chosen for the text, and then to follow through with some level of consistency. However, to have attempted to standardize the variant spellings throughout this volume would have run counter to our stated goals to allow the texture of Mande culture to emerge in all its complexity and contradiction. Variant spellings are often due to differences among regional dialects of the Mande language. However, the decision to spell a word in a certain manner reflects not only variations in the way names and terms are actually pronounced in different locales, but also the way sounds are heard by those who record them and the language in which the transcriber is literate. The use of French and English orthographies reflects the political histories of the different modern states and their current status as Francophone and Anglophone nations. Therefore, the choice of orthography is not an arcane matter for only the most specialized of linguists, but can and does have broader implications.

In Mali, for example, the choice tends to fall between two alternatives. One can use the standardized Bamana orthography developed by DNAFLA (Direction Nationale de l'Alphabetisation Fonctionnelle et de la Linguistique Appliquée) of the Malian Ministry of Education in a government effort to encourage literacy in the Bamana language. Or one can retain French orthography as it appears in much of the literature on Mande culture and on most maps, including those prepared by the Institut Géographique National. Choosing the former might be taken as a conscious anticolonialist statement, but might also have the effect of privileging an official Bamana orthography over other Mande dialects (a problem with which DNAFLA has struggled for twenty years). Choosing French orthography might avoid some confusion for those familiar with the French literature, but might be uncomfortable for the majority of our English-language readers.

In the end, our decision has been to leave the variations as they exist in moving from one chapter to the next, rather than request conformity from our authors. We have tried to supply alternative spellings when appropriate without interfering with the flow of the text. We decided to use Malian orthography in composing the maps. As a general rule, the French *ou* becomes *u* as in Segou to Segu, or *w* as in Ouassoulou to Wasulu, and *di* or *dj* becomes *j,* as in Djenne to Jenne, or Diawambe to Jawambe. We have also left to the discretion of the individual authors whether or not to use the plural marker with frequently cited terms, such as *nyamakala* (sing.) or *nyamakalaw* (pl.), *jeli* (sing.) or *jeliw* (pl.), *garanké* (sing.) or *garankéw* (pl.), etc.

In addition, we have chosen to introduce the Mande term *nyamakalaya* to a

Western audience, rather than continuing to support the use of the term "caste" to define social categories within Mande society. The applicability of the concept of "caste" to the West African context generally has been a subject of much debate, a debate that has waned in recent years. While most Africanists now agree that the term carries with it too much baggage of meaning and association from distant continents, many (ourselves included) have continued to use it, surrounded with caveats, for want of a viable alternative. With this publication, we have come to realize that translation is neither possible nor desirable. As will become apparent in the pages that follow, the term *nyamakala* is already a heavily loaded one. We have only just begun to understand the concepts and contradictions it embodies. For this process to advance, the meaning must emerge from within the Mande context itself.

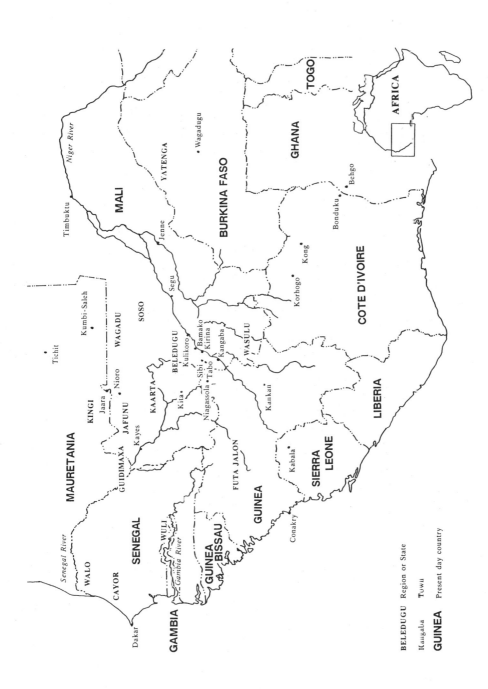

Map 1. West Africa showing regions, states and towns mentioned in the text.

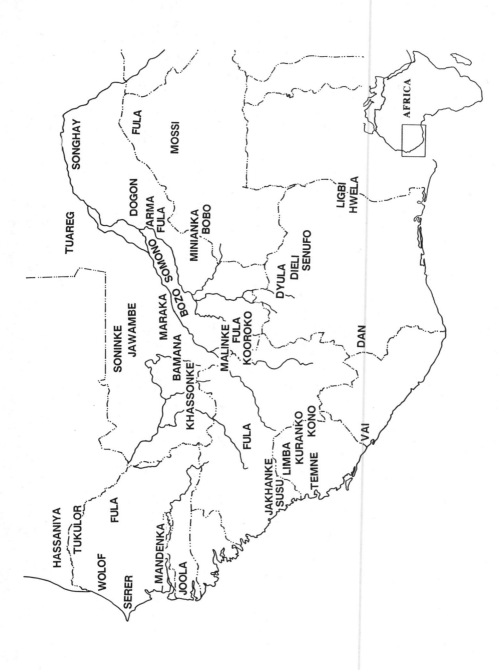

MAP 2. West Africa showing ethnic groups mentioned in the text.

Status and Identity in West Africa

INTRODUCTION

NYAMAKALAYA
CONTRADICTION AND AMBIGUITY
IN MANDE SOCIETY

David C. Conrad and Barbara E. Frank

The *nyamakalaw,* a major professional class of artists and other occupationally defined specialists among the Mande-speaking peoples of West Africa, have long been recognized for the essential roles they play in Mande society, yet they remain its most misunderstood social group.[1] Composed of primarily endogamous lineages, blacksmiths, potters, leatherworkers, and bards are accorded special but ambiguous social status apart from the *horonw,* the class of farmer "nobility." In their explorations of the identity and social history of the *nyamakalaw,* the essays in this volume reveal the often contradictory attitudes that continue to shape *nyamakala* roles in the social sphere.[2]

Historically, Mande blacksmiths (*numuw*) have been responsible for forging iron tools and weapons, and for sculpting both utilitarian and ritual objects of wood. They have also served as religious specialists and sorcerers, respected and feared for their knowledge of the occult. The wives of Mande blacksmiths continue to maintain a monopoly on the production of pottery throughout much of the region and are said to share some of the respect and caution accorded their husbands. Leatherworkers (*garankéw* and *jeliw*) have long provided the products of their craftsmanship for both Mande and non-Mande patrons, transforming raw animal skins into objects of warfare, regalia, and dress. As oral traditionists and genealogists, the bards (*jeliw* and *funéw*) are the guardians and shapers of perspectives on the past, respected for the power of their speech and their ability with music and words. It was the *nyamakalaw* who in the past were the principal spokespersons for Mande rulers and chiefs, serving as political advisors and spiritual guides to the noble classes. They continue to act as mediators in Mande society, called upon to negotiate marriages and settle family disputes.

While on the one hand acknowledged for the crucial role they play in forming and maintaining the social, political, and economic fabric of the Mande world, the *nyamakalaw* are, on the other hand, presented in the literature as decidedly lower-class citizens. Although individual *nyamakalaw* may be singled out for praise, as a group they are often described by *horon* informants with condescension, if not outright contempt. Disdained as beggars and parasites on the backs of the nobility, they are accused of appearing at weddings and other social functions only to solicit handouts. The *nyamakalaw* do not agree with these assessments of their respective social positions and responsibilities. For their part, the *nyamakalaw* stress the dependence of others on their skills, regarding whatever they receive not as gifts but as payment due for their expertise. Thus part of the ambiguity of their social status derives from these varying points of view, perspectives that to date have not been fairly represented in the literature.

This imbalance has a long history. From the time of the first European encounters with the *nyamakalaw,* their identity and social status have been subjects of great interest and confusion to outside observers. Indeed, a major subtext of this volume is a critique of the literature on Mande society, especially the colonial construction of the Mande "caste" system and the inability of this model to account for the ambiguity and contradictions of *nyamakala* status and identity. By first reviewing early Western perceptions which informed colonial attitudes, we endeavor to distinguish the misunderstandings of outsiders from the ambiguity of the social reality.

Through the Eyes of Outsiders

Some of the first Europeans who witnessed *nyamakala* activities described these artists as prosperous, respectable, and industrious members of the community. Venturing up the Gambia River in 1620, Richard Jobson distinguished three primary trades or occupations from the agricultural labor of the majority of the population. As he saw it, "the first and chiefest is the Ferraro or Smith, who holds a good repute."[3] He also described the art of leatherworkers, masons, and potters: "The next is he whom we call a *Sepatero;* one that doth make all their Gregories, wherein truely is a great deale of art shewen. . . . Another profession we finde, and those are they who temper the earth, and makes the walles of their houses, and likewise earthen pots they set to the fire."[4] Jobson also remarked on the important role of music in the lives of the peoples he encountered, though he did not identify the work of the musician as a trade or occupation. He called these musicians "Juddies, or as wee may terme them, Fidlers of the Countrey." The sound of "Juddy" is very close to some pronunciations of *jeli* ("bard" in the Mande language), and it is possible that his encounter was with bards of the Gambian Mandenka.[5] He described some of the different songs performed by these musicians, as well as the different instruments that accompany them, and noted that they were so well paid for their skills that their wives were more richly dressed than even those of the kings.[6]

Similarly, in the late eighteenth century the Scottish explorer Mungo Park noted the special status of smiths and leatherworkers as artists and supplied valuable information on the technology and manufactures of their trades.[7] Park also provided an unusually detailed description of the bardic profession:

> With the love of music is naturally connected a taste for poetry; and, fortunately for the poets of Africa, they are in great measure exempted from that neglect and indigence, which in more polished countries, commonly attend the votaries of the Muses. They consist of two classes; the most numerous are the *singing men,* called *Jilli kea,* mentioned in a former part of my narrative. One or more of these may be found in every town. They sing extempore songs, in honour of their chief men, or any other persons who are willing to give "solid pudding for empty praise." But a nobler part of their office is to recite the historical events of their country: hence, in war, they accompany the soldiers to the field; in order, by reciting the great actions of their ancestors, to awaken in them a spirit of glorious emulation. The other class, are devotees of the Mahomedan faith, who travel about the country, singing devout hymns and performing religious ceremonies, to conciliate the favour of the Almighty, either in averting calamity, or insuring success to any enterprise. Both descriptions of these itinerant bards are much employed and respected by the people, and very liberal contributions are made for them.[8]

Despite Park's assessment of part of their repertoires as "empty praise," he does call attention to the respect in which oral performers are held. More important, he provides some of the earliest evidence of the existence of different classes of bards and their distinctive repertoires. Few were as observant as Park.

In fact, unlike colonial officials who would later become preoccupied with categorizing and ranking the various occupational specialists, many of the early travelers did not distinguish between ethnic identities of those they observed, much less between types of bardic status in different locales or between variations in performance genres. Thus discussions that influenced later perceptions of the *nyamakalaw* were often based on encounters with bards of neighboring societies whose social patterns may have differed in subtle if not dramatic ways from those of Mande groups.

Early travelers journeying into the interior along the Senegal and Gambia rivers might have encountered not only Mande *jeliw,* but also bards of the Wolof called *gewel,* Fulbe oral specialists known by the Tukulor term *gawlo,* as well as the *iggiw* (sing. *iggio*) of Hassaniya communities on the northern bank of the Senegal.[9] Attempts to trace the etymology of the term "griot"—a term that has come to be used generically to refer to all of these oral artists but for the Mande bard par excellence—illustrate the complexity of linguistic and historic relationships among these peoples.[10] When seventeenth- and eighteenth-century travelers wrote about *guiriots,*[11] they were most likely rendering the French pronunciation of a local term; the question is which one. By the nineteenth century, most Europeans were using the spelling with which we are familiar today.[12] In 1882 Bérenger-Féraud argued that "griot" was a gallicized Wolof word, which he thought derived from the Cayor and Walo idiom. His alternative spellings of *gewel* as *guéroual* and *guéwoual* suggest sound patterns that might have contributed to a transition from *gewel* to "griot."[13] On the other hand, Vincent Monteil has argued that the term came from the French pronunciation of *iggio* as *guiriot*.[14] Recently, Eric Charry has drawn our attention to the similarities among all of these terms, which suggests that they may have derived from a common nonindigenous source, in part because the various languages within which they are now embedded are unrelated. He theorizes that an Arabic term (*qawal*) may have been attached to this uniquely West African phenomenon as early as the empire of Ghana, from which both term and institution dispersed following a variety of independent paths.[15] Whatever the origins of the term, or, more important, of the institution, ethnic and geographical distinctions tended to get lost in early discussions of the African social landscape.

Perhaps owing to the conspicuous nature of the bardic occupation, specialists in the oral arts generally elicited more comment than the other artists and were the ones most frequently identified as social outcasts. Little distinction was made between the bards observed as noisy street performers and those of higher social standing who not only could grow wealthy in service to the royal house, but could and did exercise a considerable degree of influence there. Despite subsequent exposure to these prominent, respected bards in Segu and elsewhere,[16] the initial impressions of griots as belonging to a sort of despised "caste" proved tenacious. As the lower-profile leatherworkers, potters, blacksmiths, and other crafts specialists went about the tasks so essential in the daily life of any Western Sudanic society, they did not go unnoticed by early observers, but in many instances the focus of attention was on their respective technologies rather than their social status.

As a result, these early sources provided a somewhat skewed perspective on which the colonial construction of *nyamakalaya* was based. The unbalanced attention to bards as opposed to other *nyamakalaw*, confusion about distinctions between different types of griots within what appears to have been a bardic hierarchy, and the fact that many of the earliest observed bards were not even Mande, all contributed to outsiders' misunderstandings regarding relationships among the different *nyamakala* groups and their place in Mande society.

The Fascination of Baobab Burial

Dramatically illustrative of the pervasive ambiguity of the bardic status, and by extension that of the *nyamakalaw* in general, is a peculiar custom of griot burial that was a source of great interest to Western observers from the late sixteenth century on. Whether the early travelers received their initial impressions of bardic status from Wolof *gewel* and Fulbe *gawlo* or from Mande *jeliw,* their universal interest in baobab burial has had an enduring impact on perceptions of bards and other *nyamakalaw* as a feared and despised people. As a sort of monster tree of the savannah appearing upside down with its roots in the air, the baobab must have seemed fitting to people who perceived of the "dark" African interior as populated with unicorns and other fantastic creatures. And the discovery that deposited in their hollow trunks were the corpses of certain "rimers"[17] and other performers whose counterparts on the European stage were generally classed with pimps, prostitutes, and other social dregs, must have gratified their most fanciful expectations of adventure. Thus, for a long time the custom of interring the bodies of deceased griots in the trunks of baobab trees became an irresistible subject for writers commenting on bardic life.

The Portuguese traveler Alvarez d'Almada (1594) may have been the first to report on the phenomenon of baobab interment in a region of what is today Senegal.[18] Jobson, following his more positive description of musicians cited above, declared that people living in the Gambia thought so little of their "Juddies" that "when any of them die, they doe not vouchsafe them buriall, as other people have; but set his dead corps upright in a hollow tree, where hee is left to consumme."[19] Other seventeenth- and eighteenth-century writers reported the curious burial custom in connection with the status of griots, including Barbot, who remarked that "these men are so much despjs'd by all the other Blacks, that they not only account them infamous, but will scarce allow them a grave when they die . . . they only thrust them into the hollow trunks or stumps of trees."[20] Long after outsiders acquired more awareness of the bardic profession, the fascination with baobab burial and its social implications continued. Mollien, Boilat, and others carried it into the nineteenth century.[21] In 1878–79, when Paul Soleillet witnessed bards of Segu collecting their fees from all and sundry, he felt compelled to remark, "Their life is blessed, but they are deprived of the honor of burial and their cadavers are placed in hollow trees."[22]

It was the apparent ambiguity of the living bards' socioeconomic status on the one hand, and their treatment in death on the other, that most stimulated the curiosity of early observers. An immediate concern of those reporting on the custom of baobab interment was to uncover the reason why the mortal remains of certain bards were not consigned to the kind of burial accorded other members of society.[23] Labat was one of those most struck by the contrast between respect shown to live, worthy practitioners of the bardic occupation and the seemingly different attitudes held toward their mortal remains. But when he asked why griots were esteemed when alive but not "properly" buried at death, he had to settle for the reply often made to inquisitive researchers of our own time, that "it was the custom."[24] Impatient with such "worthless" explanations, Raffenel believed that Jobson and others must have been near the truth when they suggested that this form of burial was performed because griots were despised in life as in death. Refusing to believe that people whose corpses were treated in such a manner could command genuine respect while alive, he argued that people must have been obliged to conceal their true feelings while the bards lived because of the importance of music and praise singing, but that after the griots' death the people's contempt was manifested in the refusal to allow proper burial.[25]

The idea that those not accorded normal burial must have been involved in occult practices introduces the element of fear into explanations of the custom. Appropriate to the thinking of their times, European observers of the seventeenth to nineteenth centuries interpreted any kind of involvement with the spirit world as a sure indication of having direct dealings with the devil. For his part, Jobson had no doubt that the "divell" had "great recourse" among people on the Gambia River, especially the "Rimers or Juddies."[26] Stressing the fear that he saw, Raffenel concluded that bardic dealings with the devil were more than a little responsible for baobab interment.[27]

It is not clear to what extent Jobson's "Juddies" and other Mande bards participated in occult matters. Blacksmiths are usually considered to be the dominant force in the practice of Mande sorcery, but perhaps griots once operated in a realm that did not infringe on that of the blacksmiths. Madrolle thought the bards he saw were sorcerers in touch with the spirit world, and whose capacities as diviners gave them the last word in all discussions.[28] The impression of some observers was that griots near the coast were much more involved in the occult than were their counterparts in the Mande heartland. Bérenger-Féraud noticed that while griots were found among peoples all along the Senegal River, as one descended the river (westward, toward the coast) they seemed to become increasingly involved with the spirit world.[29] Nevertheless, as we have seen from Soleillet's report from Segu, it was not just coastal bards whose corpses received special treatment.[30]

In view of recent revelations regarding the enormous power which the Mande attribute to the occult sciences,[31] the idea that some form of spiritual or physical pollution was strong enough to prohibit the possibility of burial in earth or water is not at all far-fetched. While blacksmiths have been identified with the use of poisons and other powerful medicines in occult practices, the assignment to bards of certain secular tasks involving poison (koroté) may help to account for the custom of baobab interment. More than a century ago, a French colonial doctor, Edouard Dupouy, studied the use of koroté in the Beledugu and Fuladugu areas of present-day Mali.[32] He reported that along with its effectiveness in truth-telling ordeals and eliminating enemies,[33] one of its most important secular uses was to poison the tips of arrows. What is of particular interest here is Dupouy's claim that the koroté he saw being used for this was handled exclusively by griots. Did the doctor glimpse an aspect of the griot occupation that has all but disappeared?[34] If so, this could help to account for the idea that of all the nyamakalaw, it was jeli corpses that would pollute the environment.[35] To this day, informants tend to associate the custom of baobab interment in the past with spiritual or physical pollution. They explain that if griots had been buried in the ground or thrown into the river or ocean, the crops would have failed or the fish would have died.[36]

As it comes to us through these European descriptions of recent centuries, the subject of baobab interment seems to touch upon an aspect of bardic life that died out sometime before the colonial era, perhaps at least partially owing to Islamic influence.[37] It is an element in their history the memory of which the bards themselves have understandably done nothing to preserve. Whatever the source of baobab interment may have been, and whatever it says about some of the historical elements of the griot population, its principal relevance for us here is that among other things it helped shape perceptions of *nyamakalaya* that have long endured. In thinking that baobab interment was associated with occult beliefs, outside observers may have been on the right track, but viewing the phenomenon through Western eyes, they were unable to fully comprehend its significance for those directly involved, and we share their fate.[38] Generations of puzzlement over the distinctive method of bidding adieu to the mortal remains of griots underline the ambiguity that generally characterizes *nyamakala* status. Now the giant, hollow baobabs that once served as receptacles for the bones of departed bards stand as enigmatic testimonials to the perceptual limitations of our understanding of Mande society.

Colonial Construction of Western Sudanic Social Hierarchy

While the early literature reflects the incomplete and inconsistent nature of multiple perspectives on the ambiguities of *nyamakala* status, as well as the complexities of the phenomenon itself, it was during the colonial period that the notion of a "Mande caste system" became codified. According to this view, Mande society could be divided into three distinct layers. At the top were the *horonw* (conveniently translated as "nobility" or "freedmen," as if to recall the feudal society of medieval Europe), including farmers, warriors, Muslim clerics, and traders. At the bottom were the slaves, and in the middle were various categories of artisans and bards. Hierarchical relationships among the different categories of individuals defined by this system were—in theory—absolute, with identity perceived to be fixed by birth. Social rank was not something that could be overturned or altered by individual agency. Those within this system were generally viewed as passive recipients of time-honored tradition, accepting of their lot.

Products of their own European background, colonial observers were committed to this sort of classification as a means of understanding the societies they were seeking to control. The cumulative effect of their efforts to classify the artisans and bards of the Western Sudan suggests wanderers in a hall of mirrors, determined to locate within a plethora of images social patterns derived from their own experience with which they could be comfortable. In some ways, it may have been easier for colonial writers to "place" blacksmiths, potters, and leatherworkers, because they had counterparts in the Western world. As already noted, mention of these artists tended to be accompanied by descriptive information on their technology and products, rather than discussions of their social status.

Colonial efforts to understand the identity of and relationships between different kinds of bards indicate the value that Europeans attached to the construction of hierarchies overall. In addition to the *jeliw* and *funéw* that are discussed elsewhere in this volume, several other kinds of oral performers were observed and variously placed within Mande as well as Fulbe, Tukulor, and other ethnic hierarchies.[39] The bards known as *mabow, gaulow,* and *tyapurtaw* were generally rated as inferior to *jeliw* and *funéw,* but confusion about their ethnic origins and occupational specializations reveals the difficulty of situating them vis-à-vis other *nyamakala* groups.

One of the most rigorous designers of hierarchical social models, Jean Cremer, scrutinized a branch of what he thought of as Fulbe society in which he found the *gaulow* to be much despised and feared, hence of the lowest status.[40] Ranking just above them in Cremer's scheme were the *tyapurtaw,* who were "somewhat less" despised and allowed to marry into blacksmith families. Next up the scale were a group called *galabé,* identified by Wane as griots who sometimes worked in leather,[41] but by Cremer simply as Futanké, which is to say people from the Futa Jalon mountain area. Above these in rank were the *jawambe* (sing. *jawando*), described as endogamous Fulbe griots. Finally, there were the *mabow,* seen as performing in a manner equivalent to Bamana *jeliw.*[42]

Meanwhile, Louis Tauxier saw a far simpler system among the Fulbe bards he studied, listing none of Cremer's griots in his version of the hierarchy. Instead, he found the Fulbe musicians, storytellers, and praise singers to be either *bambabe* or *niémmbé.*[43] Clearly, efforts to categorize oral performers failed to appreciate the fluid nature of all social labels including ethnicity. As Jean-Loup Amselle has recently observed, ethnic terms such as "Peul," "Bambara," and "Malinke" were themselves ambiguous. He argues, for example, that the Fulbe (or Peul) cannot justifiably be defined as an individual ethnic group, that *fulanité* is a product of many neighboring societies, of the ebb and flow, meeting and conflict between groups, and that one *became* a Peul, Tukulor, Bamana, etc. according to various circumstances.[44]

Thus there could hardly have been much agreement among observers trying to categorize relatively obscure groups such as the *tyapurtaw.* If, as in Amselle's view, ethnicity was a product of social circumstances, the same could be said of occupational identities. In the late nineteenth century, people referred to as *tiapatos* were remembered as having been a warrior class affiliated with both the Soninke and the Fulbe.[45] Already mentioned was Cremer's ranking of *tyapurtaw* above the *gaulow,*[46] but Zahan listed them as both the lowest class of Bamana griot, and bards of the Fulbe.[47] Labouret said they were the most despised of artisan groups, but did not indicate their occupation.[48] At the bottom of a list of Malinké griots, Humblot included a group he called *kiapourkia,* which is probably a distortion of the term *tyapurta.*[49]

Tying social categories into particularly intricate knots were the terms *mabow* or *mabubé,* on the one hand, and *jawambe* or *diawando,* on the other. The *mabow* and *jawambe* were thought to have been historically associated, but details of the relationship were as elusive as the occupations and ethnicity of the people concerned. For example, in various sources, forms of the terms *jawambe* and *diawando* appear in both upper and lower case, describing ethnicity, clan affili-ation, and occupation.

Puzzled by the *diavandous,* Raffenel concluded that they were a caste of Fulbe origin greatly resembling griots, though held in less esteem.[50] Arcin found certain "Diawando" among Soninke and Fulbe groups, describing them along with the "Finanke Bamana" and the "Selmbou Yoloff" as weavers who hardly ever did any weaving. He said the Fulbe regarded the "Diawando" as contemptible.[51] Delafosse defined "Diawambe" as both courtiers and weavers, Cremer identified the *ayawambe* as endogamous Fulbe griots, and Gaden saw the *dawambe* as "nobles" of inferior rank.[52] Tauxier said that the *diawambe* were traders, cattle raisers, and teachers, among other things, and Moreau described the "Diawandos" as *hommes d'affaires* and intermediaries.[53] According to Pageard, it was traditionally prohibited for members of the Diawambe lineage to engage in artisan or griot activity, and Urvoy described the "Diawanbes" as a branch of a Tukulor lineage who speak Fulfulde and are fanatical Muslims.[54] Bertin evidently despaired of placing the *diawambe* accurately within the Fulbe social scale, having found that while they were restricted from intermarriage with the higher proprietary ranks, neither were they allowed to intermarry with members of the artisan classes.[55]

The variety of *jawambe* identities rivals those for the *mabow,* and indeed, the two groups may have been historically connected. Two writers, Heinrich Barth and Ibrahim Bathily, collected information nearly a century apart that taken together imbues the *jawambe* and *mabow* with recognizable historical dimensions. Based on observations made between 1849 and 1855, Barth concluded that the "Jawambe" had once been a distinct ethnic group who called themselves "Zoghorân." He said they were absorbed by the Fulbe and "reduced to the occupation of mere brokers," but that in the sixteenth century they were still ethnically distinct from the Fulbe.[56] Barth's identification of the Diawambe as "Zoghorân" is supported by Siré-Abbâs-Soh, who notes that in the East the "Diawambe" are called "Dyogoran," and that this corresponds to "Dyagarani" or "Zaghrani" in the *Tarikh es-Soudan.*[57] Consistent with Barth's claim that as late as the sixteenth century the Diawambe and Fulbe were ethnically distinct, the *Tarikh* says that in 1492–93 Sonni Ali made an expedition to Gourma against two different forces, the "Z.ghrani" and the Fulbe.[58]

One route to understanding the source of the colonial view of a *jawambe-mabow* relationship lies through the work of Ibrahim Bathily. He maintained that there were once three principal "Diawando" groups: the Diawandos, the Lahtimbés (Diawando slaves), and the Kida Mabos, from whom were descended bards known as "Mabos." Bathily identified the *mabow* as members of the Kida family who were of "Diawando stock" stemming from two particular lines of descent.[59] This meshes with the findings of Pageard, who found that an important bardic family connected from early times with the "Jawambe" was the lineage of Mabo Aliou Kida.[60] Indeed, some *mabow* have claimed that their origins coincide with those of the Jawambe.[61] Later, when the Jawambe were assimilated into the amorphous populations called Fulbe, some families appear to have maintained a degree of individuality, hence the references to "Jawambe" as traders, teachers, and lesser "nobles." Others took on artisan and bardic tasks and were referred to by colonial observers in the lowercase *jawambe,* as they competed with the *mabow* in various occupations.

It was noted above that the *mabow* were among the most difficult to categorize. Their origins are no less obscure than those of other occupational specialists, but we do know that by the sixteenth century they had group recognition among local chroniclers. In 1550 the Songhay ruler Askya Dawud (1549–1582) led a military expedition into the land of Bagh.na.[62] He collected there many men and women singers called "Mabi," settling them at Kagha in their own special quarter of the town.[63] As in the case of the *funéw* described elsewhere in this volume, observers were to find that these people could be identified with a variety of occupations.

Desplagnes was convinced that weaving was the primary *mabo* craft. He believed that they were originally a mountain tribe, part of which settled as subservient weavers among sedentary Fulbe, while others remained independent.[64] Gaden pointed out that *mabade* means "to sing," and concluded that in early times the primary duty of the *mabubé* (Bamana *mabow*) was to encourage warriors by altering their genealogies and praising their ancestors.[65] Despite the importance of this service, Gaden reported that the chiefly lineages of warriors and herdsmen among the Fulbe viewed all *mabow*, regardless of their ancestry or occupation, as lesser worthies, an attitude reflected in the aphorism "Stupidity kills as many *mabow* as a natural death."[66]

Some observers acknowledged that *mabow* appeared in a variety of occupational and ethnic contexts, while others searched for more limited definitions. Pageard and others found *mabubé* performing as both bards and weavers among people described as Fulbe, Tukulor, and Diawambe.[67] Tauxier saw the *mabow* as weavers only, Cremer saw them as bards, while in one book Delafosse described the *mabow* as griots and weavers, and in another as singers and musicians only.[68] Zahan's more recent findings suggest that similar to what Conrad has found for the *funéw*, while the *mabow* normally identified with specific crafts, they might have seized whatever opportunity there was to support themselves at various times and places. Zahan described the Bamana *mabow* as bards, the Fulbe variety as tanners and weavers, and those living among Tuareg as blacksmiths and bards.[69]

As we have seen, these peoples' occupations varied from one region to another, influencing local perceptions of their social status, and even what Europeans perceived as "ethnicity." Despite the complexity of this social landscape, outside observers were able to overlook contradictions such as those described above and in the chapters that follow. As a result, the notion of a Mande caste system was firmly established.

Challenging the Colonial Model

The colonial literature tended to present Mande social structure as a codified system within which the *nyamakalaw* functioned in ascribed low status roles. Until recently, the accepted profile of Mande society coincided with a preoccupation of social scientists to define social structure in absolute terms, as an established matrix of relationships into which individuals are born. This view presupposes passive acceptance of social patterns and denies that individuals have the capacity to negotiate personal identity in the construction of their social world. In this scheme of things, *nyamakalaya* is viewed as a given inheritance, a preconceived legacy determining the shape and course of people's lives.

However, recent research has revealed the extent to which the *nyamakalaw* have continually redefined their identity in response to changing social, economic, and political circumstances. Through the study of history, language, oral tradition, social roles, and identity, the contributors to this volume explore the dynamic nature of the special status of the *nyamakalaw,* the history of this phenomenon in various Mande contexts, and the role of individuals in its development in time and space. The intent here is to challenge long-held misconceptions about this distinctive social form, to begin to reconstruct its social history, and to recognize its generative capacity.

While the authors of these essays approach this subject from different academic fields and employ quite varied data, common themes emerge that transcend the particular emphases of the disciplines. Most salient is a sense of dissatisfaction with colonial models of Mande social structure. Recognizing the limitations of categories and labels as they have been defined in the past, these authors take issue with the notion of a rigid hierarchy as the dominant social framework through which the *nyamakalaw* are to be viewed. The *nyamakalaw* emerge in these pages as powerful individuals who have played an active part in the construction of their identity, capitalizing on the value of social difference. Rather than being presented in the role of subservient outcasts, the *nyamakalaw* appear as agents who stress the interdependence of their relationships with others.

In raising concerns about the viability of social labels such as "caste" to adequately reflect the complexity of the social reality, we are by extension calling into question the concept of ethnicity itself. The tendency common during the colonial period was to perceive of ethnic groups in circumscribed fashion, as discrete units. The ethnic group was typically defined as peoples who share a sense of cultural and social heritage, as reflected in shared values, common language, occupation, social structure, and ideology. Implicit in such a definition is the notion that the component parts, such as social structure and ideology, are recognizable and distinctive social features, enabling one ethnic group to be clearly differentiated from another. Recently, scholars have become increasingly uncomfortable with the rigidity of this definition, suggesting instead that while ethnic categories remain a viable means of recognizing difference, the boundaries between them are by no means absolute and immutable.[70]

Others have raised questions about motives behind ethnic categorization. For Jean Bazin, a critical review of the European literature on "the Bamana" provided an opportunity to reveal contradictions in the available stereotypes promulgated by colonial authorities.[71] Similarly, Jean-Loup Amselle has argued that African ethnic labels were tailored to suit the territorial desires of the colonizers. He suggests that it is no accident that the concept of ethnic groups as distinct social categories took shape during the colonial period.[72] Amselle proposes to replace the colonial ethnic map with a series of linked "spaces" corresponding to different kinds of social relations between peoples. The ethnic paradigm thus reconfigured becomes a matter less of restrictive labeling, and more of choosing between various semantic classifications dependent on the particular contexts and identities involved.

Recognizing multiple and often contradictory perspectives is critical to a reexamination of the issue of hierarchy and relationships between structure, power, and agency in Mande society. We suggest that *nyamakalaya* cannot be defined in terms of a fixed hierarchy of predetermined relationships. This is not to say that the emphasis on social hierarchy in the literature is altogether misplaced. The highly stratified nature of Mande society is not a figment of outsiders' imaginations. Notions of inequality and power pervade Mande exegesis of social position among *nyamakala* groups and vis-à-vis the *horonw*. Individuals are acutely aware of the social frameworks that structure their relationships with others, but how they define the nature of attendant rights and responsibilities depends on a whole range of factors. The question is not whether social hierarchy exists, but from what perspective the relationships are to be viewed.

With this in mind we can move on to understanding how individuals play on the politics of power and difference that inform virtually all social interactions. In Bonnie Wright's penetrating study of status, identity, and power in Wolof society, she argues that

> the West African caste system, rather than being composed of hierarchically ranked groups, is really best understood as a set of groups differentiated by innate capacity or power sources. The inequalities of the system are less matters of rank than of culturally defined realms of power, and the conjunction of all these realms constitutes the social universe.[73]

In trying to understand the nature of griots' power, Wright asks how it is that a group so far down the social ladder can successfully demand payment from their supposedly higher-ranking superiors. Her answer is a conceptual framework that resonates with our understanding of Mande society: that Wolof society grants griots the power of speech, while nobles retain the power of action, setting up a dichotomy that is both mutually exclusive and interdependent. As articulators of identity in the public domain, griots are essential for the success of their patrons, tying together pieces of their past and—by implication—their future potential. Blacksmiths, potters, and leatherworkers, like griots, have both the capacity and the right to transform the raw materials of their particular domains. Whether or not they choose to develop that capacity and exercise their right does not change the fact of their inheritance, nor does it provide easy access to others who may wish to enter that domain.

Clearly, such a complex system of patronage and role playing could not have emerged without agents among both the *nyamakalaw* and the *horonw,* performing according to their own and each other's expectations of their behavior. When the concept of agency is applied to the *nyamakalaw,* two different senses of the word come into play, "agency for" and "agency of."[74] The first usage captures the perspective with which the *horonw* would be most comfortable: the notion that the *nyamakalaw* serve as agents acting on behalf of the *horonw.* Thus when a *nycmakala* is sent as an emissary in the process of marriage negotiations, *horonw* expect that the *nyamakala*'s primary responsibility is to communicate the wishes and protect the interests of the patron family. *Nyamakala* informants, in contrast, tend to emphasize the creative aspects of what they do, which is more in line with the definition of agency in the sense of causing something to happen. As mediators they call on a variety of verbal and diplomatic skills, knowing how and when to exert social pressure to secure a successful outcome. They expect to be remunerated appropriately. It is often differences in opinion as to the value of their skills and services that feed into conflicting attitudes toward *nyamakala* social position.

Similarly contrasting perspectives can be found in appraisals of the relative value of farming (*horon* activity par excellence) and the various trades practiced more or less exclusively by the *nyamakalaw,* where we might expect the exchange of goods and services to be more straightforward. While both *horonw* and *nyamakalaw* recognize the traditionally symbiotic nature of their interdependence, they each tend to see their own participation as the more essential aspect of the equation. In a discussion of the relationship between *horonw* and *numuw,* a blacksmith elder argued that the farmer had to have tools forged by the blacksmith before he could plant for, let alone reap, a successful harvest. A senior potter echoed his sentiment by saying: "If a *numu* dies of hunger, a Malinke will die of that same hunger."[75] However, the same aphorism could be effectively reversed by a *horon* to draw attention to the dependence of all *nyamakalaw* on the grain *horonw* labors supply.

In practice, the interdependence of the *nyamakala-horon* relationship has undergone tremendous change in recent decades. With the increasing availability of imported goods, *horonw* have not had to rely entirely on local craftspersons for tools and other items. Blacksmiths, potters, and leatherworkers have had to look elsewhere to find clients for their products, and many now have fields which they cultivate alongside those of their *horon* neighbors. Nevertheless, whatever the economic reality may be, perceived inequalities in their mutual economic dependence continue to extend into the social realm. Only when we accept such contradictions and ambiguities implicit in *nyamakalaw* perceptions of themselves and in how they are perceived by others, can we begin to understand the nature of their special status and attempt to construct a more dynamic model of their social history.

The chapters in this volume are organized into a series of interrelated themes, with the caveat that any one essay might easily be slipped into another group. We begin with a section entitled "The Paradox of Word and Meaning," in which the authors address the problem of defining concepts with multiple and contradictory meanings. The very term *nyamakala* is one of the most ambiguous terms imaginable, and quite appropriately so, as Charles S. Bird, Martha B. Kendall, and Kalilou Tera suggest in their discussion of different etymologies. For example, one etymology associates the *nyamakalaw* with garbage or refuse, implying pollution of both a physical and spiritual nature. On the other hand, *nyamakala* is also said to refer to these specialists' exceptional ability to protect themselves from the consequences of dealing with the powerful materials and ideas essential to their respective trades. These are just two of various semantic possibilities available for interpreting the meaning of the term *nyamakala*. More important, Bird, Kendall, and Tera remind us that the manner in which people classify themselves and others is no mere academic exercise, but a process with significant social consequences. They argue that different individuals choose to define their identity and that of others in particular ways for particular reasons. It is therefore the choice between the various etymologies that is more significant than any one translation. Thus, searching for the "true" meaning of the term through etymology (or any other means) is futile unless located within a particular context, where actor and audience are clearly recognized.

Actions, like words, can also be variously defined, in that the same act can be interpreted differently depending on the identities of those present. In her essay, Barbara G. Hoffman points to a fundamental imbalance in our views of griots' words and actions because they have been filtered through the eyes of either *horonw* or Europeans, leading to misunderstanding of griots' relationships to their patrons as well as the source and nature of their power over nobles. She points out that *horon* criticisms of griot behavior are most often of those services specifically requested—talking, singing, and dancing. In Hoffman's view, ambivalent notions about griots are primarily due to the ambiguity of their speech. She argues that because nobles cannot decipher the meaning of griot speech, they associate it with the realm of the unknown, with occult powers to which they have no access and from which they have no protection except through the agency of the griots themselves. Hoffman suggests that underlying the resentment voiced by nobles toward griots is admiration and envy for their powers that must be recognized before we can begin to understand their place in Mande society.

Patrick R. McNaughton's essay draws attention to the seemingly dichotomous roles of blacksmiths in Mande oral lore as both sorcerers and cultural heroes. In these legends, smiths are attributed with the invention of ironworking techniques as well as a host of other momentous and creative acts in the origins and civilization of the world. On the other hand, they are also identified with potentially dangerous powers of sorcery in the person of characters such as the blacksmith–sorcerer king Sumanguru Kanté, some of whose acts may appear to us as heinous crimes against humanity. McNaughton argues that Mande people would not necessarily share our assessment. He argues that it is the failure of our conceptual categories to accommodate ambiguity in such concepts as good and evil, sorcery and power, that leads us to oversimplify the ambiguity of Mande attitudes toward smiths.

The emphasis of the second group of essays, "Retracing Steps in Search of Social History," is on exploring the past for clues concerning the identity and origins of the various *nyamakala* groups. Tal Tamari's analysis of linguistic terms in different languages suggests a diversity of sources and change in the development of *nyamakala* identities over time and space. Her discussion implies that distribution patterns of these terms reflect extensive movement and interaction of both specialists and their clients, a picture far more pluralistic than the literature has allowed.

According to David C. Conrad, heritage appears to have been especially important for *funéw* in the creation of their identity. To support this claim, he draws our attention to characteristics of the Fosana legend as told by *funé* informants throughout the Mande world. The *funéw* seem to have consciously borrowed elements from Islamic tradition while at the same time maintaining a presence within the Sunjata tradition, a kind of manipulation of oral tradition to secure their place in Mande ideological heritage. On the other hand, the diversity of regional roles played by *funéw* reveals an equally pragmatic ability to turn their hands and oral skills to anything. Conrad further argues that contradictory notions are inherent in the qualities and attributes viewed as essential to *funé* identity. Not only are they identified with the submissive qualities of humility and professed poverty, they are also perceived as spiritually powerful because of the Prophet's blessing. It is the combined effects of these paradoxical attributes which have made it so difficult to pigeonhole them and which the *funéw* have been able to play to their advantage.

Heritage and distinctive identity seem to be equally important for Mande leatherworkers, whether near or far from their ancestral homes. Barbara E. Frank found that Mande leatherworkers projected an entrepreneurial image, extending their network among other Mande and non-Mande peoples, developing new markets for their expertise by providing their services to a wide range of patrons. Through restrictive marriage patterns and by invoking distinctive origins, they maintain the separateness of their identity from client populations. Thus a Soninke *garanké* in a Malinke town in Mali and a Mandingo *garanké* in Sierra Leone may have more in common with each other than either has with his host community. They seem to share a sense of past that reaches beyond occupational specialization and ethnicity. If we accept that some aspects of identity are negotiable depending on the context, it is significant that leatherworkers have chosen to preserve their *nyamakala* identity so consistently over time and space.

The third group of essays focus on "The Power of Agency and Identity," the manner in which individuals have responded to particular circumstances in such a way as to change the dynamics of their social environment. Robert Launay's study of the Dieli of Korhogo, for example, suggests that caste might more effectively be viewed as process than as category—the process of creating and maintaining monopolies over certain technologies as well as that of creating and maintaining a distinctive identity. He argues that the anomalous identity of the Dieli is the result of deliberate social action by none other than the Dieli themselves. In this respect, the Mande caste system becomes a flexible, ever-changing structure that enables rather than prevents individual agency. According to Launay, more important than determining where the Dieli came from is how they have invented and reinvented themselves according to particular local needs.

Similarly, Adria LaViolette's work among the women potters of Jenne suggests that the alliance of the *nyamakalaw* there with the Somono rather than the

Bamana may represent a conscious choice for the best social and economic opportunities. Most important, she draws our attention to the role of women in the process of creating and manipulating the social order to their advantage, challenging our views of women as passive participants in a world controlled by men. LaViolette argues that the creating and contesting of *nyamakala* (or *nyenyoBe*) identity must be seen as available to women as well as men in the construction of their identity.

While most of the present volume encourages a rethinking of our notions of collective *nyamakala* identity, implicitly attributing its negotiable character to the actions of individuals, our final contribution concludes with an assessment of the roles of particular individuals. In his essay, Cheick Mahamadou Chérif Keita pays tribute to two contemporary bards, who he suggests have contributed positively toward the building of a modern nation-state, establishing its image and forging a new identity that acknowledges and even competes with its glorious heritage.

Directions for Future Research

It is hoped that this volume will do more than simply add another layer to our understanding of Mande society. For us, the process of bringing these essays together has raised as many questions as it has answered, thereby drawing attention to potential avenues for future inquiry and reflection. One such issue deserving of further attention is the relationship between *nyamakala* identity and initiation societies. Another area of study should address the question of why occupations such as weaving, dyeing, and masonry were not associated with *nyamakala* status. In addition, variations of *nyamakalaya* in different geographical and cultural settings have not received the attention they deserve.

While the issue of personhood is implicit in our discussions of how *nyamakalaw* have collectively negotiated their status and identity, we would like to hear more from the perspective of particular individuals. Chérif Keita's aristocratic view of contemporary griots offered here is just one example of the kind of personal assessment meriting further encouragement, involving participation from all elements of the social milieu.

Perhaps most conspicuous by its absence in the literature is the issue of gender as it relates to notions of status and identity within *nyamakalaya* (Adria LaViolette's contribution to this volume being a notable exception). The wives of blacksmiths have received some attention because of their occupational specialization as potters, but any mention of their social position has generally been framed by that of their husbands.[76] There are no more than scattered references to other female *nyamakalaw*. For example, the specialization of the wives of *garankéw* in the tattooing of lips and gums is mentioned only in passing, and there is little about the special repertoire of women griots.[77] Also virtually unexplored are the attitudes of women toward their own *nyamakala* identities as female *numuw, jeliw, garankéw,* or *funéw.* Relatively little is known about their roles in the social lives of others, specifically their functions during rites of passage such as births, baptisms, initiations, marriages, and funerals.

The overall tone of this volume is positive, emphasizing how *nyamakalaw* as individuals turned their peculiar social status to their own advantage. A primary goal has been to present the point of view of *nyamakalaw* themselves, since their voices have tended not to be represented in the literature. At this stage, it seems important to provide a counterbalance to literally centuries of "bad press" on the *nyamakalaw.* Nevertheless, it must be kept in mind that the *nyamakalaw* represented here are those for whom *nyamakala* status is a mark of distinction in the most positive sense of the phrase. They proudly speak of their birthright as *nyamakalaw.* However, it is possible that not all *nyamakalaw* would share this assessment of their social standing. Moreover, it is difficult to predict the path that the next generation of *nyamakalaw* will take in the construction of their own identity and what a new generation of African scholars will contribute to the debate.

Notes

We would like to thank Ivan Karp, Richard Handler, Adria LaViolette, and Robert Launay for their helpful comments on this introduction.

1. In its strictest sense, "Mande" is a linguistic term that includes the interrelated Bamana, Malinke, Dyula, and Soninke language groups. These fall within Greenberg's "Western" Mande classification and are generally thought of as the "core" Mande peoples geographically and culturally. More southerly Mande groups include the Konyaka, Loma, Kpelle, and Koranko. We use the term "Mande world" in reference to a geographical and cultural sphere dominated by peoples for whom one of the Mande languages is their mother tongue, but which may be said to include as well those with whom they interact, the Wolof and Fula (Fulani, Fulbe, Peul) of the West Atlantic language groups, and the Senufo, Minianka, and Dogon of the Gur peoples, among others (Greenberg [1966:8]).

2. Several of the chapters in this volume are based on papers presented on two panels dedicated to the study of *nyamakalaya* that were organized by the editors for the 1988 African Studies Association meeting in Chicago. The chapter by Bird, Kendall, and Tera is one of those, as are the offerings by Tamari, Hoffman, Launay, and Keita. An earlier version of Frank's chapter was presented at the 1987 ASA meeting in Denver. The contribution by LaViolette is based on a paper presented at the 1989 ASA meeting in Atlanta. The chapter by Conrad was written specifically for this book, and subsequently an excerpt from it was presented at the 1991 meeting of the Canadian Association of African Studies in Toronto. McNaughton's contribution appeared previously in *Anthropological Linguistics,* and an earlier version of Keita's paper appeared in *Ufahamu.*

3. Jobson (1623:152). "Ferraro": Portuguese *ferreiro* = ironsmith.

4. Ibid., 154–55. "Sepatero": Portuguese *sapateiro* = shoemaker. Jobson's "Gregories" were the leather amulets commonly known as *gris-gris,* one of the more significant items produced by *garanké* and *jeli* leatherworkers. It is interesting that Jobson does not specify the gender of the masons and potters he apparently observed. Throughout the region

today, masonry is generally restricted to men, while pottery remains a monopoly of women.

5. Pointing out that Jobson used Portuguese terms, David Gamble suggests that his word "Juddies" "is not derived from the Mandinka *jeli,* but from the Portuguese *Judeus* (Jews), which was applied to 'griots' because they were outcasts" (private correspondence, April 1993).

6. Jobson (1623:133–37).

7. Park (1799:282–85).

8. Ibid., 278–79. Park's *Jilli kea* is apparently an alternative spelling of *jeli-kew* (*ké* = man), and the "other class" of performers whom he identified as Muslims were most likely *funéw* (see Conrad's contribution to this volume). His separate discussion of these oral performers suggests that he did not identify them as belonging to a clearly defined social group along with blacksmiths and leatherworkers.

9. H. T. Norris (1968:53). According to Paul Hair (1967:247–68), fifteenth-century sources reported that "the first blacks are found at the Senegal River." He also notes that Fulfulde speakers had been encountered on the Gambia River by the sixteenth century.

10. See Tamari's contribution to this volume.

11. Saint-Lô (1637:87); La Courbe (1685) in Cultru (1913:43); Labat (1728, II:242); Barbot (1746:55); Durand (1802:221).

12. Mollien (1820:77). To our knowledge, the earliest usage of "griot" located so far appears in Lamiral (1789:269). We thank both Eric Charry and David Gamble for this information. That not all travelers heard things quite the same way is evident from Caillié's spelling of the term as *guéhué* (1830, I:63).

13. Bérenger-Féraud (1882:266). Replacing French with English orthography, *guéwoual* becomes *gewal,* while the alternative *guéroual* is closer to the *guiriot* favored by earlier writers.

14. Monteil (1968:778).

15. Charry (1992:Chapter III, esp. 62–69).

16. Mage (1868:307–308); Rançon (1894:78).

17. Jobson (1623:133).

18. Cited in Mauny (1955:74).

19. Jobson (1623:137).

20. Barbot (1746:55); see also Saint-Lô (1637:87); Dapper (1686:235); and Labat (1728, II:330–31). Joseph du Sorbiers de la Tourrasse (1897:94) gruesomely describes a hyena's disposal of a griot corpse that it pulled from a hollow tree.

21. Mollien (1820:80); Boilat (1853:315); Marche (1879:17); Bérenger-Féraud (1882:268); Soleillet (1887:11). Numerous twentieth-century writers have also discussed the subject. See especially Mauny (1955:72–75) and Silla (1966:731–70); also Valtaud (1922:251); Aujas (1931:293–333); and Herpin (1955:41–47).

22. "Leur vie est heureuse, mais ils sont prives des honneurs de la sepulture et leurs cadavres sont places dans les arbres creux" (Soleillet [1887:407]).

23. Al-'Umari's description of burial practices in fourteenth-century Mali implies that at one time, bards were not the only ones who were deemed unworthy of proper burial: "It is their custom not to bury their dead unless they be people of rank and status. Otherwise those without rank and the poor and strangers are thrown into the bush like other dead creatures" (1337–38:266).

24. Labat (1728, II:331). What he saw as embarrassment on the part of his informants when he questioned them on this subject might just as well have been manifestations of displeasure at a foreigner inquiring into secret matters.

25. Raffenel (1846:19). Raffenel's opinion was probably influenced by an awareness that *gewel* of the Senegambia were treated with circumspection because of the perception that they had the power to mock with impunity, with their insults turning to open abuse if a sufficient reward was not forthcoming. See Gamble (1957:45) and also Wright (1989) for

an insightful analysis of the nature of the griots' power over their patrons based on research among the Wolof.

26. Jobson (1623:150).

27. Raffenel (1846:18–19).

28. Madrolle (1895:95).

29. Berenger-Féraud (1897:375). Contrary to Madrolle's opinion, he said that they were responsible for recognizing and chastising sorcerers, rather than being sorcerers themselves. For this writer any bard, regardless of cultural affiliation, social status, or geographical location, was a "griot."

30. Scleillet (1887:407). Turning away from the European point of view, the question arises as to whether the placement of corpses in hollow trees implies *lower* or just *different* status for the deceased. Our concern here is mainly with the effect of baobab burial on European attitudes toward *nyamakalaw* because of the way it affected later perceptions. The custom needs to be thoroughly examined from the indigenous perspective, taking into account not only funerary practices throughout the Sudanic region, but also symbolism associated with the baobab tree. We are especially grateful to Peter Weil for his comments in a panel discussion at the annual meeting of the African Studies Association in Seattle, 1992. Baobab burial was apparently not always limited to bards. According to Father Knops (1959:91–92), contempt toward certain Senufo artisans, especially woodworkers associated with occult practices, was manifested after their death when their bodies were smoked for twenty days to dry them out, and then interred in the trunks of hollow trees.

31. McNaughton (1988:40–72).

32. Edouard Dupouy (1885:153–54).

33. Both of these uses concur with Sarah Brett-Smith's recent findings in the same region (1983:47–51). She found that various kinds of poison are still particularly important among the Bamana, who resisted Islam longer than other Mande peoples.

34. Additional questions arise, such as: In the days before Western Sudanic armies were fully or even partially equipped with firearms as was the case in the Mali Empire, to what extent were poison-tipped arrows required for warfare? If poisoning arrow heads was a *jeli* specialty, were they all identified with it, including the women, or was the task confined to a limited group?

35. If poison was used in the quantities required to treat the arrows of at least some units of the armies of the Western Sudan, it would suggest an extensive industry that could have largely died out in the areas in question before foreign observers had any opportunity to report on it. Although blacksmiths were apparently involved with poison for occult purposes and although they were surely the ones who manufactured the iron arrowheads, their delicate, indeed dangerous, circumcision duties (McNaughton [1988:66–70]) would not seem to be compatible with the preparation and application of so much poison.

36. In 1990, an elderly woman remarked that in the past, living griots were not allowed near the village pond, presumably for fear of contamination (Batomi Dena from Somalo [Mali], in Cross and Barker [1992:80]).

37. We have not seen any mention of when baobab burial was discontinued in the Mande heartland. In Senegal in 1955–56, road builders in Dakar cut down "l'arbre aux griots," in which they found many skeletons, several of which were described by an eyewitness as "rather recent" (Flutre [1958:223]). It was not until 1961 that the griots of Senegal succeeded, after a serious confrontation with authorities, in having the custom entirely eliminated on the grounds that as Muslims they deserve to be buried like others of that faith (Silla [1966:746–47]).

38. McNaughton (1988:11).

39. Zahan (1963:128); Cremer (1923, I:53–54); Wane (1969:54).

40. Cremer (1923, I:53–54).

41. Wane (1969:54).
42. The Fulfulde (Fulbe/Peul language) plural of *mabo* is *mabubé.*
43. Tauxier (1937:141). Descriptions by Gaden (1931:12) and Labouret (1934:106–107) were similar to Tauxier's, minus the *niémmbé.*
44. Amselle (1990:73–75).
45. Moreau (1897). André Arcin heard that the term *tiapato* referred to Mauretanian descendants of a certain distinguished military leader named Koli (1907:262 n. 1). The specific reference is to the *grand conquérant Koli,* who should not be confused with the Fakoli of the Sunjata epic.
46. Cremer also gives *saburbé* as the plural of *tyapurto* (1923, I:53–54).
47. Zahan (1963:128).
48. Labouret (1934:106–107).
49. Humblot (1918:525). Yaya Wane characterizes the *cupurtaaji* of Tukulor society as recipients of the universal dole. He said they do not belong to any particular caste, but have extremely evil tongues which they exercise mercilessly, especially against griots, who are their preferred victims (1969:61 n. 32). The Malinke *jeli* Yamuru Diabaté identified the *tyapurtaw* as an enfranchised slave group (interview at Keyla, Mali, February 4, 1976).
50. Raffenel (1846:204).
51. Arcin (1907:261).
52. Delafosse (1912, I:135); Cremer (1923, I:54); Gaden (1931:12); Wane described the *jawambe* as praisers and counselors at the lowest level of the proprietary class (1969:31, 33).
53. Tauxier (1937:140); Moreau (1897).
54. Pageard (1959:239); Urvoy (1942:25).
55. Bertin (1954).
56. Barth (1857, III:112).
57. Siré-Abbâs-Soh (1913:148).
58. Es-Sa'di (c. 1655:116). There are also several references to military events in 1591 involving the "Z.ghrani," where they are clearly regarded as a distinct people. For oral traditions of Jawambe origin, see Siré-Abbâs-Soh (1913:146–48), Bertin (1954), Arnaud (1912:152–53), and Sidibé (1959:15–16).
59. Bathily (1936:191–92).
60. Pageard (1959:239). In his opinion, some European writers had confused the *mabow* with the *jawambe.*
61. Bertin (1954).
62. "Bagana" (Baghana, Bakunu) is a Mandekan equivalent of the Soninke "Wagadu."
63. Es-Sa'di (c. 1655:168).
64. Desplagnes (1907:173).
65. Gaden (1931:323).
66. Ibid., 322.
67. Pageard (1959:239).
68. Tauxier (1937:141); Cremer (1923, I:54); Delafosse (1912, III:118 n. 1; 1955, II:483).
69. Zahan (1963:127–28).
70. See, for example, Gallais (1962:106–29) and Barth (1969).
71. Bazin (1985:87–127).
72. Amselle (1985:11–48); see also Amselle (1990).
73. Wright (1989:42).
74. Ivan Karp, personal communication, 1992. For an example of this concept applied to the roles of women during marriage rites among the Iteso of Kenya, see Karp (1987:137–52). Karp suggested to us that like the *nyamakalaw,* Iteso women are mediators who are simultaneously agents of and agents for, a distinction that may help to account for the existence of multiple perspectives of *nyamakala* status.
75. Interviews with Boundiali Doumbia in Gouala, Mali, May 22, 1992, and with Koloko Kanté in Kangaba, Mali, February 25, 1992.
76. In 1991–92, Barbara Frank conducted fieldwork among Mande women potters, a

project undertaken in part in response to this lacuna in the literature, of which she was made especially aware as a result of working on this volume.

77. For one discussion of female bards, see Diawara (1990:115–20). Barbara Hoffman has worked extensively with women griots, and she is now in the process of preparing some of this material for publication.

References

Al-ʿUmari. 1337–38. *Masalik al-absar fi mamlik al-amsar.* English trans. by J. F. P. Hopkins in *Corpus of Early Arabic Sources for West African History,* ed. N. Levtzion and J. F. P. Hopkins. Cambridge: Cambridge University Press, 1981.

Amselle, Jean-Loup. 1985. "Ethnies et espaces: Pour une anthropologie topologique." In *Au coeur de l'ethnie: Ethnies, tribalisme et état en Afrique,* ed. Jean-Loup Amselle and Elikia M'Bokolo. Paris: Le Découverte.

———. 1990. *Logiques métisses: Anthropologie de l'identité en Afrique et ailleurs.* Paris: Editions Payot.

Arcin, André. 1907. *La Guinée française.* Paris: Augustin Challamel.

Arnaud, Robert. 1912. *L'Islam et la politique musulmane française en Afrique Occidentale Française, suivi de la singulière légende des Soninkés.* Paris: Comité de l'Afrique française.

Aujas, L. 1931. "Les Sérères du Sénégal (moeurs et coutumes de droit privé)." *Bulletin du Comité d'Etudes historiques et scientifiques de l'Afrique Occidentale Française* 14:293–333.

Barbot, J. 1746. *A Description of the Coasts of North and South Guinea, and of Ethiopia Inferior, Vulgarly Angola.* London: Henry Lintot and John Osborne.

Barth, Fredrik. 1969. *Ethnic Groups and Boundaries: The Social Organization of Cultural Difference.* Boston: Little, Brown and Co.

Barth, Heinrich. 1857. *Travels and Discoveries in North and Central Africa in the Years 1849–1855.* New York: Harper and Brothers. Reprint, London: Frank Cass, 1965.

Bathily, Ibrahim. 1936. "Les Diawandos ou Diogoramés: Traditions orales recueillies à Djenné, Corientze, Ségou et Nioro." *Education Africaine* 25:173–93.

Bazin, Jean. 1985. "A chacun son Bambara." In *Au coeur de l'ethnie: Ethnies, tribalisme et état en Afrique,* ed. Jean-Loup Amselle and Elikia M'Bokolo. Paris: Le Découverte.

Bérenger-Féraud, L. J. B. 1882. "Etude sur les griots du peuplades de la Sénégambie." *Revue d'Anthropologie,* sér. s, 50:266–79.

———. 1897. *Les peuplades de la Sénégambie.* Paris: E. Leroux. Reprint, Nendeln: Kraus, 1973.

Bertin, Jean. 1954. "Etude sur les Toucouleurs du Bondou (Cercle de Nioro)." Archives Nationales du Mali, ID-51–10.

Boilat, P.-D. 1853. *Esquisses sénégalaises.* Paris: P. Bertrand.

Brett-Smith, Sarah Catherine. 1983. "The Poisonous Child." *RES: Anthropology and Aesthetics* 6 (Autumn):47–64.

Caillié, René. 1830. *Travels through Central Africa to Timbuctoo 1824–1828.* 2 vols. London: Colburn & Bentley. Reprint, London: Frank Cass, 1968.

Charry, Eric S. 1992. "Musical Thought, History and Practice among the Mande of West Africa." Ph.D. dissertation, Princeton University.

Cremer, Jean Henri. 1923. *Matériaux d'ethnographie et de linguistique soudanaises.* Vol. 1: *Dictionnaire Française-Peul.* Paris: Paul Geuthner.

Cross, Nigel, and Rhiannon Barker. 1992. *At the Desert's Edge: Oral Histories from the Sahel.* London: Panos Publications Ltd.

Dapper, O. 1686. *Description de l'Afrique.* Amsterdam: Wolfgang, Waesberge, Boom & Van Someren.

Delafosse, Maurice. 1912. *Haut-Sènègal-Niger (Soudan Français).* 3 vols. Paris: Emile Larose. Reprint, Paris: G.-P. Maisonneuve et Larose, 1972.

———. 1955. *La langue mandingue et ses dialectes (malinké, bambara, dioula).* Vol. 2: *Dictionnaire mandingue-française.* Paris: Paul Geuthner.

Desplagnes, Louis. 1907. *Le plateau central nigérien.* Paris: E. Larose.

Diawara, Mamadou. 1990. *La graine de la parole: Dimension sociale et politique des traditions orales du royaume de Jaara (Mali) du XVème au milieu du XIXème siècle.* Stuttgart: Franz Steiner Verlag.

Dupouy, Edouard. 1885. "Le korté, poison d'épreuve du Bélédougou et du Fouladougou." *Archives de médecin navale.* 43:153–54.

Durand, Jean Baptiste Leonard. 1802. *Voyage au Sénégal.* Paris: H. Agasse.

Du Sorbiers de la Tourrasse, Joseph. 1897. *Au pays des Woloffs: Souvenirs d'un traitant du Sénégal.* Tours: Maison Alfred Mame et Fils.

es-Saʿdi, Abderrahman. c. 1655. *Tarikh es-Soudan.* Edited and translated by Octave Houdas. 1st ed., Paris: E. Leroux, 1911; reprint, Paris: Adrien-Maisonneuve, 1964.

Flutre, L.-F. 1958. "Sur deux mots qui viennent d'Afrique: *Baobab* et *griot.*" *Studia Neophilologica* 28 (2):218–15.

Gaden, Henri. 1931. *Proverbes et maximes Peuls et Toucouleurs.* Paris: Institut d'Ethnologie.

Gallais, Jean. 1962. "Signification du group ethnique au Mali." *L'Homme* 2 (2):106–29.

Gamble, David F. 1957. *The Wolof of Senegambia.* London: International African Institute.

Giddens, Anthony. 1979. *Central Problems in Social Theory: Action, Structure and Contradiction in Social Analysis.* Berkeley: University of California Press.

Greenberg, Joseph H. 1966. *The Languages of Africa.* Bloomington: Indiana University Press.

Hair, P. E. H. 1967. "Ethnolinguistic Continuity on the Guinea Coast." *Journal of African History* 8 (2):247–68.

Herpin, E. 1955. "Le Chevalier de Fréminville à Dakar (1822)." *Notes Africaines* 66:41–47.

Humblot, P. 1918. "Du nom propre et des appellations chez les Malinké des vallées du Niandan et du Milo (Guinée Française)." *Bulletin du Comité des Etudes historiques et scientifiques de l'Afrique Occidentale Française* 1 (3–4):519–40.

Jobson, Richard. 1623. *The Golden Trade, or A Discovery of the River Gambra, and the Golden Trade of the Aethiopians.* Edited by Charles G. Kingsley. Reprint, Teignmouth, England: E. E. Speight and R. H. Walpole, 1904.

Karp, Ivan. 1986. "Agency and Social Theory: A Review of Anthony Giddens." *American Ethnologist* 13 (2):131–37.

———. 1987. "Laughter at Marriage: Subversion in Performance." In *The Transformation of African Marriage,* ed. David Parkin and David Nyamwaya. Manchester: Manchester University Press for the International African Institute.

Knops, P. 1959. "L'artisan Senufo dans son cadre Ouest-Africain." *Bulletin de la Société Royale Belge d'Anthropologie et de Préhistoire* 70:84–111.

Labat, Jean Baptiste. 1728. *Nouvelle relation de l'Afrique occidentale.* 4 vols. Paris: Chez G. Cavelier.

Labouret, Henri. 1934. *Les Manding et Leur Langue.* Paris: Librarie Larose.

La Courbe, Michel J. 1685. *Premier voyage fait à la coste d'Afrique en 1685.* Edited by P. Cultru. Paris: E. Champion, 1913. Reprint, Nendeln: Kraus Reprint, 1973.

Lamiral. 1789. *L'Affrique et le peuple affriquain.* Paris: Dessenne.

Madrolle, Claudius. 1895. *En Guinée.* Paris: H. Le Soudier.

Mage, Eugène. 1868. *Voyage dans le Soudan occidental (Sénégambie-Niger)*. Paris: Hachette.

Marche, Alfred. 1879. *Trois voyages dans l'Afrique occidentale*. Paris: Hachette.

Mauny, Raymond. 1955. "Baobab cimitières à griots." *Notes Africaines* 67:72–75.

McNaughton, Patrick R. 1988. *The Mande Blacksmiths: Knowledge, Power, and Art in West Africa*. Bloomington: Indiana University Press.

Mollien, Gaspard T. 1820. *Travels in the Interior of Africa*. Translated by T. E. Bowdich. London: Colburn. Reprint, London: Cass, 1967.

Monteil, Vincent. 1968. "Un cas d'economie ostentatoire: Les griots d'Afrique noire." *Economies et Societes* 2 (4):773–91.

Moreau, J. L. M. 1897. "Notice générale sur le Soudan: 2ème partie, ethnologie." Archives Nationales du Mali, ID-19.

Norris, H. T. 1968. *Shinqiti Folk Literature and Song*. London: Oxford University Press.

Pageard, Robert. 1959. "Note sur les Diawambé ou Diokoramé." *Journal de la Société des Africanistes* 29:239–60.

Park, Mungo. 1799. *Travels in the Interior Districts of Africa*. London: W. Bulmer and Co.

———. 1907. *The Travels of Mungo Park*. London: Dent; New York: Dutton. Rev. ed., ed. Ronald Miller, London: Dent; New York: Dutton, 1954.

Raffenel, Anne. 1846. *Voyage dans l'Afrique-Occidentale*. Paris: Arthur Bertrand.

Rançon, André. 1894. *Dans la Haute-Gambie*. Paris: Société d'Editions Scientifiques.

Saint-Lô, R. P. Alexis de. 1637. *Relation du voyage du Cap Verd*. Paris: F. Targa.

Sidibé, Mamby. 1959. "Les gens de caste ou nyamakala au Soudan Français." *Notes Africaines* 81:13–17.

Silla, O. 1966. "Persistence des castes dans la société wolof contemporaine." *Bulletin de l'I.F.A.N.* 28 (3–4):731–70.

Siré-Abbâs-Soh. 1913. *Chroniques du Fouta Sénégalais*. Translated by M. Delafosse and H. Gaden. Paris: E. Leroux.

Soleillet, Paul. 1887. *Voyage à Ségou 1878–1879*. Edited by Gabriel Gravier. Paris: Challamel aîné.

Tauxier, Louis. 1927. *La religion Bambara*. Paris: Paul Geuthner.

———. 1937. *Moeurs et histoire des Peuls*. Paris: Payot.

Urvoy, Y. 1942. *Petit atlas ethno-démographique du Soudan*. Paris: Larose.

Valtaud, M. R. 1922. "Coutume funéraire des Sérères." *Bulletin du Comité d'Etudes Historiques et Scientifiques de l'Afrique Occidentale Francaise* 5:251.

Wane, Yaya. 1969. *Les Toucouleurs du Fouta Tooro (Sénégal): Stratification sociale et structure familiale*. Dakar: Institut fondamental de l'Afrique Noire.

Wright, Bonnie L. 1989. "The Power of Articulation." In *Creativity of Power: Cosmology and Action in African Societies*, ed. W. Arens and Ivan Karp. Washington and London: Smithsonian Institution Press.

Zahan, Dominique. 1963. *La Dialectique du verbe chez les Bambara*. Paris: Mouton & Co.

I

The Paradox of Word and Meaning

I

ETYMOLOGIES OF *NYAMAKALA*

Charles S. Bird, Martha B. Kendall, and Kalilou Tera

As the medical compound ibuprofen worked its way through the regulatory bureaucracy of the Food and Drug Administration, corporations and institutions representing competing interests fought long and hard for the product's classification as either a "prescription" or a "nonprescription" drug. The chemical companies producing ibuprofen argued that since the drug had been proven safe and effective, the FDA should allow consumers the widest possible access to it, and that it should therefore be sold "over the counter." The American Medical Association, representing medical doctors, on the other hand, insisted that physicians should advise patients for their own protection on the drug's potential side effects, requiring that ibuprofen be designated a "prescription" drug and sold only under doctors' orders. Unstated, but transparent in the testimony for both sides, were serious issues of profit and control—for while it is true that consumers "benefit" indirectly when medicines are readily available in nonprescription forms, drug companies benefit directly from access to unrestricted markets; and while physicians "protect" patients by advising them on possibly deleterious consequences of taking particular drugs, their advice generally requires at least one visit to their offices, which in turn guarantees profits to physicians. From the point of view of the drug companies, the physicians' arguments for restricted access to ibuprofen threatened to slow the cash flow that the new compound promised. From the physicians' point of view, the drug companies' arguments for free access to ibuprofen threatened the physicians' economically profitable relationships with patients.

The point of this example is to illustrate that classifications have tangible and immediate consequences. Powerful interests would not battle over the application of definitions and meanings were this not the case. Control over the definitions of words equals control over the social consequences of classifications. The ability to impose particular definitions on words translates into the ability to enable or constrain particular forms of social action. Control means power, and it means it universally. Wherever we discover competing definitions of words or competing understandings of their range of applicability, we touch on competing constructions of reality. We find, in short, power struggles.

This brings us to *nyamakala,* a word with strong, and often negative, associations in many Mande languages. We have been asked to comment on where the word came from and what it means, but in order to do this, we must first make clear the nature of the task we have been assigned. Let us start from the proposition that since etymology is concerned with possible historical sources and meanings, it necessarily involves decisions among alternatives. This means that while etymology is generally understood as an intellectually neutral, scientific endeavor, it is in fact very often a covert political game with overt social consequences. This being the case, we must deliberately refrain from providing a single answer to what *nyamakala* means. Our position is that its meaning depends on group ideology and point of view.

Having said this, there are four points we would like to make concerning the etymology and semantics of this term:

1. *The meaning of the word* nyamakala *does not equal the sum of its parts.* Etymologies of *nyamakala,* whether collected from native speakers or scholarly sources, generally divide the word into two putative "constituents": *nyama* and *kala.* People following this strategy inevitably provide definitions of these constituents independently and then supply arguments for their logical juxtaposition. In a typical example, *nyama* is held to mean "natural force" and *kala* is held to mean "stick," "twig," or "straw" and, by extension, "the handle of a tool," as in *dabakala,* "hoe handle." The combinatorial justification proceeds by means of the following reasoning: people who know how to deal with this force of nature—who know how to handle *nyama,* as one would handle a tool—are *nyama*-handlers. Bards, leatherworkers, and blacksmiths handle *nyama;* hence they are called *nyamakalaw.* We note nonetheless that the explanation in question adds more semantic material than the form itself provides. The compound *nyamakala* would be, for example, the only word in any Mande language in which *kala* refers to human agents; furthermore, it would be the only construction in any Mande language in which *kala* has the abstract meaning of mastery or control.

Refinements on the meaning of *nyama* include notions that the force in question is variously (a) evil or satanic; (b) morally neutral; (c) dangerous; (d) polluting; (e) energizing or animating; (f) necessary for action; or (g) indicative of imperfect self-control. Muslims tend to emphasize the evil or polluting connotations of the term, while traditionalists (e.g., hunters and their bards) tend to promote the animating and necessitative associations. All of these semantic possibilities—and no doubt others—are available, and all are employed for particular reasons in specific contexts.

A completely different sense of the word *nyama*—and by extension a completely different sense of the word *nyamakala*—appears when *nyama* is used to refer to "garbage" or "refuse."[1] While some speakers pronounce the word for "garbage" with a final nasal sound, *nyaman,* and consider it completely different from the word for "natural force," *nyama,* others pronounce the words for "garbage" and "natural force" identically and then construct reasons why one meaning should be derived from the other. Inspired by etymological exercises

linking "natural force" to "garbage," other students of Mandekan have attempted to derive *nyama* from *nyaga,* "residue," "chaff," or "the part to be
thrown away." They explain the synchronic form *nyama* as follows: speakers
drop the *g* in the middle of *nyaga,* pronouncing it *nyaa. Ma* is then added as a
suffix meaning "having the property of" (the preceding noun). In this version
of the history of Mandekan, *nyama* means "having the property of garbage or
refuse," so that those bearing the name *nyamakalaw* constitute the lowest elements, the dregs, of society. The problem here, however, is that this interpretation provides no satisfactory explanation for the second element of the
compound: *kala.*

When we look at possible meanings for *kala* other than "handle," the confusion deepens. *Kala* can mean "powerful agent," something with the force to kill,
and, by extension, "antidote" or "remedy." This expands the logically possible
meanings for *nyamakala* to such things as (a) antidote for evil; (b) remedy against
pollution; (c) antidote for poison; or (d) remedy for garbage. We might speculate
that the functions of those bearing the label *nyamakala* are to protect other
members of the society from the dangerous and polluting effects of the objects
and activities with which they deal. But although we find *kala* in combinations
with names of maladies, such as *kono-dimi-kala,* "stomachache remedy," something to kill a stomachache, we find no speakers of the language to whom this
particular use of *kala* makes sense in combination with *nyama.* Whatever *nyama*
is, it is not on the order of an illness.

We see further problems with the etymological speculations we have outlined.
First and foremost, the division of *nyamakala* into *nyama* and *kala* is by no
means the only possibility. It is entirely plausible, for instance, that the contemporary form *kala* as it appears in *nyamakala* is the modern reflex of the earlier
derived form *ke-la,* the agentive of the verb "to make" or "to do." If this were
the case, then *nyamakala* (from *nyamakela*) would translate as "makers of,"
"doers of," or "creators of" *nyama;* but then the possibility exists that the word
nyama itself is the modern reflex of some earlier compound. It could even be
the case that *nyama* breaks down into *nya,* "means," and *ma,* "having the
property of," translating as "being/having the means to X." Or, alternatively,
assuming that *ni* equals "soul," the word *nyama* might be decomposable into
ni-ya-ma, in which case it would translate as "having the property of soul or life
force."

Note that this is just the tip of the etymological iceberg, however, since we
have suggested only the most immediate and familiar possibilities. If we were to
survey comparative forms from the farthest-flung reaches of the Mande diaspora, we could make even clearer why it is impossible to get a definitive purchase
on the meaning of *nyamakala* by examining its internal parts. Decomposing the
word in this fashion allows myriad possibilities, most of which are equally
plausible from grammatical, ethnographic, and historical points of view.

2. *The word* nyamakala *is a regionally based form. Terms referring to bards,
blacksmiths, and leatherworkers take different shapes and have different etymologies in different regions.* If we are frustrated by the failure of lexical decomposi-

tion to provide us with satisfactory meanings for *nyamakala,* then logically the next methodological step would be to survey the comparative linguistic evidence from other Mandekan dialects where bards, leatherworkers, and blacksmiths are classified together under a single term. We find the word *nyamakala* primarily in the eastern dialects of Mandekan: Bambara, Maninka, and Dyula. In the western dialects, such as Mandekakan in Senegal and the Gambia, the form of the word is *nyamalo,* the standard etymology for which is *nya* (from *nyaga*) "celebration, festival" plus *mala* (from *mara*) "to save, preserve." From these forms comes the interpretation that blacksmiths and bards are the "preservers of the rituals and celebrations" that hold the society together.

The identical meaning attaches itself to the linguistically distinct forms *nyakamala* or *nyaxamala* in the Soninke dialects of the Guidimaxa and Jafunu, where *nyaka* means "celebration" and *mala* means "to preserve." The Soninke forms radically confound our search for the meaning of *nyamakala,* however, because they involve a permutation of the consonants *k* and *m* between the Soninke dialects and the Eastern Mandekan versions of the word. If such a permutation did take place, then which form came first, *nyamakala* or *nyakamala?* If it is the case that the Soninke (and Western Mandekan) forms represent the original word, then all the efforts to associate the word *nyamakala* to the word *nyama* are completely spurious historically. If the Eastern Mandekan form came first, then the etymologies involving the preservation of ceremonies are false. Unfortunately, we do not know—and cannot know— whether *nyamakala* or *nyakamala* is the original form. And if no linguistic evidence is available to help us to establish the precedence of one form over another, then it is clear that people who promote one of these forms as *the* etymon do so for other reasons. It is certainly worthwhile to consider what those other reasons are.

3. *The range of application of the term* nyamakala *(i.e., the word's referents) varies from one region to another and from one speaker to another.* Having failed to find a single historical meaning for *nyamakala* in comparative data from the dialects of Mandekan, we next turn to an investigation of the term's synchronic application as a way of specifying its meaning. However, since the word carries considerable negative social weight—in many cases stigmatizing those to whom it refers—it should come as no surprise to discover that its applications are contested. We will discuss the contests and challenges in this section by examining *nyamakala*'s reference or denotation. In the following section we will deal with its sense or connotation, i.e., with the feelings evoked when the word is used in given contexts.

When we ask Mandekan speakers what *nyamakala* means, they often respond with a list of social types to which the term applies—lists which vary from person to person, from village to village, and from occasion to occasion. Many people tell us that *nyamakala* refers to blacksmiths (*numu*), bards (*jali*), leatherworkers (*garanké*), and Islamic praise singers (*funé*). But it is important to note that there is no specific educational system in the Mande world that reproduces this knowledge unambiguously. In some villages and with some individuals, blacksmiths are not included in the category *nyamakala;* they are considered a race apart from the other casted people. In some areas, where there are no *garanké* and where *jali* do leatherwork, *garanké* are not included on the list of *nyamakala.* In still other areas, the *garanké* are considered Soninke and therefore are not included among the local *nyamakala.* In some regions, slaves, *jon,* and their descendants, *woloso,* are called *nyamakala,* but in others this inclusion is specifically denied. The other essays in this volume make this point especially clearly.

4. *The connotations, the feelings, evoked by the use of* nyamakala *vary greatly, depending on who is speaking to whom and in what particular situation.* To many *horon* in the core Mande, the word *nyamakala* evokes moral repugnance. It is an offensive word that sticks in the throat. Here we are discussing the sense of the term, not its referents. It is important to understand that we are no longer debating whether the term legitimately applies to the *jon* or the *garanké,* but what it *means*—i.e., what feelings it evokes—when used in particular situations by particular speakers.

From the Mande *horon* point of view, the *nyamakala* represent everything that a noble must not be or do. They dabble in the occult. They lie. They act shamelessly. They comport themselves without constraint or control. They plead weakness. They beg. They manifest sexuality in public places. They dance with wild gestures. They raise their voices. They shout and yell in public. The *nyamakala* are utterly alien: they are "The Other." When one *horon* tells another that he or she is acting like a *nyamakala,* it is an admonishment. It is a way of marking boundaries between groups. It is a device aimed at ensuring the status quo.

People who classify themselves as *nyamakalaw,* on the other hand, matter-of-factly describe their behavior as their "birthright," as what they were born to do, and they do not attach the same meanings to their actions as the nobles do. A celebrated Malian *jali-muso,* for instance, told us that *nyamakalaya* had two defining criteria: (a) all casted people perform the act called *deli* with respect to the *horon,* and (b) all *nyamakala* manifest *majigi* toward them.

Did she mean by *majigi* that casted people make themselves small in order to enlarge and empower nobles? By *deli* did she mean that casted people seek the patronage of/render service to nobles? By *majigi* did she mean that casted people demonstrate respect for nobles? Or did she mean that casted people abase themselves? Act servile? Beg and importune?

The "same" act can be variously defined: service from one perspective is servility from another. The word *deli* can be used to describe seeking someone's patronage, but it also refers to begging and importuning of the most opportunistic sort. *Majigi* can be used to mean showing respect or abasing oneself. The meaning of these words depends crucially on who speaks them and why.

We might expect a *jali-muso*'s translations of *deli* and *majigi* to contrast with translations a *horon* might give them. The former understands *deli* and *majigi* from an actor's perspective, while the latter incorporates an observer's point of view. But it is more than this, for in the case at hand, the words are fraught with distinct value tones depending on the perspective taken. From the perspective where *majigi* resembles selflessness, the act is positive; from the perspective where it resembles servility, the act is negative. From this follow three things: (a) we cannot take it for granted that meanings established in one context will operate unproblematically in another; (b) we cannot assume that the way we use a word is the way everybody uses it; and (c) we must know something about the conditions under which dictionaries and scholarly texts are produced in order to evaluate the relevance of their commentaries on words.

To appreciate what a word such as *nyamakala* means, we must closely attend to those who are using the term, how they are using it, and why they use it in the way they do. In other words, we need to attend to people's *interests* in defining themselves and others in particular ways. As we tried to show with the ibuprofen example, social classifications encoded in linguistic forms are grounded in social constructions of reality. Classifications, like all cultural categories, are endlessly contested because the people who employ them have competing interests in the consequences and outcomes of particular classifications.

Epilogue: Speculations on Language, Myth, and History

In the preceding sections, we have tried to make the case that in etymology, as in all other enterprises concerned with the definition and meaning of symbols, the interpretive and the political are essentially intertwined. We deliberately refrained from specifying a single meaning for *nyamakala* either historically or contemporaneously, both because we wished to emphasize the multivocality of the verbal sign and because we wanted to demonstrate the subtleties of linguistic research. Our point is that because all words have multiple meanings, it is far more enlightening to ask what categories of people use a word and how they use it than it is to ask what the word means. It makes far more sense, for example, to ask what George Bush or Adlai Stevenson means by "liberal" than it does to ask what "liberal" means.

Having made the case for the contested nature of individual words, we thought we would try to extend the argument to other forms of linguistic representation as well. In particular, we thought it might be interesting to comment on the multiplicity of meanings in myths and histories that bear on the origins of the *nyamakalaw*.

Traditional stories of the origin of *nyamakalaya* invariably refer to Sunjata, founder of the twelfth-century Mali Empire. These chartering myths credit Sunjata with conquering Sumanguru, King of the Soso, after which he organized Mande social life into its present configuration by grouping various categories of people together, classifying them as *nyamakalaw,* and setting them in opposition to another major social type: the nobility. These stories imply that social organization in the now-Mande regions of West Africa took a radically different form before the founding of the Mali Empire. What was the earlier form like?

Contemporary bards tell us that the ancient song in praise of Mande heroes, the Janjon, was originally sung for Sumanguru, King of the Soso, also known as the Blacksmith King. In the Janjon, sung as part of the Epic of Sunjata, the praise lines for Sumanguru run:

> *Mande masa folo ni masa duguren*
> First King of the Mande and King of Yesteryear

Sumanguru, a blacksmith, was First King of the Mande? Could these lines indicate that the kings of the Mande before the Mali Empire were blacksmiths? Could the legendary battle between Sunjata and Sumanguru be an allegory for a struggle between a new social order and an old one? Could the Epic of Sunjata represent in mythic form the early days of Islam in the western savannah?

Let us consider the evidence for this, starting with some suggestive facts about blacksmiths, their social roles, and their geographical distributions. Smiths appear throughout West Africa, and where they appear, they often participate in religious and political specializations forbidden to others. In many places, smiths practice endogamy, i.e., they marry only among themselves because they are restricted from marrying with nonsmiths. In many West African mythologies, the Culture Hero—the First Person, the Founder of Society—is a blacksmith. Mande origin myths, for instance, represent the Culture Hero as a blacksmith who descends from the heavens carrying the basic equipment of organized social life: grains, tools, and knowledge. This blacksmith is described as the founder of a race, *si,* which is set apart from those of all other people. Blacksmiths in the Mande have their own distinctive caste.

Praise singers, like blacksmiths, are found throughout Africa, but casted bards, like casted smiths, are found only in the regions affected by the empires of Ghana and Mali. If we examine oral traditions concerned with the origins of bard castes, we find two essential themes: the first has to do with the founding of particular bardic clans; the second has to do with the founding of *jaliya* as an institution. The myths concerned with the establishment of *jaliya* invariably link it to Islam. In this type of mythic charter, the founder of *jaliya,* Surakata, starts out as the sworn enemy of the Prophet Mohammed, but ends up as his inseparable companion. He establishes the institution of *jaliya* precisely in order that the Prophet's praises be perpetually sung.

From the facts relating to the distribution of casted smiths and bards, we could conclude that the smiths have historical precedence, which is in fact a claim made in oral tradition. Where we find *garanké* and *funé,* we also find *jali,* but the reverse is not the case. Where we find *jali,* we also find *numu,* but the reverse is not the case. The castes of leatherworkers and Islamic praise singers thus imply a caste of bards. The caste of bards implies a caste of blacksmiths.

Local traditions often reflect this implicational scale in a ranking of the *nyamakala* groups. The smiths came first, they say, then the bards, followed by the leatherworkers and the *funé,* the Islamic praise singers.

The claim that the origin of *jaliya* is found in Islam may in fact contain the key to the processes leading to the establishment of the other castes. In this version of pre-Islamic Mande history, smiths played an eminent role in the political organization of society.

If we examine the contemporary relationship between traditional smiths and Islamic holy men, *mori,* we find a certain tension rooted in their competition for clients, usually the *horon,* seeking service for spiritual needs. This is because the functions of the traditional smith and the Islamic *mori* overlap considerably, just as they must have overlapped in the past. Where Islam spreads, so spreads the competition between blacksmith and *mori.*

It is not unreasonable to speculate that this competition, leading to and resulting from changes in the economic and political order, not only created the conditions for new castes to arise during the centuries defined by the Ghana and Mali empires, but may be the origin of the negative associations that *nyamakalaya* has today.

We do not mean to imply that the epic personage Sunjata presents himself as a symbol of Islam. There is much that argues against this. Sunjata comes out of the epic to us as the young horse-warrior who has perhaps seized power and uses the epic songs of his victims to legitimize himself. There are many traditions relating to the union of these young warriors with the Islamicized merchants forming powerful city-states such as Kong, described by Kathy Green, for instance. Sunjata's power is unambiguously centered in traditional occult practices, although many epic singers include reference to his voyage to Mecca. Maybe Sunjata seems larger than life because he *is* larger than life. Maybe he is a composite.

Consider the possibility that the heroic deeds and actions of a series of kings and strong men living in the era of the early Ghana and Mali empires got telescoped into the biography of a single individual, who may or may not have had the name Sunjata in his own lifetime. Consider the possibility that the legends of Sunjata cover a period of time longer than the lifespan of a single figure. Somewhere in the great jumble of events represented in the legends of Sunjata, we may find allusions to the processes leading to the establishment of the social category *nyamakala,* the understanding of which constitutes a challenging social historical puzzle.

Notes

This essay is based primarily on field research, but like everything we write, it has been influenced greatly by the scholarship and the ideas of our colleagues and students. We gratefully acknowledge the enormous influence on our thought of Etienne Balanghien, George Brooks, Sekouba Camara, Seydou Camara, Gerald Cashion, Youssouf Cissé, David Conrad, Penta Danté, Kelemonson Diabaté, Massa M. Diabaté, Siramori Diabaté, Yamaru Diabaté, Manthia Diawara, Germaine Dieterlen, Barbara Frank, Kathryn Green, Barbara Hoffman, John William Johnson, Lansiné Kaba, Nantenegwe Kamisoko, Wa Kamisoko, Mamadou Kanté, Chérif Keita, Mamadou Koita, Alfa Konaré, Kassim

Koné, Batourou Seykou Kouyaté, Djimo Kouyaté, Fanta Kouyaté, Robert Launay, Roderick and Susan MacIntosh, Patrick McNaughton, Claude Meillassoux, Rex Moser, Bakari Sidibé, Fadigi Sissoko, Bourama Soumaoro, Satigi Soumaoru, Mamadou Soumaré, Saloum Soumaré, Mamadou Togola, Jontan Tunkara, and Ladji Tunkara—to mention but a few.

1. When Massa M. Diabaté translates the song celebrating Sunjata's triumph over his childhood paralysis, he chooses "ordure" as the French equivalent of *nyama*. Thus Diabaté's interpretation of:

> Nyama, nyama, nyama
> Fen bee b'i dogo nyama de koro
> Nyama t'i dogola fen koro

would be rendered into English as:

> Garbage, garbage, garbage
> All things hide under garbage
> Garbage hides under nothing

We would like to underline here that though Diabaté's translation is interesting, it is not necessarily what the poet who first sang those lines intended by them, nor does his interpretation necessarily represent a contemporary cultural norm. Given the rhetorical use of indeterminacy and polysemy in Mandekan poetry, it could very well be the case that the word *nyama* in this verse was intended to resonate with ambiguity, much as Banzumana Sissoko's use of the word *sanu* resonates with ambiguity in the text presented by Chérif Keita in this volume.

II

POWER, STRUCTURE, AND MANDE *JELIW*

Barbara G. Hoffman

Before leaving for what would turn out to be over four years of fieldwork and consulting in Mali, Burkina Faso, and Senegal, I read the literature on griots, and like many of my colleagues, I found its description of the relations between West African griots and their patrons problematic. At the same time, I was intrigued by the griot's art and wanted to know more about the ways of speaking at which griots excel. Upon the advice of my mentors, I went to Mali and became an apprentice *jelimuso* (woman griot) in order to study these issues from a *jeli*'s point of view.

In this essay, I discuss some of the kinds of power I learned about as a *jeli*, and how they fit into the general schema of Mande power structures that is emerging in the literature now. I believe that understanding issues of social power in the Mande world is central to understanding what we call the social structure of that world. Until we can fathom how members of different Mande social classes view themselves, the others they interact with, and the relative influence they have over one another, we will not understand what those classes are or how they create and contest organization and structure.

The early French and British travelers who wrote of the first contacts of Westerners with griots demonstrated a marked distaste for the talents of the bards, a distaste which subsequent writers have often attributed to nobles as well.[1] Even the most recent and comprehensive studies of griots and West African caste systems, those of Irvine and Camara, emphasize the negative opinions nobles hold of griots and their art while devoting little space to the discussion of what attracts nobles to them.[2] Some of the contributions to this volume reflect similar biases: for example, Keita represents the majority of present-day griots as "opportunistic," while only a select few have "integrity"; Launay, in his essay, reports that in the Korhogo regions, Mande *jeliw* are stereotyped as "quintessential spongers" who have "a less than savory reputation." These are relatively mild examples of the typically derogatory portrayals of Mande *jeliw* one finds throughout the scholarly literature.

Irvine paints a particularly scathing picture of relations between Wolof griots and nobles, reporting nobles' criticisms of griots with regard to nearly every aspect of life, from the control of bodily functions and appetites to the fulfillment of religious duties.[3] I suspect that Irvine did not collect these statements in public, nor in the presence of griots or other *nyamakalaw* (*nyenyo* among the Wolof). Such criticisms are, in the Mande world, popular insults widely used in gossip about individuals of any caste, nobles as well as griots. However, private conversations with nobles about *nyamakalaw* in general and griots in particular nearly always elicit negative statements about particular kinds of griot behavior. These criticisms are not usually made of nobles, nor are they frequently made of other *nyamakalaw*.[4] Typical statements about griots include such comments as "Jeliw ma nyi! U bè kuma kojugu, u bè kuma lankolon fò!" (Griots are bad! They talk too much, their talk is meaningless!), "Jeliw tè donkili da, u bè mankan bò" (Griots don't sing, they make noise), and "Jeliw bè don fè kojugu" (Griots like dancing too much [they dance too wildly]). Statements such as these are often vehemently spoken with pointed gestures, as though the judgment they convey were categorical. Yet, the services most regularly requested by nobles of griots are talking, singing, and dancing. Clearly, the ideology nobles claim to hold does not match their practice.

Another revealing aspect of the relationship between nobles and griots is the asymmetry of their mutual accountability. For example, nobles almost never blame individual griots for the general character of the group. The converse is more often the case: the behavior of the individual griot is seen as a result of his/her being a member of the group of griots; therefore, the individual is neither alone in nor responsible for his/her "imperfection." Griots, on the other hand, openly criticize nobles in public as well as in private, but their criticism is usually aimed at the behavior of one individual or family, whose error is not considered the result of influence from the rest of the noble group, but rather a dangerous potential source of contamination for that group. The noble is shamed not only for his/her individual wrongdoing, but also for having failed as a noble, having betrayed, however temporarily, the noble race. Practicing griots, on the other hand, are almost never ashamed of the behavior they are criticized for; in fact, they are taught that being ashamed of or being embarrassed by that behavior is inappropriate for a griot: they are thus taught to be *ashamed* of being ashamed.[5]

I have often heard young noblewomen in Bamako being publicly rebuked by their griot elders for overstepping the bounds of nobility (*horonya*) by dancing too much like griots. To the elder, this is an infraction of *horonya* not to be tolerated, lest it catch on. On the other hand, young griot women are supposed to be loud and boisterous in public performance. When one is timid instead, she runs the risk of being scolded for acting too much like a noble, and she will be reminded, proudly, that she is a *jeli,* and should comport herself accordingly.

I was intrigued by the question of the interdependency of nobles and griots,[6] in particular, why nobles depend upon griots for the performance of certain speech-related tasks which nobles are not a priori incapable of doing, but choose not to do. One of the most interesting of those tasks is public praising, *fasa dali.*

Bird and Kendall have described the high value placed on the griot's praise song by Da Monson and Sunjata.[7] I have seen nobles empty their coin purses of a month's salary in return for their *fasa,* an act they perform not just once, but over and over again throughout the course of their lives, despite the rancor and regret they may feel afterward. What is it about public praise that has such power for Mande people?

At the outset of my apprenticeship as a griot, I thought perhaps it was something like the thrill we all get when we hear "Happy Birthday" or "For She's a Jolly Good Fellow" being sung for us. It's quite often sung by a group of people, so there is a lot of attention focused on us, a lot of eyes trained directly on us, and usually when we are least expecting it; we're caught off guard and don't really know what to do with ourselves, so a hand goes to the face as we try to put up a quick wall to hide behind and collect ourselves.

Young *jelimusow* (women griots) often react like that when their praises are sung. They are trained to channel attention from themselves to someone else, and so are taken unawares when they first find themselves on the receiving end of public praise. A young noblewoman, however, expects to find herself in that position, and works very hard to show no emotion whatsoever while her praises are sung. She sits still and calm, dignified in cool silence, not even deigning to look at "her" griot. She does not speak her appreciation of the attention thus accorded her, but declares it nevertheless with a wordless gesture, a silent gift.

What moves the noble *horonmuso* under that cool, calm exterior? I wondered. Is it the style of the singer?—hardly the off-key warbling of an office crowd singing "Happy Birthday," but oftentimes the brilliant vocalization of a practiced and expert artist. Is it the rhythm the drums play for her alone, as when she is the sole dancer in the center of the ring? Or is it the words?

I learned in time that it was all those things and more, and that what stirred the most was what could not be talked about, but could be sung softly later, at home, in the privacy of one's room. Many noblewomen love the griots' songs and sing them to themselves when no one else is around to hear,[8] repeating them quietly, like personal charms. They feel the power of the griots' words, power that moves, that enables—power that, like other power structures in the Mande world, is articulated in obscurity.

In the songs that griots sing to griots, they urge each other to be men and women of wisdom,[9] to search for knowledge of the things of darkness. To attain renown as a sorcerer is, for the Mande griot, the pinnacle of achievement:[10] *ngara-soma*[11] (heroic bard-sorcerer) is the highest compliment one can pay a practicing griot. Yet, griots are the only *nyamakalaw* traditionally excluded from the Komo power association, where knowledge of the things of darkness is highly prized as a source of power.

McNaughton describes Komo sculptures as fundamental to the association's operation in that almost all Komo activities are carried out "in consort with sculpture"—the Komo sculpture's power must work in combination with the Komo master's power in order for the activity to be effective.[12] McNaughton characterizes that sculpture's power as an example of the Mande aesthetic principle that equates clarity of form and meaning with truth, purity, and straightforwardness while the obscurity of form and meaning is associated with secrecy, darkness, and tremendous power (*nyama*).[13]

This principle operates in the evaluation of ways of speaking in the Mande world as well. Speech that can be categorized as clear (*kuma jè*) is the conveyor of truth; elaborate speech obscures it, hides all or part of its referential content, renders its meaning ambiguous, and thus dangerous.

"Nyama bè kuma la," a Mande proverb states. "There is *nyama* in speech." Interpreting the meaning of *nyama* has generated considerable discussion among Mande scholars, a discussion which McNaughton insightfully summarizes:

> At sorcery's base lies a phenomenon that generates its own fair share of ambivalence and disquiet among the Mande. It is perceived as the world's basic energy, the energy that animates the universe. It is the force the Mande call *nyama,* which I refer to as special energy or occult power, and which most Westerners would consider supernatural. The Mande, in contrast, are inclined to see it as both natural and mystical, and as a source of moral reciprocity. The missionary Father Henry said that *nyama* was hard to define; he called it force, power, and energy and then described it as a kind of fluid possessed by every living being (Henry 1910:27–28). Monteil called it a fluid common to all of nature (Monteil 1924:121). The Malian scholar Youssouf Cissé followed the colonial administrator Maurice Delafosse in saying that it meant life or endowed with life, spirit or endowed with animated spirit. Cissé added that it was the emanation of the soul, a kind of flux or flow that executes the soul's will (Cissé 1964:192–193). Labouret described it in much the same way, adding, by way of illustration, that it was the power behind human thought and will, and the force that causes rain or a lack of it (Labouret 1934:120). Dominique Zahan described it as a force that exists in all beings and inorganic matter, and is comparable to a vibration (Zahan 1963:133).
>
> The Mande believe that in concentrations, especially when they are massive and uncontrolled, this force is potentially dangerous, even deadly. People can learn to control it through sorcery, however, and thereby harness it to help them carry out their activities. Thus the linguist Charles Bird describes its essence most appropriately when he calls it the energy of action (Bird 1974:vii). *Nyama* is the necessary power source behind every movement, every task. It is a prerequisite to all action and it is emitted as a by-product of every act. The more difficult the task, the more energy demanded and the more emitted. . . . *Nyama,* then is a little like electricity unconstrained by insulated wires but rather set neatly into a vast matrix of deeply interfaced social and natural laws. But it is more than energy. When the Mande tell folk stories, recount legends, or explain things to researchers, it becomes clear that they view *nyama* as a rationale for their most fundamental behavior patterns and as an explanation for the organization of their world.[14]

Zahan, who considered the *jeli* the artisan of speech, also considered the *jeli*'s art as being particularly laden with *nyama.* For him, the *fasa* (Zahan's *pasa*) is especially powerful. It stimulates the person to whom it is addressed, wakes him/her up, makes him/her vibrate with the energy of *nyama.*[15] He even postulated a classification of types of *fasa* which he hierarchized according to their capacity to excite *nyama:*

> At the bottom of this hierarchical ladder is the *mangutu.* . . . The *mangutu* is a sort of *curriculum vitae.* . . . At a level higher than the *mangutu* we find the *ma-dyamu,* a compound word which must be translated as "*dyamu* of the person." . . . This consists of saying in one word the "concentrate" of a formula which constitutes the *burudyu* (another category of praise of which we will speak later), characterizing by veiled expressions the essence of the active and conscious element of the person, which is the *dya.*
>
> . . . If the *dyamu* "paints" the *dya* of a social group, the *ma-dyamu* paints that of an individual. Despite its great power to excite *nyama,* the *ma-dyamu* is of little importance in comparison to [the *burudyu* and *balimaniw*]. . . . The *burudyu,* as a literary genre, is an account which depicts, in a concise manner and often through veiled words and expressions, the essence of that which constitutes the splendor of the person or the object it speaks of. It is a kind of slogan of which the first word constitutes the *dyamu.*
>
> . . . The slogan valorizes the *dya.* It elevates it, beautifies it, expands it. It excites the *nyama* by elevating its tone so that the person (and, by analogy, the being) who is the object feels his energy grow, his strength increase. The *burudyu* is a provider of energy. . . . The *balemani* then is a narrative destined to trace the origin and the genealogy of a person, of an animal, of a plant, or even of an object. . . . Because of its richness, the *balemani* constitutes the literary genre most capable of exciting the *nyama* of the individual. A good griot is capable, it is believed, of rendering mad or drunk the beneficiary of his *balemani* if the person does not stop the recital in time with a gift.[16] (Translation by the author)

It is difficult to understand the social grounding of these genres' capacity to stimulate *nyama* from Zahan's description. He doesn't attempt speculation about the source of the *mangutu's* power; the *ma-dyamu* he describes as a kind of concentrated personal motto which utilizes "veiled expressions" and has "great power to excite *nyama*"; the *burudyu* is merely a longer and more powerful version of the *ma-dyamu.* The *balemani* is a sort of history in shorthand, an attempt at a genealogy which links names and places and sometimes dates. Because it is "rich," the *balemani* is the most powerful of all griot genres in its capacity to "excite *nyama.*"

Mande people, as well, have difficulty verbalizing just what it is that constitutes the *nyama* of particular bardic genres. In response to direct questions on the topic, they give answers much like Zahan's characterizations. As with so many aspects of Mande social life, a fuller understanding cannot be had for the asking; it must be won slowly, with patient observation and no little amount of experiential participation.

A key to understanding the powerful nature of bardic genres can be found in Mande conceptions of the aesthetics of power. For example, McNaughton has said that Komo power association masks "depict 'obscurity fighting obscurity' . . . , they are designed to be unclear,"[17] and it is the stuff that obscures them that is the stuff of power. The Komo mask is built upon a foundation of wood carved in a simple, clear form, not dissimilar in this respect to other types of power association wood sculptures. What distinguishes the Komo mask from other association masks is the matter that is added to it over time, the multiplying of horns and quills, the layering of clay and blood, and the quantities of dangerous force (*nyama*) that these materials bring with them. The more obscured the original form becomes, the more hidden it is, the more powerful an object the mask becomes.

Griot language (*jelikan*) (what Zahan refers to as *balemani*) derives power from a simple syntactic structure whose meaning is made obscure. I agree with Zahan that of all the verbal performance genres the griot masters, *jelikan* is the most laden with dangerous force (*nyama*), the most powerful in its impact upon the hearer, and the most empowering for its speaker. Like the Komo mask, the form which the griot uses to build his power language is simple, clean, and unelaborated. Unlike ordinary language, the syntax of *jelikan* is usually restricted to noun phrases. Examples are "Simbo ni Salaba" (Simbo and Salaba), "Gasine ni Gasineka" (Gasine and the inhabitants of Gasine), "Tukuru ni Dayida" (Tukuru and Dayida). These are conjoined noun phrases, not complete sentences; there is no formal predication upon the subject, and therefore, to many listeners, the phrases sound nonsensical. The predication is performed not with verbs and objects but through the interaction of the griot and noble in the performance context.

Like the Komo mask, this simple and basic form becomes elaborated and takes on power during usage. *Jelikan* can be inserted to one degree or another into many performance genres, even the most clear and straightforward, such as introductions; it occurs extensively in the *fasaw* (praise songs), which are rated by the Mande as particularly *nyama*-laden. In my attempts to discover what it is about praise genres that is so powerful, I found that most nobles could not decipher the referential content of *jelikan;* even more surprising, a large proportion of any individual griot's repertory of phrases is empty of referential content to him/her as well. These phrases are usually not used in isolation, but in strings which may be many phrases long. When asked the meaning of an individual phrase, *jeliw* say that it is its membership in the class of phrases that can be sung for a person of a specific clan, for a Traoré, or a Kéita, or a Diallo. Its meaning is not the sum of its parts. The obscurity of its referential content in the performance context is an important aspect of the *nyama* of *jelikan*.

The contrast between the performance context of griot language and that of another power language, the language of divining, is revealing as well. A Mande word for this language is *dibikan*—the language of *dibi*. *Dibi* is a kind of darkness that is not restricted to the night—it is a word that can be applied to any area, physical or conceptual, that is unclear, amorphous, uncertain. McNaughton reminds us of the Bamana proverb "Nothing is in obscurity, but obscurity is not empty";[18] in divining, what is in the obscurity of *dibikan* is the power to transmit messages from an unseen world.

The kind of divining that sorcerers (*domaw*) do is not typically a daytime activity. Visits to the seer's hut are usually not public. The individual may meet with the sorcerer at night in private, inside a room, by the dim light of a smoky lamp. The seer may be a truth-sayer (*ciyen-fòla*) who traces figures in the sand to seek knowledge of the future for his client. His voice is just above a whisper as he speaks of the components of the divination that he calls the years of the truth's message. What the client hears is a series of conjoined nouns and noun phrases of the type "musoya ni kele" (womanhood and combat), "jugu ni dimi" (enemy and pain). Analyzed individually, each of these nouns seems to have a relatively clear referential base; however, the client does not usually hear them as individual nouns representing discrete semantic units, but as a rapidly and softly spoken series of sounds whose form is distinguishable, but whose meaning is discernible only as a unit of speech within the entire speech event of the divination. When the truth-sayer interprets *dibikan* for his client, he does so in ordinary syntax, pace, intonation, and volume—he speaks "clear speech" (*kuma jè*). The client has no means of verifying his interpretation, however; the syntax of *dibikan* is impenetrable to the noninitiate. It is obscured by the darkness, by the quiet, by the power of ambiguous form and meaning.[19]

Griot language, formally composed of noun phrases similar in structure to *dibikan,* is not whispered in nighttime privacy but shouted and sung, most often during the sunniest hours of the day, in the midst of great crowds. This contextual inversion contributes a layer of obscurity which adds to *jelikan*'s *nyama*. Once again, the phrases are for the most part incomprehensible to the listener— another layer. They are uttered very rapidly, at times like verbal gunfire, bombarding the noble with more sound than can be assimilated, causing confusion—another layer. The few images that are seized from the barrage, the name of a great warrior from the noble's clan history, for example, or the name of a famous village, can evoke entire histories heard upon countless occasions in innumerable contexts, so that what is heard is not merely what is said by the griot at the time, but what has been heard on the same topic at different times, in different places. The *nyama* grows thicker. The griot has called the weight of extraordinary achievement from the distant past into the living present of the noble "descendant" a juxtaposition which invites comparison, thus encouraging the noble to swell with pride at the thought of being on a par with such heroism, or to sink with shame at the thought that his/her own reputation will not stand up to the scrutiny—in either case, the emotion thus stirred is literally dripping with *nyama.*

It is no wonder that Mande nobles, who are taught to fear the *nyama* of speech to such an extent that they will castigate their children for merely raising their voices, should be awestruck by the effects of *jelikan.* Nor is it difficult to understand how they could be torn between their admiration for the *jeli*'s verbal prowess and their bewilderment and fear at the powerful emotions it arouses in them. I have seen many a *horon*'s hand quake as it thrust forth a bill, sometimes accompanied by a verbal plea, "ka nyama bò" (Please take away the *nyama*). It is, perhaps, even understandable that some nobles resent the fact that the *jeliw,* "their" *jeliw,* as they say, have such power over them, power not only to stir them deeply and make them tremble, but to inspire them to part with hard-won cash or goods in the bargain. But it is incomprehensible that we, as scholars, should take note only of the nobles' anger and resentment and ignore the causes of the admiration and envy that underlie them.

The three power structures I have talked about—the Komo mask, divining language, and griot language—share several striking characteristics. They are constructed from a formally simple base. They derive their social meaning from elements of the context of their use. A much-desired effect of their use is to obscure their basic form: it is layered with physical matter as in the Komo mask, or with complex social history as in griot language; elements of the context such as time and place, elements of delivery such as volume and pitch of delivery, may muddle the message even further, as with both divining and griot language. Use of all three requires extensive training and initiation into the techniques of protecting oneself from high levels of *nyama* generated by these forms and channeling it effectively for the accomplishment of the desired goal.

In the case of the griot, that goal might generally be said to be the reinforcement of *horonya* and of *jeliya*'s place as its complement. To paraphrase one of my teachers, an accomplished bard from Kela in the heart of the Mande: to be a griot is to lower oneself in order to make others greater, even when you know you are richer, more knowledgeable, more powerful. To speak griot language to someone is to make its *nyama* enter him, to make him bigger with the honor thus bestowed.[20] In the Mande world, control of *nyama* is one of the most important means of exercising power. Unless we, as scholars, take the power of griots into account, we cannot begin to understand, much less to describe, their place in Mande social organization.

Notes

This research was conducted with the partial support of a Fulbright-Hays Doctoral Dissertation Research Abroad Fellowship and a grant-in-aid from the Indiana University Graduate School. I would like to express my gratitude to these institutions for their support and to acknowledge my indebtedness to all those who took interest in and helped to bring about the research on which this paper is based; I would particularly like to thank Charles Bird and Martha Kendall, without whom this project would never have seen the light of day, for many years of patient mentoring and intellectual inspiration. Further thanks go to Kassim Koné who, as my research assistant in the field, helped me enormously throughout my journey through *jeliya*, and as a colleague now continues to generously offer his insight and perspective. Prior versions of this essay benefited from helpful commentary from Barbara Frank, Patrick McNaughton, Bonnie Wright, and Michael Short, as well as from the three people mentioned above. None of them, however, is responsible for any of its shortcomings.

1. Typical of the comments about griots in these early writings is this from Astley's 1745 collection of travel accounts: "When these varlets miss of their expected fees, they fall a-railing, and publish in the villages as many base things as they invent against the persons, contradicting whatever they had said good of them" (1745–47:279).

2. Although not comprehensive in scope, two important recent exceptions to this

general tendency are Kendall (1982) and Wright (1989). It should be noted that the bias of Irvine's and Camara's studies is not without pragmatic foundation: Camara is himself a noble, and Irvine's host family (and presumably her adoptive social status) were noble as well.

3. Irvine (1974:142–53).

4. However, in some contexts, nobles have been known to speak of all *nyamakalaw* with a certain amount of disdain. *Horon* parents frequently berate their children for behaving like *nyamakalaw,* behavior which is held to be beneath the dignity called for by the noble status.

5. Wright notes that Wolof griots also display what seems to be a deliberate public presentation of self as "loud, mischievous, and provocative" (1989:52).

6. It should be noted that the term "interdependent" is not as accurate today as it might have been in the past. While nobles who respect their own status are completely dependent on griots for a number of functions, very few griots rely entirely on the income they receive from performing services for nobles, and even fewer maintain an exclusive relationship with one patron. Johnson notes the tendency for griots to have numerous patrons, citing the case of Wa Kamissoko, who claimed to be the client of the entire village of Kirina (1986:26). Indeed, it is not uncommon today for a griot's most regular patron to be another griot or another *nyamakala.*

7. The song, *Janjon,* was so valuable to Sunjata that he refused to give it to his ally, Fakoli, until Fakoli had undergone a series of tests which included the beheading of one of Sumanguru's generals; Da Monson besieged his rival's kingdom, causing his rival to commit suicide, in order to win the song *Dugu* (Bird and Kendall 1980:20–21).

8. No one, that is, who would hold the singing noble accountable for her griot-like behavior; among intimate friends such forms of play are common occurrences.

9. One of the most spectacular renditions of this theme I encountered was performed by the late *ngara* Siramori Diabaté before an audience of Mande bards on the occasion of the installation of a new *jelikuntigi* (chief griot) in Kita, April 5, 1985.

10. Wright indicates that among the Wolof as well, the power of the griot is considered to be so similar to sorcery that the two categories of persons are often conflated, if not confused (1989:49–51).

11. The differences between sorcerers characterized as *somaw* and sorcerers characterized as *subagaw* are somewhat elusive. Cashion states that the two are categorically different: a *soma* is a sorcerer who does good, and a *subaga* is a sorcerer who does evil (1984:99, 152). McNaughton indicates that both terms denote "masters of secret things" (1988:50) and that sorcery is "not ethically qualified by the Bamana; it is good or bad depending on the character and actions of its possessor" (1979:9–10). In everyday usage, I believe that most Mande do differentiate between the two, although perhaps not along such rigidly ethical lines as Cashion claims: children are often scolded for exhibiting behaviors that leave them open to characterization as a *subaga,* such as staring at people. In addition, I never heard anyone publicly urge others to practice *subaya,* while on several occasions I heard songs performed which encouraged the audience to participate in *somaya.* Both categories, I feel, are sufficiently ambiguous to allow for a certain amount of ambivalence on the part of Mande individuals, who negotiate their valence in the particular contexts of their occurrence.

12. McNaughton (1979:13).

13. Ibid., 42–45. See Brett-Smith (1984) for a discussion of the same aesthetic principles in operation in the creation of mudcloth designs.

14. McNaughton (1988:15–16).

15. Zahan (1963:133).

16. Ibid., 136–41.

17. McNaughton (1979:44).

18. "Clarity and Obscurity in West African Sculpture," manuscript in preparation.

19. For a brief but interesting discussion of the interpretation of divining language and for references to other sources on the subject, see Kamissoko (1986).

20. "Jeliya sindi nana yèrèmajigin le kan. K'i yéré dògòya ka mògòlu bonya. Ka ban ka fò k'i ye se ko la, k'o tò yen. K'i yéré ké duguma mògò ye. . . . N'i bé jelikan fò, a nyama bè don mògò la, a b'a bonya" (The essence of griotness is in lowering oneself. To make yourself small to make others big. Despite your own power, to leave that aside. To make yourself a ground-level person. . . . When you speak griot language to someone, its *nyama* enters him and enlarges him). El Hadji Yamuru Diabaté, June 6, 1988, Bamako, Mali.

References

Astley, Thomas. 1745–47. *A New General Collection of Voyages and Travels.* 4 vols. London: Printed for T. Astley. Reprint, London: Frank Cass & Co., 1968.

Bird, Charles S., and Martha B. Kendall. 1980. "The Mande Hero: Text and Context." In *Explorations in African Systems of Thought,* ed. Ivan Karp and Charles Bird. Bloomington: Indiana University Press.

Bird, Charles S.; Mamadou Koita; and Bourama Soumaouro. 1974. *The Songs of Seydou Camara.* Vol. 1: *Kambili.* Bloomington: African Studies Center, Indiana University.

Brett-Smith, Sarah Catherine. 1984. "Speech Made Visible: The Irregular as a System of Meaning." *Empirical Studies of the Arts* 2 (2):127–47.

Camara, Sory. 1976. *Gens de la parole. Essai sur la condition et le rôle des griots dans la société Malinké.* Paris and the Hague: Mouton.

Cashion, Gerald A. 1984. "Hunters of the Mande: A Behavioral Code and Worldview Derived from the Study of Their Folklore." Ph.D. dissertation, Indiana University. Ann Arbor: University Microfilms International.

Cissé, Youssouf Tata. 1964. "Notes sur les sociétés de chasseurs Malinke." *Journal de la Société des Africanistes* 34 (2):175–226.

Henry, Joseph. 1910. *L'âme d'un peuple africain: Les Bambara, leur vie psychique, éthique, sociale, religieuse.* Munster: Aschendorff.

Irvine, Judith T. 1974. "Caste and Communication in a Wolof Village." Ph.D. dissertation, University of Pennsylvania. Ann Arbor: University Microfilms International.

Johnson, John William. 1986. *The Epic of Son-Jara: A West African Tradition.* Bloomington: Indiana University Press.

Kamissoko, Lansina E. 1986. "L'année 1986 vue par la géomancie." *Jamana* 6:23–24.

Kendall, Martha B. 1982. "Getting to Know You." In *Semantic Anthropology,* ed. David Parkin. London and New York: Academic Press.

Labouret, Henri. 1934. *Les Manding et Leur Langue.* Paris: Librarie Larose.

McNaughton, Patrick R. 1979. "Secret Sculptures of Komo: Art and Power in Bamana (Bambara) Initiation Associations." Working Papers in the Traditional Arts, 4. Philadelphia: Institute for the Study of Human Issues.

———. 1988. *The Mande Blacksmiths: Knowledge, Power, and Art in West Africa.* Bloomington: Indiana University Press.

———. "Clarity and Obscurity in West African Sculpture." Manuscript in preparation.

Monteil, Charles. 1924. *Les bambara du Segou et du Kaarta.* Paris: Larose. Reprint, Paris: G.-P. Maisonneuve et Larose, 1976, 1977.

Wright, Bonnie L. 1989. "The Power of Articulation." In *Creativity of Power: Cosmology and Action in African Societies,* ed. W. Arens and Ivan Karp. Washington and London: Smithsonian Institution Press.

Zahan, Dominique. 1963. *La Dialectique du verbe chez les Bambara.* Paris: Mouton & Co.

III

THE SEMANTICS OF *JUGU*
BLACKSMITHS, LORE, AND
"WHO'S BAD" IN MANDE

Patrick R. McNaughton

The Mande word *jugu* has been translated variously as "bad," "mean," "nasty," "vicious," and sometimes as "evil," "wicked," and "morally wrong."[1] Its counterpart is *nyi,* which means "good," "nice," "perfect," "balanced," "composed," and sometimes "correct" or "proper."[2] Mande peoples make judgments using these words all the time, yet the ideas of good and evil as Westerners conceive of them seem rarely to come up. And that brings me to the present topic.

I have been trying to understand the role of smiths in Mande lore. It attracted me, perhaps as an escape, because the roles of smiths in Mande life seem so contradictory, and difficult for us to understand. As I considered the blacksmiths' place in lore, however, I realized I was facing the same sorts of problems, and that before comprehension could ever set in I would have to deal with the issue of interpretation. I want to begin that here.[3]

A pattern runs through our literature on Mande culture that applies a Western sense of morality to ideas and practices that Mande individuals generally view in a different way. The literature quite frequently describes sorcery as evil, in addition to terrible and terrifying. It also describes blacksmiths and sculptors as repugnant outcasts whose incessant and uncontrollable acts of sorcery make them atrocious, as well as terrible and terrifying. In this vein both sorcery and those incurable sorcerers, the smiths, are interpreted by researchers as being despised, feared, and abominable.[4]

Another vein in the literature takes a surprisingly different tack. It focuses on Mande legend and myth, where it very frequently interprets the smiths as wonderful culture heroes, grand, noble actors on ancient or primordial stages whose magnanimous enterprises bring livelihood and well-being, indeed civilization itself, to humankind.[5]

Both these veins in the literature succumb to a common mistake. They indulge in overinterpretations, or underinterpretations, depending upon our perspective. They see too much of what is not there, while not seeing enough of what is. I have written elsewhere on our perceptions of blacksmiths and sorcery.[6] In this essay I want to focus on myth and lore, in the hope of showing that here too smiths should not be cast too strongly in our shadowy light of good and evil, because, while that may reveal a great deal about us, it teaches little about the Mande.

Blacksmiths are very prominently featured in the traditions called *ladaw* that Mande individuals recall among themselves informally or tell their children and researchers more formally. These traditions are what we might call vignettes, anecdotes and little bits of information that give people pleasure, but that can also be taken quite seriously. They move in and out of another kind of Mande oral lore where smiths appear with equal distinction. I mean the combinations of narrative "stories that explain things," *manaw,* and praise songs that glorify heroes, *fasaw,* which together constitute the oral epics performed by professional bards. A brief look at some of this lore will reveal how tempting it is to regard smiths as culture heroes.

There are numerous traditions throughout the Mande diaspora that consider the advent of ironworking, and almost invariably they present Mande smiths as the inventors or discoverers.[7] I collected a few from smiths themselves, who naturally did not mind promoting their own profession.[8] A famous smith of the Fané family living near Segou told me that the prophet David was the first blacksmith. He worked iron with his bare hands, but invented tools for the weaker smiths he knew would follow him.[9]

The senior smith of a town south of Bamako cited Noah as the world's first smith, and credited him with making all kinds of tools and even some human beings. His point had less to do with the Old Testament character than it did with a simile, because he punctuated it with his next breath by saying that the oldest human beings were smiths.[10] This sort of eclectic interaction with Near Eastern religions occurs often in Mande traditions of all kinds, partly because Islam has been present for so long in the Western Sudan and partly because people use Islam or Judaism metaphorically to make various kinds of points, some of which in fact express disguised anti-Muslim sentiments.

Thus another tradition, collected by the scholar Doumbia,[11] says that six sons of the prophet Abraham, all bearing Mande last names, accidentally discovered the means for smelting copper. Subsequent experimentation resulted in the discovery of gold, tin, and iron. Yet another tradition credits an ancestor named Noun Fahiri Fané with the invention of copper and iron smelting.[12] A myth collected by Dieterlen states that Mande smiths were the discoverers of iron, which they encountered by chance while digging underground in search of two missing women.[13]

Other traditions proclaim the ancient pedigree of Mande smiths. One collected by my research colleague Kalilou Tera states that Mande blacksmiths graced the earth before the great flood of the Old Testament.[14] Other myths state that the first human being created on the earth was a blacksmith named Domajiri, who became one of humankind's great benefactors.[15]

This mythical smith is said to have invented the Mande initiation associations, or at least the one named Ntomo. The traditions also say that Domajiri invented the Ntomo association's first carved wooden mask, and from one of the wood shavings he invented the lion. Ntomo association branches are divided into grades. The first is identified with lions, which the ethnographer Dominique Zahan notes are symbols of teaching, education, and wisdom.[16]

Lore collected by the Griaule group of anthropologists describes a recently created earth as in a state of severe drought, due to pollution. The ancestral smith descended to earth and struck a rock with his hammer, as a petition to the creator god for rain. Purifying and fertilizing water immediately poured forth, beginning the series of floods that formed the Niger River.[17]

In a tradition collected by Leo Frobenius, the original ancestor of Mande blacksmiths is cast in the role of co-creator.[18] No moon existed in these primordial times, and so the first smith climbed a great iron chain that connected the heavens and earth and manufactured that celestial orb out of iron. Thus, Frobenius reported, when the crescent moon appears, people say the smith is heating the iron, and when the full moon appears, they say his work has been completed. The tradition goes on to attribute the advent of death to this act of the very first smith. After he reached the sky, the chain upon which the smith ascended disappeared, creating a rupture between heaven and earth that resulted in the diffusion of mortality among humanity.

The anthropologist Viviana Pâques collected traditions that stated that the primordial blacksmith first descended to earth with iron and a hoe.[19] Ascending to the heavens again, the smith returned a second time in the form of a vulture bearing millet, a major crop in Mande farming. Ascending a third time, the smith descended yet again in the form of a sacred fish with rain, which Pâques says was the blood and sperm of heavenly sacrifice. Thus the advent of agriculture is facilitated by the acts of the world's first blacksmith.

The scholar Doumbia documented a tradition that credits an ancient Maninka smith with domesticating cattle for the Fula.[20] The smith invited a visiting Fula to sit with him in his cavern. While the Fula was there, a large cow arrived with a calf and, asking the smith to care for the calf, simply allowed herself to become the first domesticated animal.[21]

In some versions of the Sunjata epic, which addresses the founding of the Mali Empire, blacksmiths provide the young and crippled future hero with a staff of iron so powerful that as Sunjata pulls himself up on it, he miraculously regains the use of his legs and goes on to become a tremendous hunter, sorcerer, and leader.[22] Thus smiths begin the process of empowerment that leads to a great Mande empire.[23]

We could find many more traditions of creation and invention that cast blacksmiths in such leading roles. The question is how we should interpret them. These are grand and useful things smiths are said to have done, but does that make them heroes to the Mande, as authors such as Tegnaeus and members of Griaule's group suggest?

To begin to answer that question, let's return to the legendary smith named Domajiri, whom we encountered earlier. While the accomplishments we saw ascribed to him certainly seem positive, other traditions cast him in a more negative light. They say Domajiri acquired much wisdom from the hyena, an animal that symbolizes potent sorcery and all earthly knowledge. He also learned from the vulture, a creature of great sleuth and treachery, possessor of celestial knowledge and keen senses, which allow it to derive a livelihood from carrion.[24] Both creatures are viewed with a certain trepidation by most Mande, and their alleged intelligence is considered ominous and potentially dangerous. These things too are part of the legacy this first smith left the Mande.

Other traditions state that Domajiri sired Nunkulumba, who many Mande say was actually the first great ancestor of blacksmiths. Then came NunFajiri, and after him N'Fajigi, born of a direct line from Domajiri. N'Fajigi is remembered both in lore and in his own epic as having accidentally committed the scandalous act of incest with his mother.[25]

After polluting himself in this way, he traveled out of Mande lands to seek purification. He returned with monumental amounts of arcane knowledge, and shared it by introducing powerful occult associations such as the Komo. Many traditions claim that N'Fajigi introduced the concept of occult devices, in the form of *basiw,* secret things fabricated by using arcane knowledge and herbal lore.[26] These devices are the amulets that everyone wears and the larger objects that people suspend in their house rafters or hide in their family compounds, and while they are often designed to generate good in the work, they are also often designed to generate bad. They can cause illness, crop failure, infertility, and death. They can, in short, be unpleasant constructions.[27]

A major character in the Sunjata epic is the hero's great antagonist Sumanguru Kanté, the blacksmith sorcerer king of the Soso, a people said to have lived between the ancient predecessors of the Soninke and the Maninka. Some versions of the epic claim that the Kanté clan usurped power from another clan of smiths in the Sudan, and then tried to build a large empire from a small state.[28] Their power gelled and grew under Sumanguru, who is said to have killed the leaders of nine other states and marched into the Mande wearing pants, a shirt, and a hat all made from human skin.[29]

While he possessed great military might, Sumanguru's true power was his sorcery, and so he is said to have owned great numbers of potent occult devices and to have kept an enormous magical serpent in a secret palace chamber. To keep a griot whose praise singing he liked, Sumanguru severed the man's Achilles tendons,[30] which is not a friendly way to cement a relationship.

Let's pause again and consider this new turn in the oral traditions. Now we see quite plainly at what the moon myth collected by Frobenius may have hinted. There is no shortage of misery and carnage associated with these smiths. Should they now become antiheroes in our minds, monsters instead of benefactors?

Our quandary is only deepened when we learn more about Sumanguru. He is often praised in versions of the epic with the titles "The Mande King of Yesteryear," *Mande Mansa Duguré,* and "The First and Ancient King," *Mansa Folo Folo,*[31] and excerpts from one version of the Sunjata epic praise him further this way:

> The bird who stays in the sky
> Can claw the earth.
> If he lands,
> He will dig a well in the rock.
> Patriarch of Soso, good evening.
> Stranger in the morning,
> Native in the evening.
> Hero of Kukuba and Bantamba,
> Of Nyaninya and Kamasiga,
> Good evening, good evening.[32]

These lines are rather explicit. There is nothing meager about a being whose mere descent upon the earth bores deep holes into solid rock, or whose size allows him to stay in the sky but claw the ground. And there is nothing weak or undecided about a person who not only captures a place in a day, but also makes himself a native. That euphemism is especially potent for the Mande, who make a point of remembering which clans have been associated with a place for enough centuries to be considered, at last, natives.[33] In short, these lines contain respect aplenty for the Sorcerer King, which makes it hard for us to simply write him off as evil.

When Sumanguru was defeated, according to Niane's version of the epic, he disappeared into the rocks of the mountainous area near Kulikoro, north of Bamako.[34] A blacksmith priest maintains the spot today, and cares for a powerful occult object called *Nyanan*. Other versions of the epic describe Sumanguru as drying up at this spot and becoming the *Nyanan* power device,[35] and so the place is named "The Mountain of Sumanguru," or "The Nyanan Mountain of Kulikoro." It is now something of a pilgrimage spot, visited by large numbers of people every year. Anything one asks for there will be granted, for the promise of a sacrifice.[36] Many perfectly respectable Mande take advantage of the spot, which illustrates again the need to consider the nature of "bad" in this culture.

We could continue citing the deeds and attributes of smiths in Mande lore, but this would only amplify what has already been said. Often enough the smiths are clear benefactors, whose efforts enhance individuals, communities, and the whole society. As often they perpetrate heinous acts and develop devices that can be viewed with the same mixed feelings with which Westerners regard their own nuclear energy. This makes the blacksmiths very much like other categories of people among the Mande, such as hunters, or heroes (including Sunjata), or other groups of sorcerers, all of whom are quite capable of both wonderful and horrible activities.[37] Thus we still confront the question with which we began: How should we interpret these kinds of people?

If we cast our imaginations into the epic's legendary space as the Mande do, we recognize, as the Mande do, that Sumanguru perpetrates a great many atrocities. Yet many of his allies would not have considered that bad. For quite a while the legendary blacksmith Fakoli appears in the epic as just such an ally. The nephew of Sumanguru, Fakoli is portrayed as a brilliant fighter and strategist and one of the Sorcerer King's most valuable supporters. It is not until

Sumanguru steals his wife that Fakoli condemns his uncle and becomes a leading general in Sunjata's army.[38]

Sunjata, on the other hand, can be viewed as the Maninkas' savior, having delivered them from the oppressive domination of the Sorcerer King. Yet Sunjata commits his fair share of atrocities, as do several of his allies on his behalf. Indeed, one even sacrifices an unborn baby to give Sunjata enough power to save the day.[39] And so we are faced with what commonsense interpretation tells us all along: Good and bad among the Mande are wholly relativistic and contextual. They are easy enough to ascribe to people or acts from a single point of view, but add a broader perspective and things become ambiguous.

I think this is how we should view all the legendary and actual acts of smiths, as relatively good or bad depending on their context. When smiths harness their nasty airborne *koroté* poisons, it's bad if decent citizens are attacked, good if malevolent sorcerers are attacked, and bad again if you are related to the malevolent sorcerer, who may well be quite a good person in several social contexts.[40]

Very often in the West, at least when we are at our simplest, bad acts announce bad people.[41] This seems to be because we have as part of our Judeo-Christian legacy an ethos that allows the pronouncement of good and evil quite apart from context. The Mande, like many other cultures, do not do this. For them the interpretation of good and evil is much more dependent upon points of view, both individual and historical. Thus the person, people, or historical movement represented in the Sunjata epic as Sumanguru behaved horrendously in his time, but is now praised as "The King of Yesteryear."

Perhaps because of this relativism, or perhaps for some other reason entirely, issues of good and evil seem rarely to drive the Mande. A far greater driving force can be found in the entangled issues of means and power, which many scholars think hold the place that good and evil maintain in the West.

The Mande use two words, *nya* and *se,* to describe what we would call "means."[42] These words denote ability, the capacity to succeed, the wherewithal to make something work, being capable, and possessing the means. They are words about action, and most often that action focuses on the arcane knowledge used to master powerful forces.

Charles Bird and Martha Kendall have discussed these means quite elegantly, and I have touched upon them too.[43] Through Mande principles of nature and the organization of materials, formulas called *daliluw* are derived for creating things and generating the force the Mande call *nyama.*[44] I interpret this kind of action as a melding of what the West views as science and ritual. Possessing the means to undertake such acts, or having access to people who do, constitutes a tremendous source of power for Mande individuals, and that power, much more than any concern for good and bad, animates Mande social life.

This idea of the means to power brings us back to the smiths and their place in Mande lore. The idea certainly does not explain that place, or if it does we cannot prove it. But considering the idea while contemplating the presence of smiths and the appearance of their most prominent acts helps us to interpret the smiths in lore, while the lore helps us to perceive the smiths as the Mande perceive them. Let's spend a moment to do that.

Taking blacksmiths for granted would not be easy among the Mande. Every day most people use things smiths make to aid them in maintaining or enhancing the quality of their families' lives. Smiths' products surround them both at home and abroad, in utility and art.[45]

This plethora of visible objects is punctuated by the vision of smiths themselves, working at their forges. Even the smallest communities can have three or four practicing blacksmiths, and as a general rule you need but walk a hundred yards or so, near a town square or along a main thoroughfare, to reach a smith's forge. When you do not actually see them, very often you will hear their hammers ringing in high-pitched, even patterns. Near a forge you can hear the air that rushes through the bellows and the crackling of hot charcoals, and as you pass the forge entrance you might catch a glimpse of orange or nearly white-hot iron with sparks flying off it, as the smith removes it from the coals and works it on his anvil.

Often people do more than just pass by. They stop and watch, indulging in light conversation with the smith while waiting for a new knife or for a hoe blade to be repaired. But watching does not really show them what it is to be a smith. An adze moves effortlessly, relentlessly around a piece of wood. Chips fly off, and in short order a recognizable form emerges. With expert smiths it is uncanny how quickly and precisely that happens. The skill involved, however, is not at all evident. By design but as if by a miracle, an implement or mask grows by reduction into the world of tangible objects.[46]

A similar impression derives from watching iron forging. This time objects are established by amplification. Iron is hammered out, beaten into patterns of growth as axe and hoe blades spread out on an anvil, or as the arms and hands spring from the core of an iron shaft that will soon become a torso. More effort is apparent here, because after all, people sense how much those hammers weigh, and they know the implications of the sounds the hammers make. The effort does not suggest the technique, however, as people watch iron pounded forcefully and gradually into burgeoning objects and images.

Beneath the appearance of all this creating lie the technologies of carving and forging, which are part of the blacksmiths' "means." Mande smiths carve by conceiving the finished product before beginning, then roughing it out with a large adze, and finally working it into degrees of refinement with lighter adzes and a finishing knife. Much skill is required to make exact shapes, because, in contrast to using a saw, wood does not give way before an adze in predictable fashion, unless the artisan is expert. An expert, however, can carve the most subtle shapes and do so with dispatch and ease.

Iron forging is somewhat different. Similar types of control are employed, but smiths must know how hot to heat the metal they use and then direct its semiviscous flow beneath very careful hammer blows. Repeated submerging in hot charcoal causes carbon to be absorbed into the metal's surface, giving it the strength of steel, while the core remains more supple. Quenching hot iron in water is practiced occasionally, when the product is large, such as an axe blade, so that brittleness will not pose a problem.

In short, for forging and carving both, several technical factors come into play that are understood only by practitioners. These means, the secret skills, the subtleties of procedure and a sophisticated understanding of materials, are not more detectable to Mande eyes than are the kinds of expertise that constitute concert piano playing detectable to Western eyes.

Thus, in the sights and sounds and actual objects that frame people's lives, the Mande are constantly confronted with their smiths. Thus too this inescapable presence of blacksmiths does not produce an easy understanding of their technological acts, because exegesis does not follow observation. Nor is there a simple mystification of those acts, however, even though we might assume there would be. Instead the observed technology of smiths generates a modicum of understanding and mystification both, in a complex pattern of explanation that combines traditional systems of knowledge with awe in the Mande concept of means.

I doubt that we can ever truly know the historical processes by which the Mande joined smithing and sorcery. That union, however, is a social and spiritual reality for both the institution of blacksmiths and its individual practitioners, even though many of the latter possess little or no supernatural expertise.

Regardless of some smiths' ignorance, the means owned by the institution and embodied in its skilled members generate tremendous social, political, and spiritual power through paradigms of special, secret expertise that link both the smiths' work and the smiths' image to provocative levels of affecting energy.[47] Smiths can parlay that energy into social prominence, and evidently generation after generation of smiths has done it effectively enough to garner an awesome reputation for their profession.[48] Indeed, the innovative work of archaeologists Susan and Roderick McIntosh and historian George Brooks suggests positions of considerable commercial, social, and even political power for ancient smiths in Mande regions.[49]

The result of all this is that Mande blacksmiths do not easily slip into a background space where fellow citizens never really think about them. Rather, they occupy a conceptual foreground, as other citizens consider or create a lore for smiths that matches their perceived means and power. No wonder Mande bards sing songs with lines such as these:

> If we have to play the harp, . . .
> Let's play it for the smiths.
> Ah! the world belongs to the blacksmiths.[50]

Notes

I worked in Mali in 1972 and 1978, thanks to funding by the Social Science Research Council, Yale University, and the University of Wisconsin Milwaukee. The Malian government proved a most gracious host and facilitated my work at every turn. My research assistants, especially Checkna Singare, Kalilou Tera, and Seku Camara, were invaluable. The Bamana, Maninka, and Wasuluka blacksmiths with whom I worked, especially Sedu Traoré and Seydou Camara, were unendingly patient and equally informative. My Western colleagues Charles Bird and Martha Kendall made a great many suggestions and offered considerable support. In addition, the ideas in this essay have benefited from conversations with James Brink, Kate Ezra, Barbara Hoffman, and John Johnson, to say nothing of my colleague and spouse Diane Pelrine. I gratefully thank them all here.

1. Bailleul (1981:90); Bazin (1906:177); and Bird and Kanté (1977:15).

2. Bailleul (1981:167); Bazin (1906:468); and Bird and Kanté (1977:26).

3. I have followed the standardized orthography for Bamanakan as set forth in *Lexique Bambara* (1968), except in note 14, where the transcription is from Kalilou Tera.

4. McNaughton (1988a:7–9).

5. Tegnaeus (1950).

6. McNaughton (1988a:91–21, 40–64, 156–61).

7. This is interesting in part because lore in many African societies acknowledges the foreign introduction of iron technologies. See Cline (1937).

8. I am not using the oral information that follows as a folklorist would, by analyzing specific recorded and transcribed variants treated as texts. Most of my sources have not presented their materials in that way, but rather report what they claim to have heard over and over again.

9. Kodari Fané, personal communication, 1973.

10. Dramani Dunbiya, personal communication, 1973.

11. Doumbia (1936:334–39).

12. Ibid., 339–40.

13. Dieterlen (1951:113, 115–18).

14. Kalilou Tera, personal communication, 1978.

15. Ibid.; Zahan (1960:54–75, 74, 78, 306); and Imperato (1983:29–31, 34, 42–45, 47–49).

16. Zahan (1960:54–75, 74, 78, 306).

17. Dieterlen (1957:127, 130); Dieterlen (1951:1–33); and Dieterlen (1955, 1959).

18. Frobenius (1921–31, 7:18).

19. Pâques (1964:151–52).

20. Doumbia (1936:362).

21. Ibid. Traditions collected by the Griaule school of anthropology assert that the first Dogon smith also taught human beings how to domesticate animals (Griaule 1938:50). In fact, there are numerous similarities in the roles ascribed to mythical Mande and Dogon smiths, as reported by the Griaule group of anthropologists, but it seems to me prudent to postpone incorporating the Dogon materials until we understand better the historic and ethnic relationships between the Dogon and the Mande, and have addressed more thoroughly the problems contained in that group's data interpretations.

22. Niane (1965:19–21).

23. For a version in which the iron staff fails to heal Sunjata, see Johnson (1979, I:lines 1384–1489).

24. Tera, personal communication, 1978.

25. Tera, personal communication, 1977, 1978.

26. Ibid.; Traoré (1947:23–25).

27. McNaughton (1982).

28. Levtzion (1973:48–52).

29. Johnson (1986:lines 1813–1828); Niane (1965:38, 92 n. 47 and n. 49).

30. Johnson (1979, I:lines 2681–2685); and Johnson (1986:lines 1859–1974).

31. Johnson (1986:lines 1824–1825).

32. This version was provided by Kalilou Tera, July 1977. He noted that it was a favorite of Banzumana Sissoko, "The Blind Lion," one of Mali's most renowned bards. For

published versions of the epic, the reader may consult Johnson (1979 and 1986). See pp. 237–39 of the latter text for a thorough bibliography on the epic.

33. Mande communities claim to remember the number of generations that particular clans have been part of the population. Clans remain "strangers," at least theoretically, for surprisingly long times before they are considered to have become "native." Kalilou Tera, personal communication, June 1977 and June 1978.

34. Niane (1965:66–67).

35. Johnson (1979, II:lines 3474–3519); Johnson (1986:lines 2862–2887).

36. Magnan Fané, personal communication, 1972.

37. For additional information on heroes, see Bird and Kendall (1980); on hunters, see Cashion (1984) and Cissé (1964); and on sorcerers, see McNaughton (1988a) and Sidibé (1929).

38. Johnson (1986:lines 2746–2837).

39. Johnson (1979, I:lines 1513–1532, 1802–1880); and Johnson (1986:lines 1426–1478, 1725–1768).

40. These ideas about sorcery and sorcerers are paralleled by others in Mande thought regarding cooperation and aggression. See Bird and Kendall (1980:14–16, 21–24); Johnson (1986:9–12); and McNaughton (1988a:14, 64, 69, 156).

41. For a good example of more sophisticated Western thought, the reader might consider the character of Willie Stark in Robert Penn Warren's *All the King's Men* (1946).

42. Bailleul (1981:159–60, 180); Bazin (1906:446, 451–55, 517–18); Bird and Kanté (1977:28).

43. Bird and Kendall (1980:16–19) and McNaughton (1988a:152–56).

44. McNaughton (1979b; 1982).

45. McNaughton (1979a; 1988a:22–40, 58–64, 111–45).

46. Secular sculptures such as the masks carved for youth associations can be carved with clients watching. But sacred, secret sculptures are created in private, sometimes in the bush. See McNaughton (1979b:28).

47. McNaughton (1982; 1988a; 1988b).

48. A history of such entrepreneurship would be extremely difficult to write. Yet as the field of African art history, for example, progresses, the need to explain similarities in the context, conception, and form of artworks becomes increasingly acute. In my view a key will be the systematic historical investigation of blacksmith activities throughout western West Africa. Diane Pelrine and I have embarked upon such a study.

49. McIntosh and McIntosh (1983); Susan Keech McIntosh (forthcoming); and Brooks (1986). Academic dialogue about Mande blacksmiths generally asserts that these special professionals have no political power. I would argue that we should distinguish between concepts of power and authority, because, through their secret associations such as Komo, and in the dynamics of their endogamy and various monopolies, the smiths have accrued a great deal of political power, even though they cannot hold overt political offices.

50.   An bada ke julu fola . . .
                       An y'a fola numuma.
                       Ah! numu ta ye dunya di.
The transcription is from Kalilou Tera, who shared it with me in August 1977.

References

Bailleul, Père Charles. 1981. *Petit Dictionnaire. Bambara-Français, Français-Bambara.* Avebury, England: Avebury Publishing Co.

Bazin, Hippolyte. 1906. *Dictionnaire Bambara-Français.* Paris: Imprimerie nationale. Reprint, Ridgewood, N.J.: Gregg Press, 1965.

Bird, Charles S., and Mamadou Kanté. 1977. *Bambara-English, English-Bambara: Student Lexicon.* Bloomington: Linguistics Club, Indiana University.

Bird, Charles S., and Martha B. Kendall. 1980. "The Mande Hero: Text and Context." In *Explorations in African Systems of Thought,* ed. Ivan Karp and Charles Bird. Bloomington: Indiana University Press.

Brooks, George E. 1986. "A Provisional Historical Schema for Western Africa Based on Seven Climate Periods (ca. 9000 BC to the 19th Century)." *Cahiers d'Etudes Africaines* 26 (1–2):43–62.

Cashion, Gerald A. 1984. "Hunters of the Mande: A Behavioral Code and Worldview Derived from the Study of Their Folklore." Ph.D. dissertation, Indiana University. Ann Arbor: University Microfilms International.

Cissé, Youssouf Tata. 1964. "Notes sur les sociétés de chasseurs Malinke." *Journal de la Société des Africanistes* 34 (2):175–226.

Cline, Walter Buchanan. 1937. *Mining and Metallurgy in Negro Africa.* Menasha, Wis.: George Banta Publishing Co.

Dieterlen, Germaine. 1951. *Essai sur la religion Bambara.* Paris: Presses Universitaires de France.

———. 1955. "Mythe et organisation sociale au Soudan Français." *Journal de la Société des Africanistes* 25 (1–2):39–76.

———. 1957. "The Mande Creation Myth." *Africa: Journal of the International African Institute* 27 (2):124–38.

———. 1959. "Mythe et organisation sociale en Afrique Occidentale (suite)." *Journal de la Société des Africanistes* 29 (1):119–38.

Doumbia, Paul Emile Namoussa. 1936. "Etude du clan des forgerons." *Bulletin du Comité d'Etudes Historiques et Scientifiques de l'Afrique Occidentale Française* 19 (2–3):334–60.

Frobenius, Leo. 1921–31. *Atlas Africanus.* Munich: C. H. Beck.

Griaule, Marcel. 1938. *Masques Dogon.* Paris: Institut d'ethnologie.

Imperato, Pascal James. 1983. *Buffoons, Queens and Wooden Horsemen: The Dyo and Gouan Societies of the Bambara of Mali.* New York: Kilima House.

Johnson, John William. 1979. *The Epic of Sun-Jata According to Magan Sisoko.* 2 vols. Bloomington: Indiana University Folklore Group.

———. 1986. *The Epic of Son-Jara: A West African Tradition.* Bloomington: Indiana University Press.

Levtzion, Nehemia. 1973. *Ancient Ghana and Mali.* London: Methuen & Co., Ltd.

Lexique Bambara. 1968. Bamako: Ministère de l'Education Nationale.

McIntosh, Susan Keech. Forthcoming. "Blacksmiths and the Evolution of Political Complexity in Mande Society: An Hypothesis."

McIntosh, Susan Keech, and Roderick J. McIntosh. 1983. "Current Directions in West African Prehistory." *Annual Review of Anthropology* 12:215–58.

———. 1988. "From Stone to Metal: New Perspectives on the Later Prehistory of West Africa." *Journal of World Prehistory* 2 (1):89–133.

McNaughton, Patrick R. 1979a. "Bamana Blacksmiths." *African Arts* 12 (2):65–71, 92.

———. 1979b. "Secret Sculptures of Komo: Art and Power in Bamana (Bambara) Initiation Associations." Working Papers in the Traditional Arts, 4. Philadelphia: Institute for the Study of Human Issues.

———. 1982. "Language, Art, Secrecy and Power: The Semantics of Dalilu." *Anthropological Linguistics* 24 (4):487–505.

———. 1988a. *The Mande Blacksmiths: Knowledge, Power and Art in West Africa.* Bloomington: Indiana University Press.

———. 1988b. "*Nyamakalaw:* The Mande Bards and Blacksmiths." *Word and Image* (July):271–88.

Niane, Djibril Tamsir. 1965. *Sundiata: An Epic of Old Mali.* Translated by G. D. Pickett. London: Longman.

Pâques, Viviana. 1964. "Les bouffons sacrés de Bougouni." *Journal de la Société des Africanistes* 34 (1):63–110.

Sidibé, Mamby. 1929. "Les sorciers mangeurs d'hommes au Soudan Français." *Outre-Mer* 1:22–31.

Tegnaeus, Harry. 1950. *Le heros civilisateur.* Stockholm: Studia Ethnographica Upsaliensia.

Traoré, Dominique. 1947. "Makanta Djigui, fondateur de la magie soudanaise." *Notes Africaines* 34:23–25.

Warren, Robert Penn. 1946. *All The King's Men.* New York: Harcourt Brace. New ed., New York: Harcourt Brace Jovanovich, Publishers, 1974.

Zahan, Dominique. 1960. *Sociétés d'initiation Bambara: Le N'Domo, Le Kore.* Paris: Mouton.

II

Retracing Steps in Search of Social History

ERRATA

Page	For	Read
64, line 31	nyamakala	nyàmakala
64, line 43	garanké	garanke
65, line 1	jeli	jèli
65, line 1	jelibele	cèlibèlè
68, line 2	çàgibèlè	çàgíbèlè
68, line 23	garaasa	gáráasà
68, line 33	garanké	garanke
68, line 34	garanké	garanke
68, line 34	garankéjo	garankejo
68, line 34	garankéɓe	garankeɓe
69, line 14	yèè	yèè
69, line 30	fine	fina
69, line 31	fine	fina
70, line 3	gáwulo	gáwulɔ
70, line 4	gáẃlá	gáẃlà
70, line 10	gáwulo	gáwulɔ
70, line 13	gáwulo	gáwulɔ
70, line 38	maabo	máabɔ
71, line 24	garanké	garanke
71, line 28	garanké	garanke
71, line 29	garanké	garanke
71, line 33	garanké	gáranke
71, line 35	gaari	gáari
71, line 42	garanké(jo)	garanke(jo)
71, line 42	garankéɓe	garankeɓe
71, line 43	garanké	garanke
72, line 4	sakkeɓe	sakkeeɓe
72, line 8	sakkeɓe	sakkeeɓe
72, line 16	garaasa	gáráasà
72, line 18	garkaasajo	garkasaajo
72, line 31	ga(w)ulo	gá(w)ulɔ
72, line 45	maabo	máabɔ
73, line 1	maabo	máabɔ
73, line 3	maabo	máabɔ
73, line 4	maabo	máabɔ
73, line 22	funé	fùnɛ
73, line 35	Manding *gesere*	Manding *gèsere*
73, line 35	gawulo	gáwulɔ
73, line 37	bammbaaɗo	bammbaaɗo
73, line 37	ẃammbaaɓe	wammbaaɓe
73, line 38	nyàmakala	nyamakala
73, line 38	gáẃlá	gáẃlà
73, line 41	Manding *garanké*	Manding *gáranke*
73, line 41	Soninké *garanké*	Soninke *garanke*
73, line 42	sakkeɓe	sakkeeɓe
74, line 1	garanké(jo)	garanke(jo)
74, line 1	garanké(be)	garankeɓe
74, line 1	garkassaɓe	garkasaaɓe
74, line 1	cèlèbèlè	cèlìbèlè
74, line 2	garaasa	gáráasà
74, line 4	gùlèbèlè*	gùlèbèlè
74, line 4	kùle	kule
74, line 5	maabo	máabɔ
74, line 6	ràbbkat	ràbbkat*
74, line 19	jèséré	jèsérè
74, line 20	gáwulo	gáwulɔ
74, line 22	Manding *maabo*	Manding *máabɔ*
74, line 27	Soninké *garanké*	Soninke *garanke*
74, line 27	Manding *garanké*	Manding *gáranke*
74, line 27	(Fulani) *garanké(jo)*	Fulani *garanke(jo)*
74, line 28	garankéɓe	garankeɓe
74, line 35	sakkeɓe	sakkeeɓe
75, line 13	lawɓe	lawbe
75, line 21	garanké	gáranke
75, line 23	gàranké	gáranke
75, line 32	nyàmakala	nyamakala
76, line 14	gáwulo	gáwulɔ
76, line 20	garanké(jo)	garanke(jo)
76, line 20	garankéɓe	garankeɓe
76, line 23	gáwulo	gáwulɔ
76, line 30	nyàmakala	nyamakala
76, line 31	nyàmakala	nyaamakala
76, line 35	gáwulo	gáwulɔ
76, line 41	máabo	máabɔ
77, line 5	nyàmakala	nyamakala
77, line 38	gáranké	gáranke
78, line 1	nyàmakala	nyamakala
78, line 7	nùmu	numu
78, line 12	ù-yèliba	ù-yèlibá
78, line 13	ù-yèliba	ù-yèlibá
78, line 14	garanké	gáranke
78, line 29	horon	hórɔn
80, line 19	gáranké	gáranke
82, line 32	gàwulo	gáwulɔ
82, line 32	gàwulɛ	gáwulɛ
82, line 32	màabo	máabɔ
82, line 53	jãli	jãlì
83, line 3	*el-Fattāsh*	*al-Fattāsh*
83, line 8	mabi	mābī
83, line 9	maabuube	maabuuɓe
83, line 19	*es-Sūdān*	*al-Sūdān*
83, line 41	malinke	malinké
84, line 24	*el-Fattāsh*	*al-Fattāsh*

IV

LINGUISTIC EVIDENCE FOR THE HISTORY OF WEST AFRICAN "CASTES"

Tal Tamari

"Castes"—endogamous artisan and musician groups—are found among some fifteen West African peoples. They are characteristic of the Manding speakers (Bamana, Malinke, Dyula, Khassonke, and others), Soninke, Wolof, Tukulor, Dogon, Senufo, and Songhay. They are also found among most Fulani, Tuareg, and Moorish populations, in some Dan, Minianka, Temne, and Serer areas, and in eastern Ghana.

Caste people form one of three basic social categories, the other two being the "noble" or "free," who usually constitute a large majority of the population, and the slaves—who are few among stateless peoples, but may have formed up to half the total population in certain Bamana and Soninke regions in the nineteenth century.[1] Caste people never form more than a small minority of the population: about 5 percent among the Manding and Soninke, up to 10 percent among the Wolof.[2]

Nobles are associated with political power and the main subsistence activities—farming or, in the case of the Fulani, herding. Caste people are associated with crafts and music, though they may farm, herd, and trade as well. They may not hold political office, but in other respects they have the same rights as nobles. Metalwork, bardship, leatherwork, woodcarving, and weaving are the most frequent caste professions. Bard and blacksmith women are often potters. Most craft castes have some musical activities as well. In general, nobles may not engage in the above crafts, nor perform most kinds of music. There is significant ethnic and regional variation as to the precise social, religious, and occupational roles attributed to caste people.

Elsewhere, I have argued that these widely distributed, diverse institutions developed from at most three centers, located among the Manding, Soninke, and/or Wolof.[3] This point of view is based on several different kinds of evidence, including written records, which suggest dates for the formation of certain castes;

oral traditions, which help refine chronology and suggest an interpretation of Manding caste formation; and analysis of division of labor, which in several cases shows that castes are a recent or intrusive phenomenon. The single most important kind of evidence, however, comes from language. Examination of designations for caste people used in various West African languages reveals a high rate of word borrowing, and thus, that the institutions of different peoples developed in contact with each other. Furthermore, in some cases the very meanings of words—their etymology and reference range—show that they initially applied to persons with origins outside the local community.

Two major types of linguistic study have been applied to elucidating the African past: identification of language families and the study of loanwords. The first helps evaluate early relationships among African peoples, assess the time depth of certain cultural units, and trace migrations. Knowledge of the early history of the Bantu- and Nilotic-speaking peoples has been largely dependent on this approach. A far more modest, but nevertheless significant, contribution comes from the study of loanwords. These have been used to reconstruct the diffusion of plants, animals, and other objects, population movements (through toponyms), and trade patterns. The analysis presented here differs from most other attempts to study word borrowing in that it is concerned primarily with concepts and institutions, and borrowing among African languages. Most other analyses have concentrated on relationships with Near Eastern, European, and other exotic languages,[4] and material culture.

Identification of loanwords involves studying both the forms of words and their meanings. Study of the meaning of a word includes both (a) study of usage, i.e., of the various contexts in which it is employed, and of its significations as inferred from those contexts; and (b) study of its etymology. In languages with a long written tradition, it is possible to discern changes in the meaning of a word as it evolves slowly over time, through comparison of texts dating from different periods. In languages with an exclusively oral tradition, one is limited to studying contemporary usage or transcriptions of relatively recent usage. Several West African languages present an intermediate case. Many West African populations are characterized by restricted literacy, i.e., a situation in which an elite has access to the written word and produces texts concerning a relatively limited range of topics. While not all the texts thus produced were in the authors' first languages, they almost invariably include some citations from those languages. In addition, foreign travelers, geographers, and historians were recording West African words by the eleventh century A.D. Thus, we benefit from chronological depth concerning the usage of a few, but by no means most, West African words. For languages for which there is no significant early documentation, comparison of usage among geographically dispersed populations speaking related languages, or different varieties of the same language, provides important indications as to the connotations and original meaning range of a word. Study of contemporaneous usage over a large geographical area can also add considerably to the understanding of languages for which there is early written documentation.

Etymological analysis must begin with "popular etymologies" (the origins and primary meaning of a word as interpreted by native speakers); the pertinence and plausibility of a popular etymology can then be evaluated, and alternative etymologies proposed, in the light of a word's formal characteristics. Contrary to a widespread misconception, "popular etymology" is by no means a pejorative term; it simply refers to interpretations of the origin of a word current in a culture whose members use that word. All popular etymologies are in some sense "true," because they provide information about cultural attitudes, but some also illuminate the processes involved in the formation, introduction, or generalization of the usage of the word. This is particularly true of morphologically complex languages (such as the Semitic ones) in which many processes of word formation are transparent to speakers. It is least true of languages such as English, formed as a result of creolization, i.e., the encounter of several unrelated or distantly related languages, accompanied by major changes in pronunciation; speakers of such languages have little intuition concerning the sources of the words they use, unless they have engaged in specialized grammatical or philological study. Morphologically simple languages (such as Mancing) perhaps present an intermediate case, since some processes of word formation (for example, that of compound words) are understood by most speakers, but it is all too easy to reinterpret foreign words or to advance several alternative etymologies for the same word. Needless to say, members of cultures both with highly developed written traditions and with primarily oral traditions provide etymologies for many words. Such etymologies may be integrated into poetic and mythic discourse, but they can also be advanced spontaneously in the course of ordinary conversation.

The form of words includes phonology, morphology, tones, and syllabic structure. Each language has a finite set of distinctive sounds (phonemes), syllabic patterns (nature of vowel and consonant sequences, number of syllables per word), and—for most African as well as many Asian languages—tonal patterns. Tones may have either morphological or lexical values (or both), or may be governed or modified by syntactical roles, but, in any given language, manifest a limited set of characteristic patterns and possibilities. Unusual formal features often indicate that a word is borrowed. But many loanwords present no unusual formal features, whether because their form initially coincided with that of words of the borrowers' language, or because they were integrated into that language (modified to fit its characteristic patterns). In these cases, occurrence in other languages of similar-sounding words with related meanings is often an indication of borrowing. In general, evaluation on the basis of formal linguistic criteria of the plausibility of etymologies provided by native speakers is a first step in determining whether a word has been borrowed. However, it must be followed by attempts to identify alternative etymologies, and to evaluate whether the formal characteristics of a word are at all compatible with an origin in the language in which it is used.

Linguistic analysis may provide several kinds of information about loanwords, and, indirectly, about cultural and social change: incidence of outside influence on the development of a given concept or item; identity of the peoples or languages in contact; direction of influence; and—more rarely—the approximate time at which a foreign word first came into use. Sometimes, one can be certain that a word is not native to a language, yet be unable to determine its ultimate source. In other cases, one can determine the successive changes a word went through as it passed through several languages. In general, the degree of integration of a word correlates with the length of time that has elapsed since it was first borrowed. However, some words are integrated almost immediately, whereas others may retain unusual characteristics indefinitely. The speed with which a word is integrated may in turn reflect perceptions of the persons or objects designated—the extent to which they are accepted as basic to the culture or compatible with its mores. In cases where we have proposed approximate dates for borrowing, our arguments are based on the geographical distribution of words or the presence of traits characteristic of languages with which they are no longer in contact. Finally, analysis of the meanings of terms having a common origin may point to changes in the characteristics of the referents or their environments (social, cultural, or natural).

In general, the proportion of loanwords in a language or in a given thematic area probably does not fully reflect the significance of cross-cultural influence. The meaning of an existing, native term may be extended or modified to apply to an adopted item or institution, or a new word may be invented. However, these factors are partially offset by two others: a word may be assigned a meaning very different from the one it had in the donor language, or it may replace an existing word. In these cases, word borrowing indicates cultural influence, but does not prove change in the specific item, concept, or institution in question. Thus, there were probably more cases of acceptance of endogamous specialists from other linguistic communities than ones in which they conserved a designation similar to their original one, but not all instances of word borrowing reflect outside influence in the development of an institution.

In an earlier chapter, Charles Bird, Martha Kendall, and Kalilou Tera draw out the various meanings that native speakers attribute to *nyamakala,* the Manding term for "caste people," and show how these meanings are manipulated in social life. This chapter, too, includes extensive discussion of native interpretations of designations for caste specialists. Here they are studied as clues to the development of Western Sudanic civilization. Every native interpretation is culturally significant, but as we have seen, only some illuminate early phases in the development of a word.

The linguistic data presented here provide additional documentation for several recurrent themes of this volume. In particular, they show the importance of occupational change and intercultural contacts in the development of endogamous specialized groups. These processes are evidenced, largely on the basis of ethnographic data and oral traditions, in other chapters. Thus, the data support Barbara Frank's views on *garanké* (Soninke leatherworker) migrations; Robert Launay's stress on Manding-Senufo contacts in the development of specialized endogamous groups in northern Ivory Coast; Launay's contentions that the *jeli* and *jelibele* of Ivory Coast, who specialize primarily or exclusively in leatherworking, developed from bard-leatherworkers. The hypothesis that the term *fúne* is of Arabic origin lends support to David Conrad's view that this group, now associated with a variety of occupations, was initially associated with Islam.

Linguistic Analysis[5]

Collective designations. Only four West African languages have collective designations for caste people. These four languages—Manding, Soninke, Wolof, and Fulfulde (Fulani and Tukulor)—distinguish a total of five terms: Manding *nyàmakala,* Soninke *ñaxamala,* Wolof *ñeeño,* Fulfulde (Fulani and Tukulor) *nyeenyo/nyeenyɓe,* and Fulfulde (Tukulor only) *nyaamakala.* There are strong reasons for believing that these five terms have developed from only two etymons: Manding *nyàmakala* and Wolof *ñeeño.*

Similarity of form provides a first indication of borrowing: Wolof *ñeeño* and Fulfulde singular *nyeenyo,* Manding *nyàmakala* and Tukulor *nyaamakala* have virtually identical pronunciations. The Manding and Soninke terms are distinguished primarily by syllable order: the second syllable of the Manding word corresponds to the third syllable of the Soninke one.

The genetic relationship of Manding and Soninke makes it difficult to determine the direction of borrowing. However, the fact that *nyàmakala* can receive a plausible etymology in Manding, whereas *ñaxamala* cannot receive one in Soninke, indicates that the terms are probably of Manding origin.

Several different etymologies of the Manding term *nyàmakala* have been proposed. According to the three most frequently given popular etymologies (each of which is acceptable from a purely linguistic point of view), *nyàmakala* is a compound word formed from two nouns. According to the commonest etymology, the first element in this compound word is *nyàma,* "life force," and the second element, *kàla,* means "receptacle" or "handle." The next most frequent etymology assigns the same meaning to *kàla,* but claims that the first element is *nyàman,* "garbage" or "detritus." According to a third, relatively rare etymology, *nyàma* means "life force," but *kàla* means "antidote," that which is capable of countering the effects of something else. As the Manding believe that most beings have *nyàma* and that the *nyàmakala* bards, blacksmiths, and other endogamous specialists are most able to manipulate this force, the first etymology seems most likely. The term *nyàman* seems ill suited to express the respect in which blacksmiths and some bards are held.[6] A fourth etymology, which attempts to derive *nyàmakala* from *nyàmankolon,* "good for nothing," does not seem convincing, even from a purely linguistic point of view. The term *nyàmankolon* is itself composed from *nyàman,* "garbage," and *kólon,* "old, worn out, empty," each of which is frequently used both as an independent word and as an element in compound words; it seems arbitrary to suppose that each has been shortened and modified to produce *nyàmakala.*

According to the popular etymology most frequently cited by the Soninke, *ñaxamala* is also a compound word, whose first element is a noun meaning "feast," while its second element, *mala,* is a verb meaning "to cling, to be obnoxiously present"; caste people are thus defined as ones who eagerly attend feasts, where they may claim gifts. To me, this etymology is not convincing, as it emphasizes a purely negative aspect of caste persons' behavior, and furthermore, one that is not equally true of all castes. According to another etymology, the first element comes from Manding *ŋaara* (sometimes pronounced *naara?*), meaning "talented person, one who has great powers." The second element would be the Moorish word *mʿāllem,* "scholar, learned person."[7] This etymology seems implausible on linguistic grounds, as it does not correspond to any paradigm of Soninke word formation. Furthermore, why juxtapose two words that share a common reference to spiritual or religious power, but are drawn from culturally distinct universes, to define a single social category? Another set of considerations makes this etymology seem positively bizarre. Manding speakers may use the term *ŋaara,* "talented one," to express respect for caste persons. The Moorish word *mʿāllem,* "scholar," also means "blacksmith" (see below). Thus, Soninke *ñaxamala* would be formed from a Manding generic designation (or quasi-designation) for caste people and a Moorish term for blacksmith!

The Fulfulde word *nyeenyo/nyeenyɓe* could have been formed through nominalization (by addition of class suffixes) of the Fulfulde verbal root *nyeeny,* "to be skillful, resourceful." However, it seems more likely that the Fulfulde term is borrowed from Wolof, given that another Fulfulde term appears to be borrowed from Wolof and strong sociological evidence that many Fulani and Tukulor caste people are of Wolof ethnic background. The singular form of the Fulani word corresponds exactly to that of the Wolof word. *-ɓe* is the plural suffix of the class of persons in Fulfulde.

Nyaamakala—a term the Tukulor use less frequently than *nyeenyo*—clearly comes from Manding *nyàmakala.* According to Henri Gaden and Yaya Wane, *nyaamakala* derives from the Tukulor phrase *nyaamde kala,* "to eat from any trough," i.e., to act in an extremely undignified manner.[8] *Nyaamde* is the verb "to eat" and *kala* is borrowed from Arabic *kull,* "each, every." However, *nyaamde* has not been transformed into *nyaama* in other Tukulor words or expressions, and it is very unlikely that a standard syllabic structure (as in *nyaamde*) would have been transformed into a rare one, found only in loanwords. Again, a highly pejorative meaning does not seem adequate to express the status of blacksmiths and higher-ranking bards.

The Senufo term *fē-ʈɛ̄ɔ̀/fē-ʈēébèlè* is not a collective designation for caste people. It is a compound word formed from the terms *fēlīgē,* "peculiarity," and *çē̄ɔ̄,* "human," and thus means "strange, peculiar people." As such, it applies to all those who do not obtain their living primarily from farming, including traders and noncaste artisans.[9] The fact that the Senufo do not have a term which allows them to collectively distinguish the endogamous artisans from other categories of the population is a linguistic indication that caste-based hierarchical relationships are weakly developed.

Smiths. I have identified eighteen terms for smiths, in use in ten different languages. As many as twelve terms may be native to the languages in which they are used. Manding, Dogon, Hassaniya (Moorish Arabic), and Tuareg each have two terms, while Senufo has five terms. The Manding terms *nùmu* and *càgi* apply to two distinct groups. *Nùmu* is the general term for metalsmith, current throughout the Manding world, but some populations of northern Ivory Coast distinguish between *nùmuw,* who are primarily blacksmiths, and *càgi,* who are primarily jewelers, working in copper and gold. Similarly, Dogon *irunɛ/irũ* and *jémenɛ/jemõ* are not synonymous. The term *fɔ̰nɔ̃ɔ̀/fɔ̃nɔ̰bèlè* applies to smiths who work largely or exclusively in iron. The other four terms apply to four distinct groups, each of which works a different combination of the lighter metals. The Moorish terms *ṣunnāᶜ* and *mᶜāllem/mᶜāllemīn* apply to one and the same group, but each term emphasizes a different aspect of its role. The northern Tuareg call their blacksmiths *enad/enaden,* whereas the Tuareg of the desert-edge zones call theirs *gargassa.*

The linguistic properties of twelve of these terms (Manding *nùmu, càgi,* Soninke *tage,* Wolof *tëgg,* Fulfulde *baylo, bayillo/wayilɓe, wayluɓe,* Senufo *fɔ̰nɔ̃ɔ̀/fɔ̃nɔ̰bèlè,* Minianka *tũtũ,* Dogon *irunɛ/irũ,* Songhay *zèm,* Moorish *ṣunnāᶜ* and *mᶜāllem/mᶜāllemīn,* Tuareg *enad/enaden*) are compatible with an origin in the language in which they are used. Three terms—Soninke *tage,* Wolof *tëgg,* Minianka *tũtũ*—may be onomatopoeic, suggesting the sound of hammering. The Fulfulde (Fulani and Tukulor) term derives from a verbal root, *way/wade,* meaning "to have a certain aspect or form." It is thus related to the verb *wailude,* "to form, to shape," and connotes modification of the appearance of the metal as a result of heating and hammering by the smith. According to Geneviève Calame-Griaule, the Dogon word *irunɛ/irũ* is probably derived, by dissimilation, from **inunɛ,* "man of iron." The word **inunɛ* itself is probably derived from *inu,* "iron," and *inɛ,* "person, human being."[10] The Moorish word *ṣunnāᶜ* is derived from the classical Arabic *ṣāniᶜ,* pl. *ṣunnāᶜ,* "artisan, worker," and indeed, the Moorish blacksmith engages in several crafts in addition to metalwork. *Mᶜāllem/mᶜāllemīn* derives from classical Arabic *muᶜallim,* "teacher, guide," and thus expresses the belief that blacksmiths have great knowledge and powers. The word *ḥaddād,* the most usual designation for blacksmith in classical Arabic and in most modern Arabic dialects, is not used by the Moors. The northern Tuareg designation for the blacksmith, *enad/enaden,* literally means "the other." It thus aptly expresses the blacksmith's eccentric social position, and allows noble Tuareg—who fear his occult powers—to avoid naming him.

Manding *càgi* may be ultimately borrowed from Arabic, but there are no indications that it was borrowed from another West African language. Classical Arabic *ṣāʔigh,* pl. *ṣuyyāgh, ṣuwwāgh,* means "jeweler"; except in initial position, the glottal stop is replaced by a semivowel in most North African dialects. *Càgi* could have been obtained from either *ṣāʔigh* or *sayigh* through dropping of the glottal stop (which has no equivalent in most Manding dialects) or the weak middle syllable, followed by restitution of the standard syllabic structure CVCV and metathesis (with transfer of the second vowel to the second syllable).

The remaining six terms show signs of borrowing from other African languages. Senufo *çàgibèlè*, "jeweler," is clearly derived from Manding *càgi*. The tonal scheme (low-high) is unusual for Senufo nouns but corresponds to the definite form of the Manding word. *-bèlè* is the plural suffix for the class of persons in Senufo. The tonal schemes of *sūmbóróbèlè*, "blacksmith," and *cēdúmbèlè*, smith specializing in the lighter metals, indicate that these terms are either compound words or borrowed.[11] The breach of vocalic harmony in *cēdúmbèlè* also indicates that the term is either compound or borrowed, while the breach of consonantal harmony (the presence of *d* in an intervocalic position) shows that it is compound. The term *cēdúmbèlè* may be derived from the Manding words or phrase *cè dún* (people [object]—to eat), expressing the belief that members of this group are sorcerers, and thus consume human souls. The term *cēdúmbèlè* would thus literally mean: persons who eat other persons' (souls).

The Dogon term *jémɛnɛ/jemõ* seems to be borrowed from Songhay *zèm*, often pronounced [*jeːmi*]. Calame-Griaule specifically rejects the Dogon popular etymology, according to which *jémɛnɛ/jemõ* derives from *jemɛ́*, "the man with the leather bag."[12] Thus, the Dogon designate by a borrowed term those whom they believe to be the descendants of their first and only true blacksmiths! This is strong evidence that the Dogon did not independently evolve caste institutions, but rather acquired them from (or modeled them upon) those of other, neighboring peoples.

Tuareg *gargassa*, "blacksmith, artisan," has obvious affinities to Songhay *garaasa*, "leatherworker," and Fulfulde (Fulani) *garkasaajo/garkasaaɓe*. The fact that the term *gargassa* is used only by the southern Tuareg suggests that it may be borrowed from Songhay. It would have undergone a semantic shift, however, being applied no longer to leatherworkers in particular, but to all caste artisans. Among the Tuareg, artisans form a single endogamous group. They may perform any kind of craft work, but have a monopoly on metalwork only—as it is the only craft never exercised by nobles. Fulani *garkasaajo* must be borrowed from Tuareg *gargassa*, as it is identical to it in form (except for the addition of the singular and plural suffixes, *-jo* and *-ɓe*), and its phonological as well as syllabic structures are unusual for Fulfulde. All three terms may be indirectly related to Manding and Soninke *garanké*, "leatherworker," which is the source of Fulani *garanké*, *garankéjo/garankéɓe*.

Reviewing these data, one may make the following additional observations: (1) All West African languages (except, perhaps, Tuareg) have at least one native term for blacksmith or metalsmith. This implies either that West African peoples became familiar with ironworking before they acquired castes, or that they evolved blacksmith castes independently of one another. (Nonlinguistic data show that the first interpretation is the right one.) (2) Most Senufo terms for metalsmiths are nonnative. This is strong evidence that endogamous artisan groups developed among the Senufo essentially under outside influence.

Bards. I have noted twenty-three terms for bards, in use in nine different languages. This reflects the fact that there are a large number of distinct bard groups, whose social status and musical repertoires vary greatly. Wolof, Dogon,

Dan, Moorish, and Tuareg each have one term for bard, but Manding has six, Soninke three, Fulfulde five, and Songhay four. The twenty-three terms derive from at most nine etymons.

Manding *jèli* is the source of Soninke *jaare*, Dan masc. *yæmi*, fem. *yæḍɛ*, pl. *yæbo*, and Fulfulde *jeeli(ɓe)*. *Jèli* is a typical Manding word—syllabic structure CVCV—whose first attested usage goes back to the mid-fourteenth century, when Ibn Battuta reported that it was the designation for "poets" at the Malian court.[13] *Jèli* cannot be linked with certainty to any other Manding radical, though popular etymologies link it with both *jòli*, "blood," and *Joliba*, the river Niger.[14] Soninke *jaare* derives from *jèli* through reinterpretation of the Manding term; l → r; *-re* is a Soninke suffix indicating occupation. *Jaa-* has no meaning in Soninke, but the structure of the Manding term was transformed to bring it into line with a Soninke pattern of word formation. The Dan term is derived from the southern Manding form *yɛ̀ɛ̀*. *-mi*, *-ḍɛ*, and *-bo* are, respectively, the Dan masculine singular, feminine singular, and plural suffixes. The Fulani term *jeeli(ɓe)* is identical to the Manding one, except for the longer first vowel and occasional addition of the class suffix *-ɓe*. The fact that this term may be used without class suffixes is itself an important indication that it may be borrowed.

Fùne, finɔna, fine, fina, and similar words occur only in the Manding languages. They may be considered dialectal variants of a single term, and refer to "talkers" who do not accompany themselves on any musical instrument. In Muslim societies, they specialize in poems praising the Prophet, saints, or marabouts, but in pagan societies, making insults is often considered their main professional activity! *Fùne* may be derived from the Arabic *fannī*, "technician, artist." The interdialectal instability of the vowels is an indication that it is formed from a non-Manding word; so is the tension, in some variants, between lax and tense vowels (rare in Manding, which tends toward vowel harmony). But whether or not this hypothesis is correct, the term must be an old one; it is found throughout the Manding-speaking world, from Senegal to Sierra Leone to Ivory Coast, in Mali and Guinea. The Kuranko term *musa kule fine* is either a compound word or, more likely, a phrase, in which *fine* appears as one of the elements; *kule* is probably the name of another caste, or possibly of a servile group.[15]

The syllabic and phonological structures of the Soninke term *gesere* are typical of that language, but no etymology has been suggested by Soninke speakers or others. Manding *gesere* and Songhay *jèsérè* (both initial consonants are pronounced [g]) are nearly identical in form. The fact that Manding and Songhay *gesere* often speak Soninke among themselves is an indication that borrowing is from Soninke rather than in another direction.

Songhay *zémmùkóẁ*, "bard," is probably derived from the verb *zémmù*, "to praise"; *-kóẁ* is a suffix of agency. However, it could also be related to Manding *jàmu*, "clan name, honorable name." Songhay *zàmu*, meaning a poem sung by a woman in honor of her husband and his clan, is said, by the Songhay themselves, to come from Manding *jàmu*.[16] However, as the tones of *jàmu* and the first constituent of *zémmùkóẁ* are not the same, the similarity is best explained by a common heritage of the two languages, or as due to ancient rather than recent borrowing.

The Wolof word *géwél* is the source of Manding *gáwulo, gáwule,* Fulfulde *gawlo/awluɓe,* Songhay *gáwlá,* Moorish masc. *īggīw/īggāwen,* fem. *tīggiwīt/tīggāwāten,* and Tuareg *ag'gou/ag'gouten.* The Fulfulde singular term is virtually identical to the Wolof one: it has merely added a singular class suffix. The alternation of initial consonants, g → ', is a characteristic pattern in the formation of Fulfulde plural nouns. The fact that most Tukulor *awluɓe* have Wolof clan names is further evidence that the group and its name are of Wolof origin.

Manding *gáwulo, gáwule* and Songhay *gáwlá* are borrowed from Fulfulde rather than directly from Wolof. Their forms are closer to the Fulfulde than to the Wolof word. Diphthongs are rare in Manding and nearly always indicate borrowing; the w in *gáwulo, gáwule* is a purely orthographic device, introduced to bring the written form of this and similar words into line with that of the vast majority of Manding words, constituted by a succession of open syllables.

The Moorish Arabic term for bard, masc. *īggīw/īggāwen,* fem. *tīggiwīt/tīggāwāten,* is borrowed from Wolof *géwél.* It conserves the same core (gVw), and differs from it only by the addition of prefixes and suffixes and syllabic restructuring. That the feminine form prefixes *t-* indicates that the term came to Moorish Arabic through Tuareg. Both Semitic and Berber suffix *-t* to indicate feminine gender, but only Berber prefixes *t-* to nouns. This implies that the word, and the group it designates, appeared in Mauritania when Tuareg was still the dominant language there, i.e., no later than the seventeenth century.[17]

Southern Tuareg *ag'gou/ag'gouten* seems to be identical to the Moorish Arabic masculine forms; indeed, it must have been this, or a similar, Tuareg term that gave rise to the forms now used in Moorish Arabic. Feminine forms for "bard" have not been recorded among the southern Tuareg, presumably because no sufficiently complete dictionary exists. The northern Tuareg have no endogamous specialized bards.

The Fulfulde terms *maabo/maabuuɓe* and *bammbaado/wammbaaɓe* appear to be native to that language. *Bammbaado* derives from a verb meaning "to carry (a baby) on one's back." This etymology seems acceptable from a sociological as well as a linguistic point of view. It aptly expresses the relationship of dependence between members of this category of bards and the noble families that are their patrons. *Maabo* is the designation of bards specialized in epic poetry, and seems to have given rise to the verbal form *maabuude,* "to praise." Epic poetry is always accompanied by praise of the listeners' ancestors.

Manding (specifically Bamana) *maabo* and Songhay *maabe* derive from Fulfulde *maabo.* Long vowels are rare in Bamana, and the term can receive no etymology in either Manding or Songhay.

The Dogon term *gɔ̀:gɔ̀:nɛ* derives from the verb *gɔ̀:,* "dance; beat (heart)." It applies to all singers and dancers, and some masks, not just to endogamous bards. This is an indication that, although they receive considerable attention in myth, endogamous bards are a relatively recent addition or are marginal to Dogon society. An existing Dogon word has been applied to an intrusive or newly emergent social category: no Dogon word unambiguously designates this, and only this, category.

According to a linguistically acceptable popular etymology, Soninke *kusatage* is a compound word, formed from Kusa, the name of a Soninke population, and *tage,* the Soninke word for blacksmith. *Kusatage* would thus literally mean "blacksmiths of the Kusa Soninke."[18] Castes are often associated with several occupations, and, as I have shown elsewhere, they sometimes modify their professional emphases, or change occupations completely.

The Bamana of Segou use the word *surasegi* to refer to some woodcarvers who also have musical activities. This word derives from a non-Bamana designation for woodcarvers (*sakke*), to which another, unidentified term, *sura,* has been prefixed.[19]

The term *nyamakala,* applied by some Fulani populations to certain Manding-speaking bards, is obviously derived from the Manding collective designation for caste people, *nyàmakala.* We have already seen that the syllabic and phonological characteristics of these words are incompatible with those of Fulfulde.

Leatherworkers. I have identified ten terms for leatherworkers, used in eight different languages. Fulfulde (Fulani and Tukulor) has four designations for leatherworkers; each of the other languages studied—Manding, Soninke, Senufo, Dogon, Songhay, and Temne—has one. These ten terms correspond to up to eight different etymons, but six terms at most were originated by the speech communities that use them.

The term *garanké,* used by both the Manding and the Soninke, is compatible with the phonological and syllabic structures of both of these languages. However, the patterns CVNCV and CV(V)CVNCV are far more frequent in Soninke than in Manding. Examination of other Soninke words that exhibit these syllabic structures suggests that *garanké* may be a primitive term. Yet according to Soninke popular etymologies, *garanké* could be derived from the verbal-nominal root *gara,* "to dye; dyeing," or from the place name Gara by addition of the locative suffix *-nke.* It should be pointed out, however, that no place called Gara can now be identified.

Manding popular etymologies, which attempt to derive *garanké* from Garan (place name) + *-kɛ* (masculine suffix), Garan (place name) + *-ka* (suffix of derivation, meaning "person from"), or *gaari* ("thread") + *ké,* "to make," account less well for its form. Furthermore, the first etymology does not correspond to any known pattern of word formation: *-kɛ* is not normally suffixed to place names (as distinct from ethnic ones) to form words. However, if Manding borrowed from Soninke, it must have done so quite a long time ago. The term is known to all or almost all Manding populations, implying that it came into use sometime before the definitive breakup of the Mali Empire, i.e., before 1600.[20]

Fulani *garanké(jo)/garankéɓe* is obviously derived from Manding and Soninke *garanké.* The syllabic structure of this term is clearly incompatible with that of Fulfulde; *-jo* and *-ɓe* are Fulfulde class prefixes.

The Tukulor term *galabbo/alauɓe* is formed from Galam, the name of an area of Senegal with a strong Soninke majority. Thus, it literally means "people from Galam." Therefore, the very meaning of the term implies that it designates non-Fulfulde-speaking strangers.

Fulfulde *sakke(jo)/sakkeɓe,* "leatherworker," is clearly related to Soninke *sakke,* "woodworker." However, it is not possible, at this stage, to indicate direction of borrowing, since these words are not entirely characteristic of either language. Possibly, each language has borrowed and reborrowed from the other, slightly modifying the terms each time. Fulfulde *sakkeɓe* speak Soninke, while *sakke* associated with the Soninke speak Fulfulde!

Senufo *cèlìbèlè,* "leatherworker," comes from Manding *jèli,* "bard." The tonal scheme of the Senufo word corresponds to that of the Manding one; *-bèlè* is the Senufo plural suffix for the class of persons. It is understandable that a Manding word meaning "bard" has come to signify "leatherworker" in Senufo, since leatherworking is a secondary activity of many Manding bards. Furthermore, some groups called *cèlìbèlè* by the Senufo call themselves *jèli,* pl. *jèloni.*

We have already evoked the relationships among Songhay *garaasa,* "leatherworker," Tuareg *gargassa,* "artisan-blacksmith," and Fulani *garkaasajo/garkasaaɓe,* "leatherworker" (see above).

Wolof *uudé, wuudé* and Dogon *jàũ* do not seem to be related to any other terms.

Woodcarvers. I have identified eight designations for woodcarvers, used in six languages. They are derived from only three etymons—Fulfulde *labbo/lawɓe, sakke* (possibly Fulfulde or Soninke), and Manding *kùle.* Terms derived from *labbo/lawɓe* are used by many peoples without developed caste institutions to designate Fulfulde-speaking woodcarvers.

Fulfulde *labbo/lawɓe,* Wolof *lawbe,* and Manding *la(w)ube* are obviously related. According to a linguistically acceptable popular etymology, the Fulfulde term is derived (by nominalization) from the verb *law, lawde,* "to hollow out" (a recipient, a piece of wood). The Wolof and Manding terms are virtually identical in pronunciation to the Fulfulde plural. Diphthongs are not found in Bamana, except in loanwords. We have encountered the diphthong *a(w)u* once before, in *gá(w)ulo, gá(w)ulɛ,* "bard," another term borrowed by Bamana from Fulfulde.

The Manding term *kùle* has given rise to Senufo *gùlèbèlè; -bèlè* is simply the Senufo plural suffix. The tonal scheme of the Senufo word corresponds to that of the Manding one. The Minianka call the endogamous woodcarvers that work for them *kule,* simply conserving the Bamana term.

As we have seen, the Soninke word for woodcarver, *sakke,* is related to a Fulfulde word for leatherworker. Soninke *sakke* is also the source of two other terms for woodcarver—*segi* and *surasegi*—used only by the Bamana of the Segou area. The fact that *segi* and *surasegi* speak Soninke, as well as oral traditions, proves that *segi* comes from *sakke,* and is not of independent origin. The pronunciation of *sakke* has been modified, omitting the doubled consonant and bringing it into line with the standard Bamana syllabic structure.

Weavers. I know only three terms for endogamous, professional weavers: Fulfulde *maabo/maabuuɓe,* Wolof *ràbbkat,* and Manding *maabo.* The Fulani and Tukulor *maabo/maabuuɓe* and Manding *maabo* are really musician-weavers: in most Fulfulde-speaking areas, bardship is thought of as the primary activity, and weaving as a secondary one, but in some Manding areas, *maabo* are thought of primarily as weavers. We have already seen that Manding *maabo* comes from Fulfulde *maabo/maabuuɓe*. The Wolof term *ràbbkat* is formed from the verb *ràbb*, "to weave," by addition of a suffix of agency. Thus, consideration of the vocabulary for caste weavers adds only one item to the set of etymons from which the vocabulary for caste people is formed.

Potters. In most West African societies, pottery is made by blacksmith and/or bard women. However, the Tukulor distinguish one group, the *buurnaajo/buurnaaɓe*, whose women are potters and whose men have no specialized activity. Two etymologies have been proposed for this term. According to Henri Gaden, it comes from the Wolof expression *dom-u-dambur*, "person dependent on the *bur*," *bur* being the title of a Wolof ruler. The Tukulor term thus would have conserved the element *bur*.[21] According to Yaya Wane, on the other hand, *buurnaajo/buurnaaɓe* derives from the verb *buurnoyaade*, "to fire pottery."[22] Although the second etymology accounts more fully for the form of the term, the first etymology may be the right one: *buurnaaɓe* have Wolof clan names, indicating that they may indeed be of Wolof origin.[23]

Summary of Linguistic Data

Results of the above analysis are summarized in the following lists. Only two of the Manding terms, *càgi* (smith/jeweler) and *funé* (a type of bard), bear indications that they might have been borrowed from Arabic. One Soninke term, *kusatage* (a type of bard), appears to be derived from *tage*, also a Soninke term, but one originally used for blacksmiths. Terms which are likely to be native to the languages in which they are used are marked with an asterisk(*).

Collective designations: Manding *nyàmakala**, Soninke *ñaxamala*, Wolof *ñeeño**, Fulfulde (Fulani and Tukulor) *nyeenyo/nyeenyɓe*, Fulfulde (Tukulor only) *nyaamakala*.

Smiths: Manding *nùmu**, *càgi*, Soninke *tage**, Wolof *tëgg**, Fulfulde (Fulani and Tukulor) *baylo, bayillo/wayilɓe**, *wayluɓe*, Senufo *fɔ̀nɔ̀ɔ̀/fɔ̀nɔ̀bèlè**, *sūmbóróbèlè, càgíbèlè, cédúmbèlè, kpḛ̀g̰bèlè*, Minianka *tūtū**, Dogon *irunɛ/irū**, *jémɛnɛ/jemɔ̃*, Songhay *zèm**, Moorish *ṣunnā^c**, *m^callem/m^callemīn**, northern Tuareg *enad/enaden**, southern Tuareg *gargassa*.

Bards: Manding, *jèli**, *fùnɛ, gesere, gáwulo, gáwulɛ, surasegi*, Soninke *gesere**, *jaare, kusatage*, Dan *yæmi, yædɛ/yæbo*, Wolof *géwél**, Fulfulde (Fulani and Tukulor) *maabo/maabuuɓe**, *bammbaaɗo/ẁammbaaɓe**, *gawlo/awluɓe*, Fulani *jeeli, nyàmakala*, Dogon *gɔ̀:gɔ̀:nɛ/gɔgɔ:ū̃**, Songhay *zémmùkóẁ**, *jèsérè, gáẁlá, maabe*, Moorish (masc.) *īggīw/īggāwen*, (fem.) *tīggiwīt/tīggāwāten*, Tuareg *ag'goul/ag'gouten*.

Leatherworkers: Manding *garanké*, Soninke *garanké**, Wolof *uudé, wuudé**, Fulfulde (Fulani and Tukulor) *sakke/sakkeɓe*, Tukulor *galabbo/alauɓe*, Fulani *garanké(jo)/garankébe, garkasaajo/garkassaɓe,* Senufo *cèlèbèlè,* Dogon *jàũ*,* Songhay *garaasa.*

Woodcarvers: Manding *kùle*, lawube, segi,* Soninke *sakke,* Wolof *lawbe,* Fulfulde (Fulani and Tukulor) *labbo/lawɓe*,* Senufo *gùlèbèlè*,* Minianka *kùle.*

Weavers: Manding *maabo,* Fulfulde (Fulani and Tukulor) *maabo/maabuuɓe*,* Wolof *ràbbkat.*

Potters: Fulfulde (Tukulor) *buurnaajo/buurnaaɓe.*

We have also identified the following clusters of related terms. The fact that similar-sounding words, with connected though not always identical meanings, occur in unrelated or distantly related languages proves that borrowing has taken place, even in those cases where it is not possible to propose etymologies or determine the direction of borrowing.

1. Manding *nyàmakala,* Soninke *ñaxamala,* Fulfulde (Tukulor) *nyaamakala:* collective designations for caste people; Fulfulde (Fulani) *nyàmakala* bards.

2. Wolof *ñeeño,* Fulfulde (Fulani and Tukulor) *nyeenyo/nyeenyɓe:* collective designations for caste people.

3. Manding *jèli,* Soninke *jaare,* Dan *yœmi, yœɖe/yœbo,* Fulfulde (Fulani) *jeeli(ɓe):* bards; Senufo *cèlìbèlè:* leatherworkers.

4. Soninke *gesere,* Manding *gèsere,* Songhay *jèséré:* bards.

5. Wolof *géwél,* Fulfulde (Fulani and Tukulor) *gawlo/awluɓe,* Manding *gáwulo, gáwule,* Songhay *gáwlà,* Moorish (masc.) *īggīw/īggāwen,* (fem.) *tīggiwīt/tīggāwāten,* southern Tuareg *ag'gou/ag'gouten:* bards.

6. Fulfulde (Fulani and Tukulor) *maabo/maabuuɓe,* Manding *maabo,* Songhay *maabe:* musician-weavers.

7. Manding *càgi,* Senufo *càgíbèlè:* smiths.

8. Soninke *tage:* smith; *kusatage:* bard.

9. Songhay *zèm,* Dogon *jémenɛ/jɛmõ:* blacksmiths.

10. Soninke *garanké,* Manding *gáranké,* Fulfulde (Fulani) *garanké(jo)/garankéɓe:* leatherworkers.

11. Songhay *gáráasà:* leatherworker, southern Tuareg *gargassa:* artisan—primarily blacksmith, Fulfulde (Fulani) *garkasaajo/garkasaaɓe:* artisan—primarily leatherworker.

12. Fulfulde (Fulani and Tukulor) *labbo/lawɓe,* Manding *lawube,* Wolof *lawbe:* woodcarvers.

13. Soninke *sakke:* woodcarvers, Fulfulde (Fulani and Tukulor) *sakke/sakkeɓe:* leatherworkers, Manding *segi:* woodcarvers, *surasegi:* bard-woodcarvers.

14. Manding *kùle,* Senufo *gùlèbèlè,* Minianka *kule:* woodcarvers.

Thus, we have identified a total of sixty-seven terms, formed from thirty-three etymons. If we exclude words for smiths, for which native forms exist in almost all languages, we are left with a total of forty-nine terms, formed from at most twenty etymons. Yet, we have probably not identified all cases of word borrowing. It may be impossible to identify loans made long ago, whether from other African languages or from Arabic, as these may by now be completely integrated. Furthermore, the fact that a term is native to a language is not necessarily an indication that the group or institution it designates is also native. Some languages, for example Dogon, may extend the meaning of an existing term, or forge a new one from a native root; though if the term refers to both caste and noncaste persons, this in itself constitutes an indication that the institution is either nonnative or emergent.

Historical Interpretation

The elevated proportion of loanwords among the terms used for designating castes brings out the importance of cultural exchange in the formation of this vocabulary, and thus, in the development of the caste institutions themselves. The significance of linguistic data for historical reconstruction becomes further apparent when one considers the vocabulary of each language or ethnic group.

Five out of six Wolof designations for caste people are formed from Wolof radicals. The only non-Wolof term (*lawɓe*) applies to woodcarvers, who, though they supply essential craft goods, are not integrated into Wolof society.

Three out of seven Soninke terms are likely to be of foreign origin. Two of these terms (*jaare, sakke*) apply to marginal groups, but the fact that the Soninke collective designation for caste people (*ñaxamala*) is probably of foreign origin indicates that there has been significant outside influence on the development of Soninke concepts pertaining to caste.

I have identified thirteen terms for caste people in use among Manding-speaking peoples. Of these, five (*nyàmakala, nùmu, jèli, fùnɛ, gàranké*) are common throughout the Manding world, while eight have restricted distribution. Four of the basic terms (all except *gàranké*) and two of the regionally restricted terms (*kùle, càgi*) are of Manding origin or, at any rate, are not borrowed from other African languages. The six other regionally restricted terms all apply to marginal groups; five of them are known only in the Segou area. Thus, linguistic data imply that the Manding have ancient and well-developed caste institutions, but that in one area (Segou) they have increased in complexity as a result of foreign contacts.[24]

Six out of ten terms used by the Tukulor seem to be of foreign origin or otherwise denote the foreign origin of those to whom they apply; the same is true of seven of the eleven terms used by the Fulani. Only two of the foreign-derived terms (*jeeli, nyàmakala*) apply to marginal groups. In particular, collective designations for caste people, all terms for leatherworkers, and the designation of one major bard group (*gawlo/awluɓe*) seem to be of foreign origin. This indicates that outside influences have had a major structuring effect on the development of Fulani and Tukulor caste institutions.

At least five (probably six) of the seven Senufo designations for endogamous artisans are of foreign origin. This indicates that Senufo caste institutions developed essentially under foreign influence.

At least three of six Songhay terms are borrowed: the three loanwords refer to three different categories of bards. This indicates significant outside influence on the development of Songhay endogamous musician groups.

One of four Dogon designations for caste people (*jémɛnɛ/jɛmõ*) is borrowed, while another term (*gɔ̀:gɔ̀:nɛ/gɔgɔ:ũ,* "bard") applies to nonendogamous as well as endogamous musicians. This implies that though the Dogon have highly elaborate myths about caste people, their caste institutions are neither particularly ancient nor well developed.

The Moorish and Tuareg term for "bard," (masc.) *ĭggĭw/ĭggāwen,* (fem.) *tĭggiwĭt/tĭggāwāten,* is borrowed, as is the southern Tuareg term for blacksmith. This indicates that the Moorish and Tuareg endogamous musician category developed under foreign influence, and that outside factors may have had a considerable impact on the development of the endogamous blacksmith groups as well.

Examination of vocabulary also allows one to trace some lines of influence. Fulfulde speakers are major "recipients" of foreign caste institutions, but this did not prevent them from bringing some caste institutions to other peoples. Thus, Songhay *gáwlà* and *maabe* bards and Bamana *gáwulo/gáwulɛ* bards have come to these peoples through the Fulani. The Fulani are also the source of all or nearly all West African woodcarvers—in particular those designated by terms derived from *labbo/lawɓe.* The Songhay, who are major "recipients" of caste institutions, have "contributed" one caste group, the *jémɛnɛ/jɛmõ* blacksmiths, to the Dogon. The Soninke have contributed caste leatherworkers to the Fulani and Tukulor (*garanké(jo)/garankéɓe, galabbo/alauɓe*) and probably to the Manding. They have also given bards (*gesere*) to the Manding and Songhay. The Wolof have provided bards to the Fulani, Tukulor, Manding, Songhay, Moors, and Tuareg (*gawlo/awluɓe, gáwulo, gáwulɛ, gáwlà, ĭggĭw/ĭggāwen, ag'goul/ag'gouten*). They have also contributed a group of potters to the Tukulor (*buurnaajo/buurnaaɓe*) and influenced Fulfulde speakers' perceptions of caste people (collective designation *nyeenyo/nyeenyɓe*). The Manding language is the source of nearly all the designations for caste people in use among the Senufo, Dan, and Minianka, two terms in use among the Soninke, including the collective designation for caste people (*ñaxamala*). Manding is also the source of two Fulani designations for bards (*jeeli, nyàmakala*) and a Tukulor collective designation for caste people (*nyàmakala*).

It is important to note that a language or ethnic group may serve as a "transmitter" for a specialist group it did not itself originate. Thus, the Fulfulde term *gawlo/awluɓe* is borrowed from Wolof, but the closely related terms Songhay *gáwlà* and Bamana *gáwulo, gáwulɛ* came into these languages through Fulfulde rather than Wolof.

Vocabulary analysis brings out another important process in the development of caste institutions: castes have often modified their vocational emphases, or even changed occupations entirely. These modifications are facilitated by change in ethnic affiliation, but may also take place without it. Thus, Senufo *cèlìbèlè,* leatherworkers, developed from Manding *jèli,* bards; Manding *máabo,* for whom weaving is a primary activity, developed from Fulfulde (Fulani and Tukulor) bards, for whom musicianship is primary. Fulfulde-speaking Soninke-associated *sakke* woodcarvers are somehow related to Soninke-speaking, Fulani-associated leatherworkers. Manding *surasegi* musician-woodcarvers developed from *sakke* and *segi* woodcarvers. Tuareg *gargassa* artisans, who are primarily ironworkers, have links to Fulani *garkasaajo/garkasaaɓe,* who are primarily leatherworkers. The Soninke *kusatage* bards developed from the Soninke *tage* smiths. These, and another case of semantic shift (Manding *nyàmakala,* collective designation for caste people, → Fulani *nyàmakala,* a bard group), can be read off easily from the vocabulary clusters summarized in the previous section.

I have shown that the Manding terms *fùnɛ,* "talker, religious singer," and *càgi,* "smith-jeweler," could have been borrowed from Arabic. If so, they are by no means the only words borrowed by West African languages from Arabic to describe West African institutions. The Manding and Soninke terms *hɔ́rɔn, hoore,* "freemen," "nobles," are both borrowed from Arabic, while some Manding-speaking populations use the term *kàbila,* which comes from the Arabic word for "tribe," in addition to *jàmu,* to signify "clan."[25]

It is appropriate that the term *fùnɛ* be formed from an Arabic word, since its original meaning seems to have been "person specialized in the recitation of Muslim religious poetry." An Arabic origin for the term *càgi* could mean that some of imperial Mali's jewelers were of North African or Middle Eastern background, or were regarded as working in foreign styles; the jewelry (but not ironworking) techniques and styles of many West African peoples closely resemble Oriental ones. However, these instances of linguistic borrowing do not imply that, in general, caste institutions developed as a result of North African or Middle Eastern influence. Key terms such as *nyàmakala* not only show no signs of Arabic linguistic influence, but they do not correspond to Arab, Muslim, North African, or Middle Eastern concepts. Rather, the presence of a few Arabic loanwords in the Manding vocabulary pertaining to caste reflects the overwhelming importance of Afro-Arab contacts in the savannah and desert-edge zones in the Middle Ages.[26] One should not assume, either, that terms of Arabic origin, such as *hɔ́rɔn* and *càgi,* necessarily replaced native African terms; as I have shown elsewhere, Manding caste institutions began to take shape during one of the peak periods of Afro-Arab contact.[27] The Moors and Tuareg designate blacksmiths by terms different from those used by other Arabic- and Berber-speaking populations; this implies that their ideas about ironworking have been modified through contact with Sudanese peoples.

In general, we must rely on other kinds of evidence (written records and oral traditions) to help us establish the chronological framework of caste history. Occasionally, however, linguistic data provide clues as to the date of appearance of a caste. Thus, we have seen that Soninke *ñaxamala* is probably borrowed from Manding, while Manding *gáranké* is probably borrowed from Soninke. As these terms and the corresponding social categories are found among all or virtually all the far-flung Soninke and Manding populations, this implies that borrowing occurred several hundred years ago (before 1600 in the case of the Manding). The fact that the feminine form of the Moorish Arabic term for bard carries the prefix *t-* implies that this term came into usage in the region corresponding to Mauritania at a time when the Berber-speaking community was still dominant there (i.e., well before 1700). In contrast, the completely nonintegrated character of Fulani *jeeli* and *nyàmakala* implies that these are recently borrowed terms (or alternatively, that they are perceived as foreign words, describing foreign institutions).[28]

So far, we have considered data pertaining to peoples whose caste systems are well developed and/or for which we have relatively full lexical data. However, several of the terms studied above are also found among other West African peoples, underlining the importance of cultural interchange and of castes' geographical mobility. The term *nùmu* (obviously related to Manding *nùmu*) is found as a designation for the endogamous blacksmith groups associated with several Voltaic-speaking peoples of eastern Ghana.[29] The Susu of Guinea have endogamous bards called *yèliba;* this term is obviously related to *jèliba* or *yèliba* (lit.: great bard), the usual designation for bards in some Manding languages. The Temne of Sierra Leone have *ù-yèliba* endogamous musicians. They state that *ù-yèliba* is borrowed from Manding or Susu; *u-* is a Temne class prefix. The Temne term *ù-káránké* is obviously related to Manding *gáránké* (the Temne have few or no direct contacts with Soninke speakers), but it is not certain that the Temne *ù-káránké* are endogamous.[30] The Serer term *kawul,* "bard," is obviously related to Wolof *géwél.*[31] The Joola, like so many Senegalese peoples, are familiar with the *lawbe* woodworkers.[32] The Mossi of Burkina Faso call Fulfulde-speaking woodworkers *seta,* pl. *setba*—a term that may well be related to Soninke *sakke,* which has the same meaning.[33]

The conceptual implications of *nyàmakala* have been amply discussed in this volume. Analysis of the etymologies (popular or not) of other terms also helps us get closer to the meaning of "caste" for West African societies. The term *galabbolalaube,* being formed from the name of a foreign land, implies that the people whom it designates are not considered full members of society. Perhaps all caste people are, to some degree, contrasted to the majority population, not only as different in status and behavior, but as outsiders looking in: endogamous specialists living among the Senufo may be contrasted to Senufo (Senari), while ones associated with the Bamana may be opposed not only to "nobles" (*horon*) but to Bamana (members of the ethnic group). The etymology of *cédúmbèlè* proposed above implies that members of this group are expert sorcerers; and, possibly, given that the constituents of the term are Manding rather than Senufo, that the *cédúmbèlè* themselves have promoted this image, perhaps in order to coax the Senufo farmers into granting them maximal privileges. On the other hand, the Fulfulde designation for one group of bards—*bammbaadolwammbaabe,* "carried on the back like a baby"—implies a caring though unequal relationship. I have rejected the popular etymologies of Soninke *ñaxamala,* Fulfulde *nyeenyolnyeenybe* and *nyaamakala* as linguistically unsound and too pejorative to be historically true. Nevertheless, they express a frequent attitude toward caste people: as perpetual receivers, they are inferior to nobles, the eternal gift-givers.

Examination of the vocabulary pertaining to the endogamous (or quasi-endogamous) specialists goes a long way toward modifying a monolithic vision of caste. First, it shows that the number and attributions of castes vary considerably among different languages, dialects, and even speech groups—corresponding to different ethnic groups, populations, and localities. Second, it shows that castes were dynamic entities: the presence of numerous loanwords indicates that they were mobile in space, while numerous cases of semantic shift (cccurring with or without word borrowing) demonstrate that the characteristics of castes evolved over time. Even the meaning of "caste" does not remain constant throughout West Africa. Manifestly, a people who has a collective term for the endogamous specialists does not perceive them in quite the same way as one that merely has names for individual professions, or characterizes the specialists as "nonmajority" or "nonfarmers." These semantic differences correlate to differences in social organization, as the essay by Robert Launay makes clear.

These findings have wider implications for the interpretation of West African history and cultures. Above all, they support the view that one may indeed speak of a Western Sudanese civilization, embracing the Western Sahara, Sahel, savannah, and indeed part of the forest zones. This civilization is characterized by significant variations, but also by significant commonalities—including the presence of endogamous artisan and musician groups. Some of these resemblances are due to common origins, but in the case of the endogamous specialists, they are primarily due to continued cultural interchange. This interchange has led peoples as initially diverse as the Moors and Tuareg, West Atlantic speakers, Voltaic speakers, Mande, and Songhay to share the basic outlines of their social structure. The case of the Moors is particularly telling, since they reached the southern Sahara only in the fifteenth century. Northern Moors, who have fewer contacts with Sudanese peoples, do not always have endogamous specialists. The contrasts between northern and southern (Sahelian and Sudanese) Tuareg are equally telling. Not only the vocabulary for endogamous specialists but also that for designating serfs differs among these groups. The verbal and conceptual categories of a once Mediterranean people have given way to Sudanese ones. To speak of ethnic permeability is an understatement. Peoples as widely separated as the Wolof and Songhay share elements of a common vocabulary and culture.

Furthermore, these findings support the view that Western Sudanese civilization should be seen as part of a Eurasian ecumene. Examination of the vocabulary of social categories shows cases of borrowing from Arabic only (*hɔrɔn, càgi, fùnɛ*), but a comprehensive examination of words of Arabic origin in West African languages would reveal that many ultimately come from Latin, Greek, or Aramaic. The nature of the items borrowed shows that the medieval Arab impact in West Africa must have been a very deep one, affecting abstract concepts, technology, and urban professions as well as religion and spirituality.

Conclusion

We have identified sixty-seven designations for caste persons, in use in eleven languages; they are formed from at most thirty-three etymons. The forty-nine designations for nonsmiths come from only twenty etymons. The five collective designations for caste people, twenty-three terms for bards, ten terms for leatherworkers, eight terms for woodcarvers, and three terms for weavers come from only two, nine, eight, three, and two etymons respectively. One of the etymons for each of the categories of bards, leatherworkers, woodcarvers, and weavers is also included among the etymons of another vocational group.

Four out of five basic Manding terms, three out of four basic Soninke terms, and all five basic Wolof terms are native to those languages (or at least are not borrowed from other West African languages). In contrast, several key Fulfulde (Fulani and Tukulor) terms (including the collective designations for caste people, all terms for leatherworkers, and one term for bard) are borrowed, as are most Senufo designations, three out of four Songhay terms for bards, the Moorish and Tuareg terms for bards, and the few Minianka and Dan terms. These data suggest that Manding, Soninke, and Wolof caste institutions may have each evolved independently, but that caste institutions of other peoples were heavily dependent on those of other groups for their development. No caste system, however, followed a completely independent path; the Wolof rely on the services of Fulfulde-speaking woodcarvers, the Bamana of Segou have provided a home to several Fulani- and Tukulor-associated castes, and the Soninke have accepted both Manding bards and Fulani woodcarvers. Most interesting, the Soninke collective designation for caste people (*ñaxamala*) seems to be borrowed from Manding, while the Manding designation for leatherworkers (*gáranké*) seems to be borrowed from Soninke. The Manding and Soninke played a critical role in the development of West African caste systems, contributing vocabulary to the Fulani, Tukulor, Senufo, Minianka, Dan, Susu, Temne, and several other peoples. Northern Mande (Manding and Soninke) appear as "donors," whereas southern Mande (Dan) appear as "recipients."

Throughout this essay, we have restricted ourselves, insofar as possible, to examination of the vocabulary for designating caste people. However, in a few cases, we have had to refer to social or sociolinguistic facts—for example, clan names, the language(s) caste people speak—to determine the validity of alternative etymologies or the direction of borrowing. Several of our interpretations could have received additional support from oral traditions or analysis of social structure. Thus, language history can draw on social history. But a reconstruction of the history of West African castes is hardly possible without an examination of the relationships among words. We have been able to show, on linguistic grounds alone, that numerous designations for caste people are not native to the languages in which they are used, and therefore, that the groups to which they apply developed at least in part as a result of foreign contacts. Oral traditions, of varying degrees of fullness and specificity, support most but not all of these claims; but oral traditions alone prove foreign origin in only a few cases.

Language classification has been a major tool—perhaps *the* major tool—in establishing the outlines of early African history. However, word borrowing has been little studied, except as a means of tracing population movements (through toponyms) and the diffusion of plants and animals. I hope to have shown its usefulness for reconstructing the history of social institutions.

Notes

Thanks are due to Mamadou Diabaté, Moustapha Sanogo, and Pierre Boutin, who respectively provided me with Maukakan, Selakakan and Senufo vocabularies. Pierre Boutin also commented on an earlier version of this essay.

1. Meillassoux (1975:15–18).

2. Pollet and Winter (1971:218); Silla (1966:755–58). A figure of about 5 percent for the Bamana is supported by my own observations in villages near the Segou area (1985, 1986) and in southern Beledugu (1988).

3. This essay is extracted and condensed from my doctoral dissertation, "Les castes au Soudan occidental: Etude anthropologique et historique" (Castes in the Western Sudan: An Anthropological and Historical Study), U.E.R. d'Ethnologie, Université de Paris X-Nanterre, January 1988. See also Tamari 1991.

4. Ba (1972), Diagne (1972), and Turay (1972) are notable exceptions.

5. African terms are cited in the official orthographies adopted by African states. When this can be misleading, as in comparing words from different languages, a phonetic transcription is also supplied, between square brackets. 6 is glottalized b; ɗ is glottalized d; Fulfulde words written as if they had an initial vowel in fact begin with a glottal occlusive; ny = ñ = ɲ. In Dogon, long vowels are represented by the sign : following the vowel; in other African languages, by writing the vowel twice; in Arabic, by a stroke over the vowel. Bamana forms of Manding terms are cited, unless otherwise indicated. For more information on the orthographic system used in this study, please refer to the author's thesis (Tamari 1988).

When two words are separated by a slash mark, the first represents the singular, the second the plural form. Words separated only by commas represent alternative pronunciations, or different dialectal forms, of the same term.

The vocabulary studied is drawn from the following sources: Bamana: *Lexique bambara-français* (1980), Bailleul (1981); Maukakan: Creissels (1982) and Mamadou Diabaté, graduate student, Ecole Pratique des Hautes Etudes: Sciences Religieuses, personal communication; Selakakan: Moustapha Sanogo, Institut des Sciences Humaines, Abidjan, personal communication; Mandinko: Schaffer (1980); Kuranko: Jackson (1977). Schaffer's and Jackson's transcriptions are not always accurate, but they provide apparently complete lists of terms for castes used by the Mandinko and Kuranko respectively. Soninke: Pollet and Winter (1971), Bathily and Meillassoux (1975); Dan Zemp (1964); Wolof: *Lexique wolof-français* (1976–81), Diop (1981); Tukulor: Gaden (1914), Wane (1969); Fulfulde: Seydou (1972) (introduction), Zubko (1980); Senufo (Tyebara dialect): Pierre Boutin, Université de Paris V, personal communication; Minianka: Jonckers (1979), Cauvin (1980); Dogon: Calame-Griaule (1968); Songhay: Prost (1956, 1977), Ducroz and Charles (1978), Olivier de Sardan (1982); Temne: Turay (1972); Hassaniya (Moorish Arabic): Pierret (1948), Norris (1968); Tuareg: Foucauld (1951), Lhote (1955), Nicolas (1953), Cortade and Mammeri (1967).

6. However, that *nyàma*, "life force," and *nyàman*, "garbage," are nearly homophonous may be no accident. Manding believe that the life forces of animals and plants may continue to cling to them even after death or during decomposition. Youssouf Cissé (1964) and Bird, Kendall, and Tera in this volume provide fuller discussions of these and other etymologies.

7. Claude Meillassoux (1973) discusses both of these etymologies and defends the latter.

8. Gaden (1914:142–43); Wane (1969:223).

9. All transcriptions and analyses of Senufo words are due to Pierre Boutin. Transcriptions correspond to the Tyebara dialect.

10. Calame-Griaule (1968:122).

11. In the generic form of the base, Senufo nouns present the following tonal schemes: low-low, middle-low, middle-middle, low-middle. The last three schemes are found only in Senufo roots. The tonal scheme -low-low is found both in Senufo roots and in loan-words. The tonal scheme -middle-high is found both in compound words and in loan-words. The tonal schemes low-high and high-high are found only among loanwords. Pierre Boutin, personal communication.

12. Calame-Griaule (1968:130–31).

13. Ibn Baṭṭūṭa, Arabic text (1355/1854–74, IV:413); French translation, Cuoq (1975:307).

14. The relationship to *jòli,* "blood," discussed by Sory Camara (1976) at some length, is not entirely fanciful. Many stories link the acquisition of bard status to the absorption of the blood of another person. However, as *jèli* is a very ancient and basic term in Manding, it is possible that it is not derived from or closely related to any other existing radical.

15. On *kùle* as a designation for woodcarvers, see below. K. J. B. Konaré (1975) states that *kùle* is a designation for third-generation slaves.

16. Bisilliat and Laya (1972).

17. The relationship of Moorish *īggīw* to Wolof *géwél* has already been noted by H. T. Norris (1968:53), who also remarked that the word must have come into Moorish through Tuareg.

18. Meillassoux, Doucouré, and Simagha (1967:13).

19. The words *segi* and *surasegi* have been reported only by Dominique Zahan (1963:126–28). However, I was able to verify that these words are known in the Segou area.

20. Oral traditions and features of social structure that support a Soninke rather than Manding origin for *garanke* are well discussed by Barbara Frank in this volume.

21. Gaden (1914:22).

22. Wane (1969:58).

23. Ibid., 59.

24. The large number of different castes represented in the Segou area is a result of contacts with Macina, but especially of the Tukulor conquest of the 1860s. Of the five terms known only in the Segou area, three (*gàwulo, gàwule; lawube; màabo*) are borrowed from Fulfulde. The two remaining terms (*segi, surasegi*) come from those of a Soninke caste (the *sakke*) which has some links with the Fulani.

25. *Hɔrɔn* and *hoore* come from Arabic *ḥurr,* which, like the Manding and Soninke terms, may be translated as either "noble" or "free." Fulfulde *dimo/rimɓe* derives from the Fulfulde radical *rim,* but has the same connotations. *Kàbila* comes from Arabic *qabīla.*

26. Maurice Delafosse (1955) claimed that almost 10 percent of the vocabulary of Manding and Soninke consists of Arabic loanwords. I read Ibn Baṭṭūṭa's description of the Mali Empire as implying that the Arab-Berber presence there was at least as important as the French or British one in most West African colonies; and of course, the Arabs and Berbers stayed far longer.

27. In my doctoral dissertation, I argued that Manding endogamous artisan and musician groups began to form in the thirteenth century, partly as a result of the Sosso-Malinke conflict. This interpretation is based on the Sunjata epic, controlled by the Arabic sources (Tamari [1988:389–448]).

28. Several early Arabic and European sources cite African words for castes. Analysis of these references constitutes a separate topic—use of conventional written records for the elucidation of language history, rather than the application of synchronic linguistics to social history. However, pending full publication of my results, the following comments may be in order. The first citation of an African designation for a caste occurs in Ibn Baṭṭūṭa's *Travels.* As we have already seen, the fourteenth-century globetrotter noted that "poets" at the court of Mali were called *jāli,* pl. *jūla*—terms similar or identical to the modern *jèli* (Ibn Baṭṭūṭa [1355/1854–74, IV:413/trans. 307]). The next reference dates to

about 1500, when the Lisbon-based compiler and traveler Valentim Fernandes (1506–10) reported the Wolof term for bards, which he spelled *gaul*, and which must therefore have been similar or identical to contemporary Wolof *géwél*. The *Ta'rīkh el-Fattāsh* (written in the 1660s) mentions that the master of ceremonies at the Songhay court of Askia Muhammad (1492–1528) was called *gissiridunka;* this term was probably composed from Soninke or Songhay *gesere*, "bard," and Soninke *tunka*, "king, leader, chief" (Ibn al-Mukhtār [c. 1665/1913:11, 94, 155/trans. 14, 177, 276]). The *Ta'rīkh al-Sūdān* (written in the 1650s) states that in 1549, a Songhay ruler captured some *mabi* musicians—generally identified with the Fulani *maabo/maabuube* (Al-Saʿdī [c. 1655/1911:102/trans. 168]). African terms reported by Arab travelers are analyzed in an all but forgotten article by Delafosse (1913), African words cited in the *Ta'rikhs* are analyzed by John Hunwick (1970–71).

29. Bravmann (1974:75–79).
30. Turay (1972).
31. Crétois (1974, III:345).
32. Thomas (1959:30–46).
33. Pageard (1961).

References

Al-Saʿdī. c. 1655/1911. *Ta'rīkh es-Sūdān*. Edited and translated by Octave Houdas and Edmond Benoist. 1st ed., Paris: E. Leroux, 1911. Reprint, Paris: Adrien Maisonneuve, 1981.

Ba, Oumar. 1972. "Glossaire des mots mandé passés au Poulâr du Foûta Toro." Paper presented at the Conference on Manding Studies, School of Oriental and African Studies, University of London.

Bailleul, Père Charles. 1981. *Petit dictionnaire bambara-français, français-bambara.* Avebury, England: Avebury Publishing Co.

Bathily, Abdoulaye, and Claude Meillassoux. 1975. *Lexique soninké (sarakolé)-français.* Dakar: C.L.A.D.

Bisilliat, Jeanne, and Dioulde Laya. 1972. *La tradition orale dans la société songhay-zarma: Les zamu ou poèmes sur les noms.* Niamey: Centre Nigérien de Recherche en Sciences Humaines.

Bravmann, René A. 1974. *Islam and Tribal Art in West Africa.* Cambridge: Cambridge University Press.

Calame-Griaule, Geneviève. 1968. *Dictionaire dogon. Dialecte tɔrɔ. Langue et civilisation.* Paris: C. Klincksieck.

Camara, Sory. 1976. *Gens de la parole. Essai sur la condition et le rôle des griots dans la société malinké.* Paris and the Hague: Mouton.

Cauvin, Jean. 1980. *L'image, la langue et la pensée.* Vol. I: *L'exemple des proverbes (Mali).* Vol. II: *Recueil de proverbes de Karangasso.* St. Augustin: Anthropos-Institut-Haus Völker und Kulturen.

Cissé, Youssouf Tata. 1964. "Notes sur les sociétés de chasseurs malinke." *Journal de la Société des Africanistes* 34 (2):175–226.

Cortade, Jean-Marie, and Mouloud Mammeri. 1967. *Lexique français-touareg. Dialecte de l'Ahaggar.* Preface by G. Camps. Paris: Arts et Métiers Graphiques.

Creissels, Denis. 1982. *Document lexical maukakan (parler manding du Maou).* Grenoble: Université de Grenoble III.

Crétois, Léonce. 1972–77. *Dictionnaire sereer-français. (Différents dialectes).* 6 vols. Dakar: C.L.A.D.

Cuoq, Joseph. 1975. *Recueil des sources arabes concernant l'Afrique occidentale du VIIIe au XVIe siècle. (Bilad al-Sudan)*. Preface by Raymond Mauny. Paris: Editions du CNRS.

Delafosse, Maurice. 1913. "Mots soudanais du Moyen-Age." *Société de Linguistique de Paris* 18 (4):281–88.

————. 1955. *La langue mandingue et ses dialectes (malinké, bambara, dioula)*. Vol. 2: *Dictionnaire mandingue-français*. Paris: Paul Geuthner.

Diagne, Pathé. 1972. "La Mandiguophonie nord-soudanienne comme facteur d'unification ouest-africaine." Paper presented at the Conference on Manding Studies, School of Oriental and African Studies, University of London.

Diop, Abdoulaye-Bara. 1981. *La société wolof. Tradition et changement. Les systèmes d'inégalité et de domination*. Paris: Karthala.

Ducroz, Jean-Marie, and Marie-Claire Charles. 1978. *Lexique soney (songay)-français. Parler kaado du Gorouol*. Paris: L'Harmattan.

Fernandes, Valentim. 1506–10. *Description de la côte occidentale d'Afrique (Sénégal au Cap de Monte, Archipels)*. Edited and translated by Théodore Monod, Avelino Teixeira da Moto, and Raymond Mauny. Bissau: Centro de Estudos da Guiné Portuguesa, 1951.

Foucauld, Charles de. 1951. *Dictionnaire touareg-français. Dialecte de l'Ahaggar*. 4 vols. Paris: Imprimerie Nationale.

Gaden, Henri. 1914. *Le poular: dialecte peul du Fouta sénégalais*. Vol. 2: *Lexique poular-français*. Paris: Ernest Leroux.

Hunwick, John. 1970–71. "African Language Material in Arabic Sources—The Case of Songhay (Sonrai)." *African Language Review* 9:51–73.

Ibn al-Mukhtār. c. 1665/1913. *Ta'rīkh el-Fattāsh*. Arabic text and French translation by O. Houdas and M. Delafosse. 1st ed., Paris: E. Leroux, 1913. Reprint, Paris: Adrien-Maisonneuve, 1964.

Ibn Baṭṭūṭa. 1355/1854–74. *Voyages d'Ibn Baṭṭūṭa (Tuḥfat al-nuẓẓār fī gharā'ib al-amṣār wa-ʿadjā'ib al-asfār)*. Arabic text and translation by C. Defrémery and B. R. Sanguinetti. 1st ed., Paris: Imprimerie Nationale. Rev. ed. by Vincent Monteil, Paris: Editions Anthropos, 1969.

Jackson, Michael. 1977. *The Kuranko: Dimensions of Social Reality in a West African Society*. London: C. Hurst and Co.

Jonckers, Danielle. 1979. "Notes sur le forgeron, la forge et les métaux en pays minyanka." *Journal de la Société des Africanistes* 49 (1):103–24.

Konare, Kanyumen Jean Bosco. 1975. "De Sabouciré à Tombouctou, 1878–95. Contribution à l'étude des résistances africaines à la pénétration française." Thèse de 3ème cycle, Université de Montpellier III.

Lexique bambara-français (bamanankan ni tubabukan danyègafe). 1980. Bamako: DNAFLA.

Lexique wolof-français. 1976, 1977, 1979, 1981. 4 vols. Dakar: CLAD.

Lhote, Henri. 1955. *Les Touaregs du Hoggar (Ahaggar)*. 1st ed., 1944. 2nd ed. rev., Paris: Payot.

Meillassoux, Claude. 1973. "Note sur l'étymologie de *nyamakala*." *Notes Africaines* 139:79.

Meillassoux, Claude, ed. 1975. *L'esclavage en Afrique précoloniale*. Paris: François Maspero.

Meillassoux, Claude; Lassana Doucoure; and Diaowé Simagha. 1967. *Légende de la dispersion des Kusa (Epopée soninke)*. Dakar: IFAN.

Nicolas, Francis. 1953. *La langue berbère de Mauritanie*. Dakar: IFAN.

Norris, Harry Thirwall. 1968. *Shinqiti Folk Literature and Song*. Oxford: Clarendon Press.

Olivier de Sardan, Jean-Pierre. 1982. *Concepts et conceptions songhay-zarma*. Paris: Nubia.

Pageard, Robert. 1961. "Note sur les Setba." *Etudes Voltaïques*, n.s.:57–60.

Pierret, Roger. 1948. *Etude du dialecte maure des régions sahariennes et sahéliennes de l'Afrique occidentale française*. Paris: Imprimerie Nationale.

Pollet, Eric, and Grace Winter. 1971. *La société soninké (Dyahunu, Mali)*. Brussels: Editions de l'Institut de Sociologie, Université Libre de Bruxelles.

Prost, André. 1956. *La langue soñay et ses dialectes*. Dakar: IFAN.

———. 1977. "Supplément au dictionnaire soñay-français (parler de Gao, Mali)." *Bulletin de l'I.F.A.N.* 39 (3):584–657.

Schaffer, Matt. 1980. *Mandinko: The Ethnography of a West African Holy Land*. New York: Holt, Rinehart and Winston.

Seydou, Christiane. 1972. *Silâmaka et Poullôri; récit épique raconté par Tinguidji*. Paris: A. Colin.

Silla, O. 1966. "Persistance des castes dans la société wolof contemporaine." *Bulletin de l'I.F.A.N.* 28 (3–4):731–70.

Tamari, Tal. 1988. "Les castes au Soudan occidental: Etude anthropologique et historique." Thèse de doctorat, Université de Paris X-Nanterre.

———. 1991. "The Development of Caste Systems in West Africa." *The Journal of African History* 32 (1991):221–50.

Thomas, Louis-Vincent. 1959. *Les Diola. Essai d'analyse fonctiohnelle sur une population de Haute-Casamance*. 2 vols. Dakar: IFAN.

Turay, A. K. 1972. "Manding and Susu Loanwords in Temne." Paper presented at the Conference on Manding Studies, School of Oriental and African Studies, University of London.

Wane, Yaya. 1969. *Les Toucouleurs du Fouta Tooro, stratification sociale et structure familiale*. Dakar: IFAN.

Zahan, Dominique. 1963. *La Dialectique du verbe chez les Bambara*. Paris: Mouton & Co.

Zemp, Hugo. 1964. "Musiciens autochtones et griots malinké chez les Dan de Côte d'Ivoire." *Cahiers d'Etudes Africaines* 4 (3):370–82.

Zubko, G. V. 1980. *Dictionnaire peul (fula)-russe-français d'environ 25,000 mots*. Moscow: Langue russe.

V

BLIND MAN MEETS PROPHET
ORAL TRADITION, ISLAM, AND *FUNÉ* IDENTITY

David C. Conrad

The Mutability of *funéya*

Among the artisan and bardic groups collectively known in the heartlands of
Mande society as *nyamakalaw,* the role of the *funé* is the least clearly understood.
The occupations of professional artisans and bards are known to have varied at
different times and places according to local requirements and conditions. The
available evidence suggests that among these groups, in the frequency and variety
of their role changes, the *funéw* have been the most protean of *nyamakalaw.* At
the same time, the primary, or at least most consistent, function of the *funéw* in
times of historical record has been specialization in an area of the oral arts
associated with Islam.

Arab travelers and geographers who recorded miscellaneous bits of information about early Mande society make no mention of anyone resembling the
funéw as we now recognize them. However, the sketchiness of the Arab sources
makes it impossible to accept this as an indication that their occupational
specialty did not exist by the fourteenth century, which encompasses the period
described by the most informative of the Arab writers.[1] It will be shown below
that in addition to the claims made in the oral traditions, the *funéw* themselves
insist that their ancestors' affiliation with Islam commenced sometime after the
arrival of Muslims in ancient Ghana (locally known as "Wagadu"). We may
never be able to confirm this with direct evidence, subject as we are to the
disadvantage of being obliged to rely on oral tradition for our earliest information about the *funéw,* with the first eyewitness reports not appearing until the
eighteenth- and nineteenth-century explorers and colonial administrators began
publishing their accounts.[2] Work in progress is gradually uncovering evidence
in support of the *nyamakala* claim, to be discussed below, that ancestors of some
people known as *funéw* originated in Wagadu. Confirmation of a proto-*funé*
presence in Wagadu would take us a notable step toward accepting the not
unreasonable claim that a Muslim bardic vocation arose at that time.

The broad occupational scope of the *funéw*, which in some cases seems to blur their identity and in others to define it, was apparent to some of the earlier observers. In the 1880s it appeared to Dr. Tautain that Bamana *funéw* had no particular vocational specialty, but performed whatever tasks were not covered by *numuw, jeliw,* or slaves. He specified that they often served as agents of the chief, collecting his taxes, carrying messages, or serving as guards and informants (Tautain said "spies"), while their women worked as dyers.[3] Henri Labouret saw the *funéw* as social undesirables occupying the lowest level of a *nyamakala* hierarchy, working as canoe-makers and calabash-menders,[4] and André Arcin reported that they belonged to a class of weavers that hardly ever did any weaving.[5] Leather goods were usually produced by *garankéw,* and as Barbara Frank points out in this volume, *jeliw* sometimes practiced that craft, but Leynaud and Cissé interpret their evidence from oral tradition to describe the *funéw* as leatherworkers, saying nothing of the *garankéw.*[6] Meanwhile, descriptions of the *funéw* as messengers, agents, and "diplomats" (i.e., go-betweens) are of very limited value,[7] because any *nyamakala* could and did perform these duties. Nevertheless, such tasks are within the range of genres of the oral arts with which the *funéw* have often been identified. In one place Maurice Delafosse describes them as religious mimes and magicians, and elsewhere as bards of inferior caste.[8]

In recent times, reports from a wide variety of observers and informants reinforce the impression of regional roles for the *funéw,* roles that are defined according to local need, or to the absence of preferred vocational opportunities. Germaine Dieterlen refers to the *fina* (i.e., *finaw* or *funéw*) as basket-makers,[9] while Mamby Sidibé identifies them simply as mendicants, without specifying any craft or art with which *nyamakalaw* are usually associated.[10] The Mandinka *funéw* of the Kita area are described by Nicholas Hopkins as musicians and mimes,[11] and Sory Camara calls the *funé* a type of bard that plays no musical instrument.[12] Dominique Zahan stresses their bardic role,[13] and an apparently puzzled Hugo Zemp falls into line with those who consider them to be griots of "inferior caste."[14] A present-day view of *funéw* in some places as bards of "inferior status" is supported by distinguished Mande-born scholars with an inside perspective such as Lansiné Kaba, as well as by nonliterate local informants.[15] In view of their highly mutable perambulations throughout the temporal and spatial dimensions of the social order, Bokar N'Diaye's description of today's *funéw* as "an intermediate caste between those of the artisans and those of the musicians"[16] acknowledges the *funé*'s ability to turn their hands to virtually anything, depending on what opportunities present themselves. A similar attitude is reflected in the bard Tayiru Banbera's remark, based on his observation of daily life in the region of Segu: "But to say that the *funéw* have some particular kind of work that they do, no! They do not perform any special tasks."[17]

At times the descriptive terminology leaves much to be desired, but there is no evidence that the widely diverse occupations attributed to the *funéw* by different observers at various times and places since the late eighteenth century are the result of inaccurate observations or careless reporting. Instead, it seems clear that the *funéw* of relatively recent centuries, perhaps displaying a flexibility that goes back to their origins, have tended to function as vocational itinerants. That is to say, they have been versatile, pragmatic opportunists crossing occupational boundaries of the *nyamakala* world to seize whatever opportunities might be presented either by large-scale historical change at various times and places or, less permanently, by the vicissitudes of daily life on a limited local level. Among the possible interpretations to be noted below of the basic theme of the *funé* ancestral legend in which the poor blind man hosts the apostle of God, it will be suggested that it legitimizes and consolidates the ideal *funé* role in Mande society.

While the basic tradition stresses the *funé* ancestor's hospitality to Muhammad, the group's ability to practice various occupations is acknowledged in miscellaneous anecdotes describing tasks such as serving as a messenger or guardian. Were these tasks not being performed for the Prophet, they would instantly lose their luster. The messenger theme, for example, appears in a variety of forms. In a fragment of a story told by a *garanké,* Muhammad sends Fosana on a mission to Yemen to help sick people and orphans, promising that the *funé* ancestor will be rewarded with "the writings of the angels."[18] A more complete tale told by a *jeli* has Tiramakan, one of Sunjata's most important generals (and in this story, a descendant of Muhammad), providing sixteen warriors for the battle of Kaybara, one of the Prophet's most important campaigns. The sole survivor of the sixteen, ashamed that he too was not killed, must be persuaded to go on living, and to send one of the four master bards to announce the names of the fallen warriors. Fosana the *funé* ancestor is the first one approached, but in a tale in which the *jeli* ancestor is the central character, he goes against the jack-of-all-trades image of daily life, refusing the task and a golden reward on the grounds that it is better to refuse wealth than to be the bearer of bad tidings.[19] In this case Fosana plays only a secondary part, but the tale nevertheless locates the normally humble role of messenger within the orbit of the Prophet's activities. In another story, as Muhammad departs on a journey, Fosana is left behind in the menial role of guardian to the Prophet's wife, but nevertheless contrives to achieve glory:

> They came to another place, and Muhammad said to Fosana,
> "I have a wife I want to leave with you while I continue my travels."
> Muhammad left his wife and went on a journey.
> Fosana was tempted to couple with her,
> But he remembered that she was in his trust.
> He went into the bathing hut and cut off his genitals.
> He said, "One's manhood depends on his sex.
> Our chief Muhammad trusted his wife to me,
> And though I wanted to couple with her,
> I could not let it happen."
> Muhammad was traveling far away, but he saw what Fosana had done.
> He cast a spell to preserve the sexual parts.
> When the Prophet returned from his journey he said,
> "Fosana, I saw what you did.
> I choose you as the most trustworthy of my people."[20]

Performing various ordinary tasks but prepared to make any sacrifice for the Prophet, Fosana acquires a luster as a very special early convert and companion of Muhammad that tradition beams onward through time, as it seems from our latter-day perspective, to later generations of *nyamakalaw,* thus burnishing the image of his *funé* "descendants." The tale functions as a form of praise for the *funéw,* reminding the *horon* ("noble") audience of their responsibilities as hosts (*jatigiw*) to those whose ancestor selflessly provided for the apostle of God. Bard and audience alike are perfectly aware of the hyperbole involved, just as they are when a praise song is performed to laud the deeds of a heroic warrior ancestor. But in these cases, as the *jeliw* relate stories of the *funé* "ancestor," they confirm and support the claims to special privileges of their fellow *nyamakalaw.* Muhammad's blessing of the *funé* ancestor in the lines of one *jeli's* discourse reveals much about the *nyamakala* attitude toward the nature of these claims: "May God give you the power to be taken care of by other people."[21]

The questions of how, why, and when this group evolved within the Mande social system are thorny ones that cannot be satisfactorily answered here, because much more research concentrating on the *funéw* will have to be undertaken before substantive conclusions can be reached. Meanwhile, however, it is possible to review some oral sources for what they may have to tell us, and to suggest some potentially fruitful directions to be pursued in future research. The focus below will be on what received variants of the bardic tradition can reveal about how the *funéw* themselves, as well as their *nyamakala* peers, view this occupational group. Their view is of course deeply colored by the *funé* relationship with Islam, while at the same time it exhibits a distinct, though less vibrant, consciousness of the predominantly non-Muslim themes of the Sunjata tradition. Questions regarding the interpretation of oral sources and the translation of written ones are discussed as we go along. A special effort is made to let the voices of our informants be heard more than they usually are. Translations of especially informative and colorful lines from original transcripts are offered in appropriate places, and an appendix contains samples of two interviews with *nyamakalaw.*

The *funéw* and Islam in Oral Tradition

On the routes followed by some of the earlier European observers, *funé* involvement in both the oral arts and Islam was apparent. The *funéw* observed by Major Laing in the early 1800s were conspicuous as public speakers, though Laing did not describe their topics of discourse.[22] An earlier traveler, the intrepid Scottish physician Mungo Park, provides details of apparent *funé* discourse that he heard in the 1790s, without mentioning the term *funé:* "The other class [of 'singing men'] are devotees of the Mahomedan faith, who travel about the country, singing devout hymns and performing religious ceremonies, to conciliate the favour of the Almighty, either in averting calamity, or insuring success to any enterprise."[23] Park's description sums up what local informants regard as the ideal *funé* role, the occupation that basically defines their place among the *nyamakalaw*. Over time, the extent to which *funéya* involves Islamic matters has apparently fluctuated with the level of intensity of Muslim devotion in various localities. Not surprisingly, the primary *funé* role of Islamic bard, as it is traditionally claimed to be, is most clearly defined and practiced in Mande cultural regions where Muslim tradition has been firmly established.

If, within the *nyamakala* system of values, to specialize in Islamic discourse was historically the *funé* "ideal," this should not be taken to imply that it was so for material reasons. The sources available to me reveal no evidence that *funéw* were ever richly rewarded for their services as were, for example, some *jeliw* of Segu.[24] Near the turn of this century, a French priest observed five artisan/bardic groups plying their crafts among the Sarakolé (Soninke) in the Sahelian area around Nioro. One of many colonial-era observers who interpreted *nyamakalaya* as signifying "caste impurity," the priest describes the *Finé* that he saw as the most despised of all:

> These days, their only specialty is to read the Quran, and to always live as dependents of a prosperous family. On important occasions, they recite verses from the holy book, for example when the head of the family returns from a journey, when they shave the head of one of the children for the first time, etc. They do not farm at all, and are always very poor.[25]

It is not certain that such observations represent the truth about a significant proportion of the *funé* populations during the colonial period or any other. Nevertheless, any evaluation of *funé* motives for seeking the Islamic "ideal" of their profession must take their spiritual goals seriously.

The Gambia is apparently one place where the *funé* role can still be regarded as an "exclusively" Muslim vocation. As Gordon Innes describes it, whereas a *jeli* (*jalo* in Gambian Mandinka) would attend upon a chief, a *fino* (pl. *finolu*) attends upon a Muslim scholar. The *fino* knows his patron's family history, and is well acquainted with the Quran and with Islam generally: "A *fino*'s performance is usually of a homiletic nature, concerned with proper behavior and supported by copious quotations from the Koran."[26] Also addressing the Islamic orientation of the Gambian "Finas," Seni Darbo says they specialize in singing the Hadiths, poems said to have been written by Muhammad, and in reciting the 201 names of the Prophet. These *funéw* play no instruments, and unlike the *jeliw* of traditional society, they are not attached to any family or class, but will perform for any interested Muslim.[27] Despite their lofty spiritual orientation, the social status of these *funéw* is no less ambiguous than that of *jeliw, numuw,* and *garankéw,* in that the respect accorded them by "the older generation" for their scholarly accomplishments does not exempt them from endogamy and certain taboos.[28]

Though often less conspicuous among the Bamana and other Mande societies in places other than the Gambia, the *funé* affiliation with Islam is usually at least nominally present. They are still Muslims even if, in some locations, their Islamic scholarship or related vocational functions give way to some genre of the secular oral arts, craft specialties, or to what most of them now prefer to do, farming.

Regardless of what non-Islamic occupational niche they might have been occupying at a particular time or place, local explanations of their identity and origins almost invariably include variants of an oral tradition connecting them with the life and times of Muhammad, through a legendary ancestor distinguished for his personal relationship with the Prophet.

In present-day Mali, when bards are asked about their own ancestors or about the forebears of any of the *nyamakala* peoples, they are likely to respond with stories from Arab tradition mixed in varying proportions with elements from local African culture. Islamic antecedents are also claimed for the noblest of all Mande heroes, Sunjata, through the recitation of descent lists that include certain Muslim names inserted ahead of whatever non-Islamic ones have survived in the collective bardic memory. Among the Muslim names are occasional recognizable figures from Arab tradition, one of which is Bilāl ibn Rabāḥ, the black former slave who became Muhammad's first muezzin, known to the Mande as "Bilali."[29] Stories of Bilali are not as common as those of the bardic ancestor Surakata, but a few traditionists, including some Muslim blacksmiths, are fond of relating how Sunjata's ancestor helped Muhammad at the battle of Khaybar.[30] Currently, the general bardic awareness of Bilali appears to have dwindled, as many have ceased to make the connection between Muhammad's caller-to-prayers and the name in Sunjata's genealogy.[31] As for the *jeliw,* their adopted ancestor originated as Surāqa ibn Mālik ibn Ju'shum, in Arab tradition an enemy of Muhammad who subsequently becomes an early convert to Islam.[32] Awareness of Surakata is much more acute among today's Malian oral traditionists than is that of Bilali. Memories of the encounter between Surakata and Muhammad have been reinforced by readings of the original story on Radio Mali.[33]

The process through which characters from Islamic literature came to occupy important roles in Mande oral tradition could have begun very early on. The respected Arab geographer Al-Bakrī wrote in the year 1068 that there were significant Muslim populations already occupying towns of the Mande peoples and their neighbors in the western Sahel,[34] and in subsequent centuries Islam would become a common though not universal aspect of Mande culture.[35] During the centuries when Islam was being integrated into Mande society and gradually becoming an African religion,[36] Mande bards were assimilating elements of Islamic tradition. Some of the stories told by Muslim clerics and by pilgrims returning from Mecca had particular appeal for Mande audiences and were easily adapted to indigenous narrative repertoires. The Prophet Muhammad, as well as characters from his life and times, was borrowed by Mande bards and woven into the fabric of their most important myths and legends.[37] In modern times, regular radio broadcasts and increased mobility providing more opportunities for direct experience of the Islamic heartland through the pilgrimage to Mecca have doubtless served to inject fresh infusions of Arab texts into nonliterate Mande discourse.

Standing somewhere between the counterpart legendary ancestors Bilali and Surakata in terms of his depth of characterization and legendary significance within the collective bardic memory is a character called Fosana, whom the *funéw* claim as their ancestor. An Arab prototype for the Mande Fosana has been more difficult to discern than the ones for Bilali and Surakata. This is partly because "Fosana" is a Mande praise name for Abū Ayyūb Al-Anṣārī, the historical character who provides the basis for Fosana's identity. Like Bilāl ibn Rabāḥ and Surāqa ibn Mālik, Abū Ayyūb was a companion of the Prophet. He is known to Mande informants by a variety of distortions of his name, including Aba Ayuba Lazarihu, Abbah-Yuba-Lazariyu, and Abai Bulaziru.[38]

Details of the Fosana tradition typically change from one oral account to the next. The basic historical point giving rise to the tradition is that upon arriving in Medina, the Prophet did actually lodge in the house of Abū Ayyūb Al-Anṣārī.[39] In Mande discourse, "Aba Ayuba Lazarihu" provides food and shelter or performs some other service for Muhammad, thereby acquiring the praise name Fosana (*fisa* = "better")[40] as well as the Prophet's blessing for himself and all his descendants. The ancestor Fosana's status as Muḥammad's *jatigi* (host) during the critical period of the *hijra* constitutes the basis of *funé* identity and the position of *funéw* in the social order. Nevertheless, the legendary Fosana is a composite that includes features unrelated to the historical Abū Ayyūb Al-Anṣārī. For example, Mande tradition describes Fosana as a blind man, although Abū Ayyūb Al-Anṣārī was not blind.

Mande anecdotes about Fosana characterize him in a variety of ways, but they all establish him as a contemporary of Muhammad. Seni Darbo identifies the legendary "Fina" ancestor only as Fisan, a poet who specialized in poems written by Muhammad, citing no Arabic source for this conclusion.[41] In sifting Islamic tradition for elements contributing to Fosana's composite character, it is possible to correlate various figures appearing in stories about Muhammad with the general image of Fosana as he is revealed in Mande legend.

Fosana's character and the stories about him constitute a collage of loosely connected incidents from the Prophet's life and times. The related sources in Muslim tradition are anecdotes and fragments of stories that for one reason or another have struck a chord of interest among the *funéw*, the *jeliw,* and whoever else contributed to Fosana's legend. In the case of Bilāl ibn Rabāḥ, his black skin, his heroic devotion to Islam, and his direct association with Muhammad provided him with the right credentials to be adopted as legendary progenitor of ancient Mali's ruling lineage. Surāqa ibn Mālik was equally qualified, in the view of Mande *jeliw,* to be their own distinguished Islamic forebear.[42] That the composite image of Fosana derives from not one but several miscellaneous characters and incidents from the Prophet's life and times may be due to the usual distortions in the long chain of transmission characteristic of oral tradition. But as already noted, our nonliterate informants' knowledge of these texts is periodically reinforced nowadays by radio broadcasts and increasingly direct experience of the Islamic heartland. Therefore, the extensive range of elements selected for the Fosana legend could be a matter as much of choice as of chance. The Fosana composite probably owes something to *funé* acquaintance with Arab tradition being more extensive than any held by other Muslim *nyamakalaw.*

Generally speaking, the more secular *jeliw,* wishing to acquire for themselves and their patrons whatever advantages might be accruing through a claim to early Islamic antecedents, apparently had enough exposure to Islamic tradition to form a legendary affiliation with the character obviously suited to their needs. The *funéw,* owing to their more thorough exposure to the literature, had more to choose from. What appears to be a less cohesive, more fragmented discourse may actually be a function of their more informed position vis-à-vis Islamic tradition and Arabic language, originally acquired through close relationships with Muslim clerics (or "marabouts"). The *funéw* had more opportunities to select widely from the literature both written and oral, some texts read by those acquiring various degrees of literacy, others heard repeatedly from Muslim clerics with whom they were associated. In the process, the contents of their discourse would ebb and flow as it proved more or less adaptable to their continually evolving legendary ancestor, and hence to their own image.

The present effort to uncover the basis for the Fosana tradition mainly employs two written sources, one of which is Ibn Ishāq's *Sīrat Rasūl Allāh.* Muhammad, son of Ishāq, son of Yasār, was born in Medina about A.H. 85 (c. A.D. 707/708), and died in Baghdad in A.H. 151. Early in life, Ibn Ishāq became an authority on apostolic tradition. Collecting and arranging his corpus of material, he drew on a great many sources very close to Muhammad's own time, among which was ʾUrwa b. al-Zubayr b. al-ʾAwwām (A.H. 23–94), a cousin of the Prophet. ʾUrwa was in close contact with the Prophet's widow ʾĀisha, and according to Ibn Ishāq's translator, A. Guillaume, the many traditions that are handed down in ʾUrwa's name by Ibn Ishāq and other writers justify the assertion that he was the founder of Islamic history.[43] So for our purposes, Arab tradition according to Ibn Ishāq is about as close as we can get to the Prophet's own time.[44] The contents of the Guillaume translation indicate that these traditions were disseminated widely enough to find their way into Mande lore.

Another useful source for clarifying Fosana's traditional origins is a fragment of Arabic manuscript, the text of which was partially preserved by P. Humblot, a French colonial administrator. Humblot acquired what he calls the "Tarikh du griot de Téliko" ("Chronicle" or "History of the Bard of Teliko") sometime before 1918 from an unnamed bard living near the heart of old Mande in the village of Teliko, District of Kankan, in the north of what is now the Republic of Guinea.[45] Textual evidence indicates that the scribe who recorded the *tarīkh* (and may have partially authored it) was more knowledgeable about Islamic literature than he was about Mande oral tradition. Significantly, the author was ignorant of the most famous *jeli* in Mande tradition, Sunjata's bard Bala Fasséké Kouyaté.[46] This suggests that most *jeli* influence had been virtually submerged beneath Muslim discourse, and that the author may not have been a native son of Mande. The *tarīkh* identifies the Kouyaté ancestor as "Baba Fasséli, a genie who came out of the caves." While the topical orientation of the text is a combination of Islam and Mande, the author appears to have been a Muslim cleric of some kind. At the same time, the modes of expression, as they appear in the French translation, are distinctly bardic. They represent a style familiar in Mande genealogical recitation evoking such phrases as "Qui peut dire" or "Qui se dit: Je suis 'Kamara,' ce mot signifie. . . ."[47] Thus the manuscript is an interesting combination of Muslim literacy and indigenous oral convention. It conveys the impression that variants of it might have survived for periods of time in both written Arabic form and the oral repertoires of marabouts or Muslim bards.

The *tarīkh* of Teliko could be a product of the kind of maraboutic textual manipulation encountered by Mamadou Diawara in the region of Kingi, where the sixteenth-century Soninke kingdom of Jaara was located. Diawara describes instances in which marabouts and oral traditionists would collaborate in efforts to "conserve" oral texts. The marabout would write down in Arabic a genealogy recited by an oral traditionist. As the marabout wrote he would, true to his calling, sprinkle the text with Arabic expressions and references to Allah and the Prophet Muhammad. Subsequently, oral traditionists wishing to refresh their memories would consult the marabout, as would notables seeking confidential information about their own genealogical traditions. There can be no doubt that more than just references to Allah and Muhammad were added to these texts. Diawara notes one instance where a marabout attached to a prominent clan was combining oral performance with literacy as he took nearly an hour of recitation to get through his two pages of Arabic script.[48] This is one way in which distinguished local ancestors acquired Arab antecedents, as in the case mentioned earlier of Bilāl ibn Rabāḥ becoming a forebear in Sunjata's lineage.

The scribe who produced the manuscript seen by Humblot preserved a discourse in which a substantial amount of material from Arab tradition is preceded in the text by material derived from Mande. Whatever the author's identity, the text of the *tarīkh* of Teliko provides outstanding evidence of the Muslim Mande interest in contriving distinguished antecedents from the life and times of the Prophet for all inhabitants of Mande, i.e., Malinke, Bamana, Fulbe, Maraka, or *nyamakalaw*. It commences as no less than a "history" of the origin of man from Adam, in a way very similar to the traditional beginning of the "book of the biography of the apostle of God" with "Muhammad's pure descent from Adam,"[49] though the genealogies are much shorter. Once those are disposed of, the list of familiar Mande *jamuw* and their Arab antecedents begins.

Though more widely scattered and less immediately recognizable in Arab tradition than are the sources for Bilali and Surakata, the elements incorporated into the *funé* ancestor's character offer some useful insights into that group's own idea of their position within the social order. But far from being a window looking backward into the rapidly fading traditional *funé* world, the Fosana legend is more like a mirror (distorted in varying degrees), reflecting glimpses of the ideal public image of *funéw* that once protected their interests, one which evolved over many generations of exposure to stories from Arab texts and assimilating various elements from them into Mande tradition. As we consider some variants of the "Fosana" or "Blind Man" tradition (though he is not always called Fosana, nor is he always blind), it is possible to discern elements that point to some sources in Arab tradition that probably influenced the legend of the *funé* ancestor.

Stories of the *funé* ancestor reflect aspects of this group's social status, associating their condition with Muhammad's humble origins and the empathy he showed later in his life for people of lesser privilege. A useful example of Mande bardic assimilation of Arab themes occurs early in Fadian Soumanou's account of *nyamakala* ancestors, where he explains what happens after (as he believes) Muhammad's mother dies in childbirth. Soumanou's anecdote draws on impressions of Muhammad's infancy, as well as on Western Sudanic folklore that appears to originate with the Fulbe pastoralists, whose tales of famine include the motif of milk miraculously produced to save the infant that will grow up to be the hero. A variant collected before 1910 tells of a drought-induced famine in which a maternal ancestress was unable to feed her child, whose life was saved when it sucked milk from the tail of a friendly python.[50] In Soumanou's story of Muhammad's infancy, it is said that people in all the lands of Africa asked their women how this orphaned "little man of God" might be saved. Meanwhile, the infant nourishes himself by sucking on his own finger. Among the African women who come to see him is Fulamatu, who has only one breast. In this form the name indicates a Fula identity, but it is probably a variant of "Fatamata" (from "Fatima"), an archetypal female figure appearing regularly in the narratives.[51] Here the woman is said to be the maternal ancestress of the Turé clan, married to an Arab so poor that they are ashamed to visit the baby Prophet because of their "nudity." Nevertheless, when Fulamatu puts one of her feet inside the door of the room where the infant lies, a second breast appears on her chest, she takes the child in her arms, and it begins to suckle.[52]

While this story does not directly concern the Fosana theme, it is of interest here because its counterpart in Arab tradition is readily recognizable, and because it demonstrates the sort of detail that strikes a vital note among Muslim people of the Mande. Overlooking the fact that at this stage of Muhammad's life it was his father who had died rather than his mother,[53] the interest for Muslim Mande people in this case derives not only from their interest in the Prophet's life but from the fact that poverty, famine, and infant mortality have been among life's most familiar realities. According to Ibn Isḥāq, Halima, the apostle's foster mother, herself told the story of how, in a year of famine when she and her husband were destitute and she was nursing a son, they went searching among the women of her tribe for an extra baby to wet-nurse. As they travel without food, neither she nor their old she-camel can yield any milk, and they cannot sleep at night because of the wailing of her hungry child. When they reach Mecca looking for a foster child, they find that the apostle of God is being offered to women as a suckling, but they all refuse him because he has no father to pay them. She also spurns him, but when faced with the prospect of being the only woman to return home without a suckling, she goes back for the orphan. As soon as she takes him up, both her breasts and the udder of the she-camel are overflowing with milk, and their flocks prosper during the two years until the child is weaned.[54]

The theme of Muhammad's exalted status through poverty and humility occurs in some episodes directly related to the *funé* ancestor, expressions of which include such statements as "The Prophet gave nobility to the people of Mecca though he wore a torn shirt like a beggar," and "Muhammad humbled himself and God gave him great nobility."[55] The most important difference between the traditions of the alleged *funé* ancestor and those of other Mande occupational and kin groups is that once the Muslim antecedents are established, the descendants of Fosana are the only ones to continue, ideally at least, in an occupation fundamentally connected to Islam. There are distinct indications that this did in fact set them apart from other *nyamakalaw*, something that was probably more evident in the past than it is now. Describing the post-Islamic social order, a *jeli* of northern Guinea separates the *funéw* from all other *nyamakalaw*. He declares that anyone who can do the work can become a *numu*, anyone who can play an instrument and sing can become a *jeli*, and anyone who can sew leather can become a *garanké*. But, he says, only God can make one a *funé*. He describes Fosana as "the originator of humility" and later says,

> Only the *funé* occupation was not made into law.
> Just as they were descended from Lasiri Yugba, no one joined them.
> That is how they remained.[56]

At the same time, in the context of the Fosana tradition, *nyamakala* informants, whether *jeliw, garankéw,* or *numuw,* unhesitatingly identify the *funé* ancestor as the most favored of the Prophet's companions, agreeing that Muhammad's blind host received the praise name Fosana or Fisana. A *garanké* says:

> As for the *funéw,*
> The *funéw* came from Fosana.
> Fosana was the host of the Prophet Muhammad at Mecca.
> The *funéw* are closer to the Prophet Muhammad than all other men.[57]

According to a *jeli:*

> The ancestor of the *funé,* Fosana Camara,
> He was blessed by God,
> And our great Prophet blessed him.
> He made him the first famous man. . . .
> The Prophet said to him, . . .
> "May God give you the power to be taken care of by other people.
> May God bless you with the voice of everyone."[58]

And as a *numu* tells it:

> Muhammad said to Mali Balansari,
> "You are better than everyone."
> If you hear "Fosana,"
> The descendants of Mali Balansari took that name.
> All his descendants became known as *funélu,*

They who are superior to everyone.
And when they come to your house,
You must give them something.[59]

This does not mean that individual *nyamakalaw* personally believe that the *funéw* as a group are in fact socially superior to others in the context of daily life. In fact, one paradox of *funé* status is that they have the so-called "privilege" or even "power," as we saw it phrased above, of begging from other *nyamakalaw*, which ranks them slightly lower than whoever gives to them.[60] *Nyamakala* informants are conscious of contradictions between oral tradition and everyday life. Some would acknowledge that the Fosana legend comprises a formula prescribed for *funé* well-being. It legitimizes the *funé* occupation and place in the social order, thus allowing *funéw* to acquire benefits from those who respect the spiritual power of Islam. In Fosana's case, of paramount importance are the commendable qualities that he shares with the Prophet, including humility (especially as it is shown in the youthful Muhammad's image as an "outsider"), poverty, hospitality, insight into human character, and the strongest possible faith in, and submission to, God. His blindness to things of the temporal world highlights his spiritual vision and, incidentally, might even account for the term *fina,* with its affinities to *finyekè,* meaning "blind man." Fosana's combined virtues define the ideal—though not necessarily the reality—of *funé* existence within the context of daily life in Mande society, and they account for *funé* group identity. Otherwise, as the *jeli* Tayiru Banbera says, "It was men themselves who began these things. . . . The *funéw* derive from the customs of people, and they do things similar to what we [*jeliw*] do."[61]

The theme of poverty and humility continues in an episode of the Fosana tradition where Muhammad declares to his companions that knowledge is more important than the condition of one's apparel, but the companions claim the opposite. To resolve the issue, they journey together to a village where the well-dressed disciples are invited to lodge in the homes of notables, while the ragged Muhammad is abandoned in the village square. The *funé* ancestor, here called Mali Balansari, a blind man "who was not a native of that place," invites the one remaining stranger to his house and feeds him his last few grains of millet. The Prophet rewards the blind man with a perpetually full granary and restores his eyesight. He also commends Mali Balansari with words guaranteed, in the Mande view, to provide his descendants with a distinction that will contribute to their well-being: "You are better than everyone."[62] The sentiment behind this ideal is beautifully expressed in a poem nestled among passages of Arab tradition that directly contribute to the Fosana legend:

My people it was who sheltered their Prophet
And believed in him when all the world were unbelievers,
Except a chosen few who were forerunners
To the righteous, helpers with the Helpers.
Rejoicing in God's portion
Saying when he came to them, noble of race, chosen,

Welcome in safety and comfort,
Goodly the Prophet the portion and the guest.
They gave him a home in which a guest of theirs
Need have no fear—an (ideal) home.
They shared their wealth when the refugees came
While the share of the stubborn opponent is hell.[63]

That the story of the humble host is a well-established tradition and not an isolated story is evident from very similar accounts containing the same central elements that were collected elsewhere in Mali. From another *nyamakala* informant, in this case a *garanké* from Yaterra in the area of Kita, comes a variant in which the disagreement between Muhammad and his companions is over the issue of whether being the son of a good man is better than being the son of a well-dressed man. Muhammad argues that it is better to be well-dressed so that people will give you comfortable lodgings, and to prove his point he wears ragged clothes on arriving in Medina. When the people come rushing to meet them, the well-dressed disciples are offered pleasant accommodation, and the apparently indigent Prophet is left sitting at the mosque. In this case the blind man who offers sanctuary is Abai Bulazairu, a beggar whose wife prepares their last kilo of maize for the Prophet. Again the reward is a full granary and restored eyesight, as the villagers celebrate:

Fosana, Fosana,
His eyes have been opened,
His hunger is banished.
Fosana, Fosana, it is you who are the best in all Medina,
For you gave lodging to the Prophet.[64]

However details may vary in this episode, the key to the humble *funé* ancestor's success is the "blind" acceptance of Muhammad into his home, and the supremely generous act of offering to the Prophet his last grains of food. Some elements of the Mande episode are drawn from Arab anecdotes in which the stress is laid not on the generosity shown to Muhammad but on the act of recognizing an obscure youth traveling in a merchant caravan as the apostle of God. The recognition comes from a monk instead of an indigent blind man. The blind man popular in Mande variants was taken from elsewhere in the Arab texts and mingled with the tradition that carries the main story line. One blind man with whom the bards of Mande might readily identify would be Abū Aḥmad, because he was both a poet and a native of Mecca. From the Mande point of view he blends easily into a tradition that concerns the *funé* ancestor's role in events during the time of the *hijra,* because the Arab accounts include Abū Aḥmad among the first emigrants to Medina.[65]

Thus, while the blind man is present in Arab tradition, the recognition of the youthful apostle is credited to various monks. One of them sees Muhammad stopping in the shade of a tree, recognizes him, and says, "None but a Prophet ever sat beneath a tree."[66] As in the case of the humble lodger and the blind benefactor, the image of Muhammad left standing apart, sometimes ragged and forlorn, has, like the rejected orphan suckling the vagabond wet-nurse, struck a basic chord among Mande traditionists. Apparently contributing to this image is the story of how after the death of Muhammad's grandfather, 'Abdu'l-Muṭṭalib, the youthful Muhammad goes to live with his uncle Abū Ṭālib and is allowed to accompany him in a merchant caravan to Syria. When the caravan reaches Busra in Syria, it stops near the cell of a monk who had never before taken any notice of the merchants who often passed that way. This time he prepares a great feast for them because as the caravan approached, he saw from his cell the apostle of God with a cloud overshadowing him among the people. The monk invites the men of Quraysh to the feast and they gather at his cell, but they leave Muhammad behind with their baggage under a tree, on account of his youth. Upon the monk's insistence, the youth is invited to join the company, and the monk sees the "seal of prophethood" between his shoulders.[67]

Some Fosana episodes reflect a close affinity with the historic Abū Ayyūb Al-Anṣārī and his role in Islamic tradition. The *funé* Sadyo Camara provides one variant of the story of Muhammad's arrival in Medina on a camel. The entire town turns out to welcome him, with everyone wanting him to lodge with them. The Prophet lets his camel go where it will, intending to choose his abode according to where the camel lies down. The townspeople are dismayed when the camel directs itself not to one of the wealthy noblemen's houses but to the compound of a poor man named Aba Yiruba Lazarihu, the *funé* ancestor, whose wife prepares a meal from the last measure of grain. In this case the other townspeople bring a rich variety of food especially prepared in the Prophet's honor, but he will take only his host's humble food, declaring it must be so because his camel is a creature of God and what it chose must be God's will.[68]

This is the part of the legend in which the *funé* lay claim to Abū Ayyūb Al-Anṣārī as their ancestor, praising him as Fosana who is "better than every one." According to Ibn Isḥāq, after Muhammad lays the foundation of his mosque,[69] he receives an invitation from some people to live with them and enjoy their wealth and protection. But, declaring that his camel is "under God's orders," Muhammad says, "Let her go her way." The camel wanders past several more homes where prosperous people issue generous invitations, finally kneeling exhausted at the door of a humble mosque.[70] Once the Prophet is sure this is where the camel wants to stay, he alights and accepts an invitation to remain until his mosque and houses are built. As noted earlier, the Prophet did stay at the home of Abū Ayyūb Al-Anṣārī during this period.[71] Muslim tradition's description of this is the source of Sadyo Camara's story of Muhammad letting his camel choose the host. An additional anecdote from Ibn Isḥāq about acquiring blessings from meals prepared for the Prophet probably influenced the Mande tradition of the humble host's blindness cured by blessings won through serving the last grains of millet.[72]

Non-Islamic Elements in the *funé* Tradition

One characteristic that most distinguishes the *funéw* of recent centuries from
other *nyamakalaw* is that virtually all *funéw* are known by the surname Camara
(or Kamara). To fully understand the reasons for this would be to fit an
important piece into the puzzle of the development of *funéya* and its relationship to the rest of Mande society. Camara *horonw* (nobles), Camara blacksmiths, and Camara *funéw* are said to belong to separate kin groups carrying
the same surname. In the Teliko chronicle there is a connection made between
the alleged Arab forebear of the non-*funé* Camara and Abū Ayyūb the *funé*
ancestor which is of interest, because Camara is the only surname associated
with the *funéw*.[73] While *funéw* are now virtually always said to be Camara,
that *jamu* (family name, identity) also applies to one of the most prominent
kin groups of the blacksmith occupation, as well as to *horon* families. There
are other *jamuw* that cut across social and occupational categories, and there
are *jamuw* that in some regions are identified with a single occupation, as in
the cases of the Kouyaté and Diabaté *jeliw*. But the *funéw* are the only
nyamakalaw who are identified by a single family name.

The Camara name is also prominent among blacksmiths, the *nyamakalaw*
most distinguished for positions of power and responsibility in the daily life of
Mande. In addition to being ironworkers, diviners, sorcerers, rainmakers, heal-
ers, and sculptors, blacksmiths are exclusively the leaders of *komo,* the most
important Mande initiation association or spirit society.[74] As such, some of them
function as the principal intermediaries between the temporal and spiritual
worlds, i.e., as guardians of the indigenous belief system. If some Camara *numuw*
function in these crucial roles while Camara *funéw* are the *nyamakalaw* most
concerned with Islam, anything in oral tradition connecting early aspects of the
two Camara occupations will be of interest. Most of the avenues involving
primarily non-Islamic evidence require more direct contact with local informants
than has so far been accomplished, but we can at least begin here with material
that is presently available from oral sources.

Seni Darbo draws on his own knowledge of the oral tradition to suggest that
an important branch of the Camara came from "Tabung," which he locates at
Timbuktu. Darbo says this would account for the strong Arab influence on them,
including their early conversion to Islam. He makes the interesting claim that
during the time of Sunjata, one branch of the Camara converted to Islam and
laid down their arms because they could no longer fight in any war but a holy
one. At a period when high status was acquired and maintained by feats of arms,
says Darbo, anyone otherwise inclined was relegated to an inferior position in
society.[75] This appears to be Darbo's hypothesis rather than material gleaned
from oral tradition, and it addresses the Camara *horon* ancestors Fran and
Kamanjan, who were among Sunjata's officers, rather than Silamaka the
Camara *funé* ancestor. If such a transition in status from *horon* to *nyamakala*
did take place—and many legends claim they did—it seems possible that the

reduction in status involved a period of slavery in between (a subject to which we return below), and thus would have taken a number of generations to complete.[76]

Passages of Mande tradition describing the Camara *horon* ancestor Fran Camara occur in variants of the Sunjata epic and are mainly concerned with his activities as one of Sunjata's generals.[77] These narrative threads are fairly distinct from the ones describing origins of the non-*horon* Camara which are woven into miscellaneous episodes of Mande tradition that occasionally also appear as elements in the Sunjata tapestry. While Arab tradition accounts for the composite character Fosana and his surrogates, the legend of Silamaka is a product of Mande, though it may have developed concurrently with the Fosana tradition. Nevertheless, as can be seen in virtually all cases of legendary Mande heroes, they are now inextricably entangled with Arab elements and probably have been for many centuries.

As creative genealogists the *jeliw* are peerless, and to inject Islamic forebears into an ancient descent list or to honor a pagan patriarch from the dawn of time with a Muslim ancestor causes them not a single missed pluck of the *ngoni* strings. When Islamic antecedents became fashionable among Mande raconteurs and genealogists, Bilali and other alleged Arab forefathers were inserted into Sunjata's family tree above the ancient animist hunter-warrior ancestors of Mande, thus moving the latter forward in time and turning them into Muslims.[78] Conversely, Surakata, the Arab *jeli* ancestor, has been projected backward in time, to where he appears in the "Mande Creation Myth."[79] As for the question of how traditionists might reconcile the impoverished blind host of Muhammad in the Arabia-oriented texts with the *funé* native son of Mande in stories with a sub-Saharan bias, we are told that "Funé Fosana was the ancestor of Silamaka."[80]

Whereas the Fosana legend is much concerned with establishing Muslim antecedents for the *funé* ancestor, thereby accounting for the group's special Islamic status, the Silamaka tradition stresses an ancestor's deeds within the broad context of the Sunjata epic. This is consistent with evidence throughout the oral tradition, indicating that there was a time when the most important source of prestige in Mande was in tracing one's ancestors to Sunjata's life and times rather than Muhammad's. The Sunjata epic still describes heroic ancestral deeds through predominantly non-Muslim themes, a tradition that exists more or less side by side with the type of Islamic texts described above, though there are many instances of interaction between what are basically Sunjata characters and those borrowed from Arabia. Unlike the tales involving Arab ancestors, the relevant Sunjata episodes do not indicate a primary concern with justifying any particular social status for the *funéw*. Instead, they tend to establish an ancestral involvement—though one that is very peripheral—in events at the time of the unification of the Mali Empire, as expressed in deeds performed by Silamaka the *funé* ancestor.

André Arcin heard a tradition claiming that the Camara of northern Guinea maintained their links with Mande antecedents by tracing their descent from

Fina Silla Makha (i.e., *fina* Silamaka).[81] If Arcin's informants maintained an awareness of Silamaka's *funé* connection, the tracing of their descent from Silamaka would be of interest both in terms of the tradition's historical validity and in terms of attitudes toward a *nyamakala* ancestor. If they knew Silamaka was a *funé* and did not want to be identified with what the colonial literature describes as a "lower caste" group, they could just as well have echoed the claims of many other Camara/Kamara of northern Guinea, who enhance their own pedigrees by naming as their ancestor a hero such as Fran Camara, one of Sunjata's generals. That it was the *funé* ancestor who was invoked instead of a hero from the Sunjata epic suggests not just a preference for Muhammad's companions over Sunjata's generals as a source of prestige, but a vocational identity. Arcin's Camara informants could well have been identifying themselves as *funéw*. The Islamic and Mande ancestral spheres of activity should not be considered mutually exclusive in this or any other case.

Another account recorded in northern Guinea in 1961, more than a half-century after Arcin's, describes the migration and conversion to Islam of a Kamara ancestor called "Feni," a name that could arguably derive from "Fina" or "Fune."[82] In this case, the emigrants accompanying Feni Kamara are said to have converted to Islam, and they include familiar names from the Sunjata epic. The references in various oral texts to a legendary *funé* ancestor named either Silamaka or Camara might refer to several historical persons jumbled together during the long chain of transmission, but this does not diminish the consistency with which they stress a relationship between the *funé,* the Camara, and Islam.

In the Sunjata texts the relationships between kings and commoners do not always reflect the kind of social differentiation that characterizes *nyamakalaya* as it is familiar to us. This can be due to distortion caused by various lapses through generations of oral transmission, but we cannot dismiss the possibility that in some instances it could reflect an earlier stage of development in the social hierarchy. Hints of this are spread throughout the epic and tend to reveal themselves through scrutiny of individual characters and occupational groups. One of the most conspicuous instances of this is where Sumanguru the Soso king and Fakoli, one of Sunjata's most important generals, are identified in some variants as blacksmiths.[83] In the case of Silamaka, he is identified as both war chief and *funé,* which are not mutually exclusive roles.

The non-Islamic tradition of a *funé* ancestor has evidently been largely submerged by the Fosana legend, but it is still recognizable. A surviving text collected at the beginning of this century is of particular interest, because in addition to plainly portraying Silamaka in the status and role of a Mande *funé* instead of an Arab Anṣāri,[84] it has other clear affinities within the broader context of Mande tradition. Occurring as an episode in a fragment of a Sunjata variant, it describes a meeting in which Sumanguru welcomes Sunjata to Mande but warns him of dire consequences that would result from any hostile acts against Soso. Assisting at this meeting, says the narrator, are the Camara ancestor "Fina Manga Sylla Makha," whose name can be roughly translated as "Silamaka the *funé* (or *fina*) chief,"[85] and a chief griot called "Balafa Séga, ancestor of the Koaté," readily identifiable as Bala Fasseké Kouyaté, Sunjata's famous bard. But it is the *funé* who takes center stage in this anecdote that offers examples—as perceived by at least some traditionists—of the nature of the relationship between this "assistant," the Soso king, and a certain chief of Mande.

As the great adversaries take each other's measure, the *funé* and *jeli* "assistants" ask God for enduring good relations between Sunjata and Sumanguru. At the same time Sumanguru rests his right hand on a piece of dead wood, and that night the wood sprouts with greenery, which he interprets as a favorable omen. Accompanying Sumanguru on the road to Soso, the Camara ancestor who is here called "Fina" is asked to pray to God again, that the Soso ruler may become the greatest chief and the conqueror of Sunjata. Fina replies that everything he could ask of God in favor of both adversaries was requested the day before, but that he will pray that Sumanguru never becomes the object of ridicule by Sunjata. Satisfied with this response, Sumanguru gives Fina the standard reward of Mande tradition (and fantasy), a hundred each of cows, sheep, and gold *mithqals*.[86]

The motif of sprouting dead wood employed in this text dramatically expresses the occult power of the person who touches the wood,[87] but of potential historical value here is the implied claim that the *funéw* of Sunjata's time were among groups of the social level now known as *nyamakalaw*. That this could indicate actual social conditions of the time receives at least some tenuous support from the way in which this passage describes a secular chief/Muslim cleric relationship thought to have existed even prior to the rise of ancient Mali. The tone of the interaction portrayed in this encounter between the itinerant Muslim bard and the animist Soso king who is much attracted by the power of Islam as a source of blessings, has distinct affinities with Al-Bakrī's description of the relationship between the pagan king of eleventh-century Ghana and the early Muslims in his town, some of whom must have been Soninke.[88] While there is no denying the virtual impossibility of extrapolating confirmable historical data from oral tradition that has evolved through as many as seven or eight centuries, it is interesting that a brief anecdote such as this can present a miniature word-picture of what some of the best-informed historical research has suggested was actually the case. In the Sunjata epic, the character who ultimately succumbs to all of the occult and military power that can be brought to bear in Mande is Sumanguru. Here we see Sumanguru seeking whatever help he can get from Islam, having doubtless (in accord with routine Mande practice) already marshaled all occult power at his command. In his discussion of the circumstances of Western Sudanic chiefs who were early recipients of Islamic influence, Nehemia Levtzion produced an outline of the same kind of chiefly predicament portrayed above: "Chiefs were particularly inclined to seek the prayers of Muslims, and their highly appreciated amulets. Chiefs were under greater strains—competition over the chieftaincy, fear of plots, wars with other chiefs, or responsibility for the welfare of the whole community—than the common people whose way of life harmonized with the rhythm of the traditional religion."[89]

The anecdote about Fina the Camara ancestor evokes the *funé* of Sunjata's time in what we gather to be his ideal role, that of Islamic bard. It must be stressed that *nyamakalaw* at any time early or late in the chain of transmission may have told this story simply to associate the *funéw* with Sunjata, just as they relate the tales of Fosana as a means of establishing Islamic antecedents. With the opportunities for dropping, adding, or distorting elements of the text spanning some seven centuries, we cannot know at what point the relationship between pagan king and Muslim *funé* took the form in which it was recorded. This could have happened in the final performance before it was written down, or it could have endured through many generations of oral transmission.

Having acknowledged this, we must avoid turning a blind or overly cautious eye toward a potentially historical element, and consider the possibility that the description of the relationship between pagan king and Muslim *funé* is an archaic fragment reflecting a situation that actually existed. Fina's prayers to "Allah" are consistent with what is now regarded as an essential part of the *funé* identity, while Bala Fasséké's participation is decidedly out of character for the premier secular *jeli* of Mande legend.[90] Implicit in the reward that Fina receives is acknowledgment of his "dependent" relationship to the patron (*jatigi*), with the bard's benefactor in this case being Sumanguru. Further evidence in this text of his lack of *horonya* ("nobility") is Fina's behavior when, upon returning toward Mande with his herds, he is robbed of his new possessions by the troops of a chief (Sangara Bandigué Kouté) who mistakes him and his companions for an advance unit of Sumanguru's invading army. The error is acknowledged and, upon Fina's bitter complaint (rather than the counterattack that would be undertaken by a hunter/warrior), Sangara promises to make restitution. Fina is invited to return the next day to Sangara's house, where he will find that which he is owed. Fina finds one of Sangara's pregnant wives, and accepting this compensation he takes her along on the road back to Mande. When the woman gives birth, instead of the child's being named "Fina," it is called "Dabo," meaning, as it is translated in the received form, "qu'il n'est pas de lui." This, we are told, is the origin of the Dabo.[91]

This anecdote is woven of threads that extend in several directions through a sizable swatch of Mande tradition, and as such it contains clues that the narrator probably never intended,[92] about local perceptions of where the *funéw* fit within the overall social fabric. Essentially, this tale locates them in a narrative subtext running just below the most salient events of the greater epic context. This addresses clans of the Sunjata era known collectively as the *blaw* (or *bulaw, bilaw,* etc.) that appear to have been involved in the origins of *nyamakalaya,* though not all aspects of the relationship are clear as yet.

At this point, much about *bla* clan social status remains unclear, but it appears to derive from a fluid period in the evolution of the social order. The *blaw* are apparently entangled in questions of who arrived in Mande first, and how power and authority were resolved between early arrivals and latecomers. The subject lies outside the scope of this essay and is discussed more fully elsewhere,[93] but it can be mentioned here that among the kin groups involved, those most often named as *blaw* are the Sissoko, Dumbia, and Koroma, with Sunjata's famous general Fakoli claimed as their legendary ancestor. The *bla* clans are thought to have been in Mande ahead of certain conquering hunter/warrior groups known as *dunan* or "strangers," including the Konaté and Keita, which are Sunjata's clan affiliations. Monteil reported that the earlier *blaw* were regarded as possessors of esoteric knowledge about such things as religious ritual and land tenure, but that they fell under the domination of invading clans (*dunan*), some of whose descendants remain most eligible for chiefly office. In some cases, the term *bla* appears to differentiate the earlier people from the *mansaré* (royal lineages), whose hunter/warrior forebears are considered to have remained free through centuries of political and social change.[94] The relevance here is that female *blaw*, especially of the Camara clan, are said to answer to the name "Dabo." "Dabo" (also pronounced and/or transcribed as "Damba" or "Danba") is described variously as the name of a clan that shares the *funé* identity with the Camara, as a special name to which only *bla* women respond, and as the name of females of the Camara *funéw*.[95]

Certain clichés or motifs might appear anywhere in Mande oral tradition because they have been, and still are, heavily relied upon by bards to explain matters of deep social significance. These formula anecdotes now provide stock answers to questions about ancient times which the *nyamakalaw* could probably no longer answer in any other way if they wanted to, though such verbal instruments may have been devised originally with the intention of concealing facts about the *nyamakalaw*'s own origins. These anecdotes are West African originals, but they function in much the same way that the Arab-derived stories of Surakata, Walali Ibrahima, and Fosana do for the *jeliw, garankéw,* and *funéw* respectively, in that they appear in tales claiming antecedents that are somehow superior to the *nyamakalaw* as perceived in the colonial literature.

One of the most frequently exercised formulas is the ubiquitous Western Sudanic tale of two traveling companions (usually but not always brothers) of the distant past, lost and starving in the wilderness. Seeing that his brother is faint with hunger, the elder secretly carves a piece of flesh from his own leg to nourish his youthful sibling. Upon learning the truth of this gallant sacrifice, the younger brother begins to praise the elder, thus assuming for himself and his descendants the role of bard.[96] As a popular explanation for *senanku* (joking) relationships between clans,[97] for the existence of *horon* and bardic clans of the same *jamu,* or for how different branches of clans derive from the same root, this tale is at the heart of folklore concerning the "origins" of social stratification, with the implication being that the beneficiary of the noble sacrifice is—in varying degrees—socially inferior to the donor. One variant of this tale recalls both the dependent status of the "Fina" and the arcane *funé/bla* affiliation as expressed in the "gift of the pregnant noble wife" anecdote described above. In this case a Koroma serves his flesh to a "Fina," thus establishing a *senanku* relationship between one of the principal *bla* kin groups (Koroma) and the *funé* occupational class.[98] This is one of the ways in which traditionists express fine points of social differentiation within the broader *horon* and/or *nyamakala* categories. We also encounter direct statements, as with the distinguished bard Wa Kamissoko's outright claim that his people, the bards of Kirina, have their own griots, the "Fine" [sic] and the Kouyaté.[99]

As an explanation for arcane social relationships, the story of the starving travelers is of one genre with the less widespread but functionally similar legend in which, as we have seen, a prominent chief of Mande gives away one of his own wives, who is pregnant with the unborn ancestor of a particular kin group.[100] A claim to a sort of shirttail *horon* ancestry for the descendants of the unborn child is suggested, but also lurking therein appears to be some sort of implied message having to do with the firstcomer-latecomer groups. The subject is kinship, perhaps acknowledging that men of the dominant *mansaré* "latecomers" had married women of the preceding *bla* populations (i.e., those known as "Dabo" or "Damba"/"Danba").[101] In the texts now available, the people most often indicated as descendants of the infant born to the gift-wife and the awardee are the Dabo specifically, or an unnamed branch of the *blaw*. In some cases, as in the one outlined above, the recipient of the pregnant wife is the *funé* ancestor. The identities of the chief and the awardee change from one variant to the next, but in most cases either directly or by extension, there is some reference to the *funé* ancestor, the Dabo clan, or the *blaw*.[102]

Whatever the finer points of the original may have included, the story of the "noble" who presents his pregnant wife to a "subordinate" now addresses, to at least some degree, the relationship between the (possibly) earlier-arriving *blaw* and the later but dominant *mansaré*. As such, it is involved in the kind of "historical games" described by Kopytoff, engaged in by early and late-arriving groups in order to coexist within the same political boundaries.[103] In the tradition, the husband is a *mansa* or chief, while the wife and/or offspring are *blaw*. In the variant described above, the father of the infant Dabo, Sangara Bandigué Kouté, is probably Sangaran Madiba Konté (Madiba Konté, king of Sankaran), a prominent figure in the Sunjata tradition.[104] Other versions of the legend name Sunjata himself as bestower of the pregnant wife.[105] The *mansaré* husband/*bla* wife combination also occurs outside this anecdote, though it still involves the question of offspring, as in the case of "Nareng Mahan" (Naré Fa Maghan, Sunjata's father) and the jealous Koutouyoro Boula (Boula = *bla*), mother of Sunjata's stepbrother (*faden* or "rival brother").[106] The *nyamakalaw* enter the picture where the receiver of the pregnant wife bounty is the *funé* ancestor. The implicit claim that Dabo or *bla* offspring of *horon* chiefs passed into the *nyamakala* milieu involves both the process of Mande social differentiation and the issue of firstcomer and latecomer coexistence.

Regarding the background of *funéya* specifically, there are two principal areas of tradition that might yield useful information upon further investigation. One involves references to early ancestral links with the Soninke society of Wagadu (ancient Ghana) and/or the successor states that occupied a power vacuum between the decline of Wagadu and the consolidation of the Mali Empire. A related area of inquiry has to do with the possibility that a period of servitude was involved in the development of *funéya,* and this includes the questions of *funé* Camara kin group identity and its distinguished ancestors.

Addressing the first of these subjects is a tradition recorded by Bokar N'Diaye that links the Arab and Mande stories of *funé* origin through descendants of Fosana who arrived in the Mande heartland by stages, with one generation of praisers of God and Muhammad settling in Kumbi Saleh, which is believed by some to have been the capital of ancient Ghana. It is claimed here that the marriage of Fosana's Arab descendant to local women produced the *caste des Finah,* and that upon the destruction of the Ghana Empire a descendant and community patriarch named Ibrahima emigrated to Kaarta, which is to say the region between Nioro and Kita. One of his sons was Madiba Niakhalé, one of whose descendants was Finah-Mady (Mady the *funé*), who is the fortunate recipient in a variant of the "gift of the pregnant noble wife" motif.[107]

The credence of the Wagadu link in this account suffers from a lack of supporting variants, from N'Diaye's failure to name his informants, and from the general tendency in Mande Islamic tradition to claim that any and all ancestors followed a similar migratory pattern. However, the northern orientation is consistent with other evidence, including Seni Darbo's assertion that certain Camara forebears—including the ancestors of both Fran and Kamanjan Camara—were centered in the Timbuktu region, specifically as kings of Tabo and Sibi.[108] Though they do not say so, both N'Diaye and Darbo appear to be drawing on elements of a tradition whereby the *funéw* themselves, among other *nyamakala* informants, persistently indicate that their ancestors figured among certain Soninke populations dispersed from Wagadu, with the place names Sibi and Tabo consistently appearing in their testimonies.[109] Among non-*funé,* the bard Jeli Baba Sissoko presents his discourse on Wagadu and ancient Mali as one continuous traditional history, claiming that all *nyamakala* occupations commenced in Wagadu.[110] As Meillassoux has shown, kin group references in Soninke tradition connecting Wagadu with Mande can provide useful evidence,[111] although owing to the ease with which patronyms have been changed in the past, apparently by entire groups at times, they must be handled carefully. Persistent mention of such names as Diawara, Fofana, Diabi, Magassa, Dukuré, and Niakhalé[112] suggests some potentially fruitful avenues of investigation. Variants of the *jamu* Niakhalé, for example, are prominent in the *funé* tradition, including the story of the "gift of the pregnant noble wife."[113] Elsewhere, a brief but intriguing glimpse of *funé* activity associated with Wagadu occurs in variants of the Sunjata epic from the Nioro region, where the "Finanou" woman Niagalé Missâné (also Fina Niakalé Missansé) is in charge of Sunjata's armory ("cette femme était préposée à la garde des sabres de Soundiata").[114]

The names from Wagadu also point to the time when *funéw,* or at least their ancestors, were acknowledged by other *jamuw* than Camara. This is consistent with other indications that the period between the destruction of ancient Ghana and the rise of Mali was crucial in the development of *funéya.* It is too early to feel comfortable with any conclusions, but a pattern is beginning to emerge: At various stages during the history of the great Western Sudanic states, certain *mansaw* (in this case chiefs of the Camara *jamu,* evidently of Tabon) may have been among those who controlled very extensive populations of slaves and artisans who provided essential goods and services,including agricultural produce (from slaves), tools and weapons (from smiths), and genealogies invented to legitimize claims to power (from bards). These populations normally adopted the names of the rulers they served, which could be one way in which the *funéw* came to be generally identified as Camara. Regarded from this perspective, references to the "Kamara Fina" as bards *of* the Camara rather than bards *named* Camara are of particular interest and point to a need for further investigation of this relationship.[115]

The essence of the *funé* informants' claim to Wagadu antecedents is that their ancestors were already serving as Islam-oriented bards to Muslim clerics of eleventh-century Ghana. This cannot be accepted without further evidence, because if *funéya* developed somewhat later as a consequence of, say, the turmoil accompanying the consolidation of thirteenth-century Mali, they could have subsequently made specious legitimizing claims to distinguished forebears from the Wagadu epoch, just as they have adopted ancestors from the period of the *hijra.* At the same time, neither can we reject the possibility that there is substance to the claim. Among the first sub-Saharan peoples to be exposed to Islam were the Soninke of Wagadu. Though there were people performing bardic functions in ancient Ghana,[116] we cannot assume that the kind of bard-host relationship known to have existed later in the Mande heartland had developed in Wagadu society by the time in question. However, the arrival of Muslim clerics bringing with them a new belief system could well have been seen by some members of the artisan/bardic groups as a potential new source of livelihood. It may have been very early on that professional praisers began to orbit the agents of Islam in order to benefit by whatever opportunities might be forthcoming, soon beginning to establish their own proficiency in matters pertaining to that religion. It is this sort of occupational opportunism to which Tayiru Banbera refers, with the remark that "men, when they noticed that a certain prosperity derived from one occupation, and that it produced good things, they would see that this was preferable and continue in that way."[117]

The traditionists' persistent references to a place called Sibi are of special interest in light of a learned Muslim Soninke informant's reference to people known as "Sibi" of Tichitt, whom he describes as *captifs de cases* of the Kayamagha (king) of Wagadu.[118] The collective sources indicate that during the epoch when Wagadu was ruled from Kumbi by the Cisse dynasty, whose rulers held the title *kayamaga (magha, manga),* a very considerable part of society consisted of slaves and former slaves. It appears, too, that toward the end of that period, certain servile or formerly servile individuals occupied prominent positions in the social hierarchy, possibly including the forebears of Sumanguru, ruler of Soso, strongest of the Soninke successor states,[119] which extended right down into Mande. A thorough discussion of the question of servile background from Wagadu and the Soninke successor states must be reserved for another study, but we can note here that it is events of this epoch that give rise to the occasional references in our material to ancestors of the Wagadu era. If servitude figures in the *funé* past, it could date from this time, but so could *funé* involvement with Islam, and further research should be able to shed some light on these matters.

Owing to many colonial writers' exaggerated stress on the alleged unsavory reputations of *nyamakalaw,* one hesitates to raise the subject here. Nonetheless, in the interest of reviewing all available aspects of oral tradition concerning the *funéw,* it must be noted that despite their traditionally cultivated ties with Islam, there exists a residue of not entirely submerged evidence suggesting that at some stage of their history and in some social contexts, the *funéw* have been considered to be somehow impure. The taboo prohibiting them from sitting on the bed of a noble echoes yet another incident from Muhammad's childhood,[120] and may reflect a popular notion about the custom of *nyamakala* endogamy. However, vestiges of the lowest level of captive servitude might also lurk somewhere in the background to *funéya.* In stark contrast to the prestigious legend of the "ancestor" Fosana's personal relationship with Muhammad is a tradition heard by Tautain, attributing the origin of the *funéw* (he calls them "Finankes") to an ancestor who was the offspring of a union between a corpse and a living person.[121]

It is very unlikely that anyone but slaves would have been slandered in such a way, and if anything is to be made of this, it could suggest a period of servitude for a *funé* population at some juncture. It may be, however, that the necrophilia tradition refers only to albino human beings destined for sacrifice. In addition to being the occupational term for the group under discussion, the word *funé* means "albino."[122] This is why, when Paul Soleillet speaks of the *Founes* of Segu, he is describing people of abnormal skin pigmentation rather than bards or artisans.[123] Perhaps the necrophilia story derives from the practice of reserving albino or irregularly pigmented captives for sacrifice on critical occasions.[124] In an episode of the Bamana Segu epic, the king refers to one such group of future victims as "the dead people."[125] However, if this is related to a stage of *funé* history, it could indicate a period of servitude somewhere along the line, suggesting the possibility that at least some early *funéw* would have regarded Islam initially as a refuge as much as a source of livelihood.

At this stage of inquiry, the exact nature of original *funé* status, occupation, and spiritual persuasion—servile or free, artisan or bard, secular or Muslim— remains to be clarified. A possible hypothesis for the development of *funéya,* based on evidence now available, begins with the arrival of Islam in the Western Sudan, with some lesser worthies of society seizing the opportunity to place themselves in the service of Muslim clerics and lay the groundwork for the ideal *funé* occupation. Later these hypothetical proto-*funéw* moved with the Soninke diaspora into the Mande heartland, with some of them possibly passing through a period of servitude at some point or points along the way. If such was the case, the present *funé* kin group identification as Camara suggests that during the servile period this would have been the predominant *jamu* of their masters, whether *numuw* or *horonw.* A possibly fruitful area for further inquiry into the *funé* background comprises any oral traditions involving the Camara kin group's activities, especially north of the Niger. However, it must be clear from the above discussion that the oral sources constitute not an avenue but a maze through which to follow shadowy generations of socially itinerant *funéw* as they wander the artistic, religious, and economic milieux of Mande.

Appendix: Perspectives from *nyamakalaw* in Our Time

Regardless of how careful we are in our interpretation of oral evidence collected directly from the people of Mande, we can never be entirely certain that we are not contributing to the distortion that already forms so much of the fabric of tradition. Historians endeavoring to shed a ray of light on the most distant epochs must generally resign themselves to lamentably feeble (and often very questionable) results, due in no small part to the vast temporal distances between today's oral informants and the events of which they speak. As most scholars who work with such material are aware, these pitfalls and limitations must be kept constantly in mind in order to achieve useful results with a minimum of error.[126]

Many researchers now deposit tapes of their collected oral texts at the Archives of Traditional Music in Bloomington, Indiana,[127] but transcripts of interviews in translation are rarely accessible. Some interviews are granted on conditions of confidentiality which must be honored, and those which are not would usually be of very little interest to any but a few specialists. But as it happens, two of the most interesting and nonconfidential interviews in my experience provided evidence for the above essay. Portions of those interviews are offered here with the idea of giving readers a somewhat clearer (though far from perfect, owing to problems of translation) impression of how the original words of some of the more articulate and thoughtful of the Mande bards come to us.

Both of these interviews contain fragments of oral traditions or references to them. When a *nyamakala* is asked a question about people and events of the past, the response will usually include a bit of oral tradition. This is the pigment with which *nyamakalaw*—as people of speech and of the power that accompanies it—paint their word pictures of the past and interpret the daily lives of their people. But as will be seen from the two samples offered here, modes of expression vary greatly from one traditionist to the next.

A fundamental difference between the two samples is that "Interview I" is the result of a single meeting with an informant who never relied primarily on the bardic occupation for his livelihood. During the one session, Sadyo Camara probably responded to the questions with most of what he knew about those topics, knowledge derived as much from the consequence of simply having been reared in the traditional *funé* milieu as from any special effort to become a savant. In contrast, "Interview II" consists of a distinguished bard's remarks in the first of seven sessions that included more than ten hours' recording over a period of two weeks, of an epic narrative running to nearly eight thousand lines. Tayiru Banbera was a professional *jeli* for much of his life, having acquired his knowledge and skills through years of apprenticeship with bards of the previous generation, especially a griot named Duguné, of Joforobo.[128]

It can be seen that of the two traditionsts, Sadyo Camara leans most heavily on oral tradition for his responses to questions, and appears to be more accepting of its claims. This is owing not to any lack of acuteness on his part but to the circumstances of the interview, and the nature of the questions to which he was responding. In his kind effort to accommodate the interviewer's questions, he was concerned mainly with relating what he knew of the tradition, rather than offering his own comments. For his part, Tayiru Banbera had reason to believe that this was only the first of many meetings, and that he would have plenty of time to perform his narrative. For that reason, and because he was a veteran performer of his material, he was more willing and able than was Sadyo Camara to share some of his own thoughts about the subjects on which he was being questioned. His remarks make it plain that oral tradition does not necessarily reflect the views and attitudes of the narrator. This is especially true when a knowledgeable and experienced raconteur dwells in an urban area, has traveled widely, is a relatively devout Muslim, or has in other ways been exposed to a significant amount of nontraditional influence.

In the process of collecting oral traditions and conducting interviews with *nyamakala* people in Mali, it is not unusual to find that their personal views of Mande society do not run in the traditional vein preserved in discourse passed down to them from previous generations. Tayiru Banbera has a large repertoire of popular anecdotes concerning the alleged origin of various social groups and their customs, many of which he inserted into the discourse that I recorded. But in the interview that preceded those performances, part of which is presented here, he exhibits a distinctly nontraditional attitude toward the entire concept of social differentiation.

The interview with Sadyo Camara concerned only the *funéw,* so it is reproduced in its entirety. The Tayiru Banbera session was about twice as long, beginning with questions on the *nyamakalaw* in general and the *jeliw* in particular before turning to the *funéw,* so only the *funé* material is included here. Neither text is what could be justifiably described as typical, because not all informants provide as much colorful material and interesting insight. However, the general tenor of the beliefs and sentiments, both traditional and otherwise, are not uncommon among the *nyamakalaw.* Most bardic testimony would lean more toward that of Sadyo Camara than that of Tayiru Banbera, but to Tayiru's skepticism of the message of his own tradition, compare the remarks of another *jeli:* "In everything concerning the origin of the world there are many lies. No one wrote things down in books in Africa. Here it is the mouth-to-mouth system. They pass the news from mouth to mouth."[129]

The relative degrees of knowledge and expertise displayed by the two informants reflect their individual circumstances, rather than those of the *funé* and *jeli* groups in general. One encounters many *jeliw* less knowledgeable than the *funé* Sadyo Camara, and there are *funéw* (not to mention *numuw* and *garankéw*) who are able to narrate their own versions of Mande epic.[130] Generally, however, the *jeliw* have had the most extensive repertoires.

Sadyo Camara of "Interview I" was a *funé* originally from Nyamina. A handsome, dignified individual in his sixties who preferred to speak French with me, he lived in the Dar Salam quarter of Segu at the time of recording. My notes recall that this gentleman made a sincere effort to answer my questions to the best of his ability, and that he did not appear concerned with the customary Mande practice of concealing at least some of his knowledge, though he may well have done so. The interview was arranged by Moulaye Kida, director of the Segu archives, and it took place in the reading room next to his office in the presence of only one other person, my assistant Ibrahima Diawara.[131]

Tayiru Banbera of "Interview II" is a *jeli* who resides in the village of Ngoin, seven kilometers east of Segu, though in 1976 he also had a part-time residence in Segu. During his younger days Tayiru achieved distinction as one of the most knowledgeable and skilled raconteurs of Mali. He was about forty-five years old at the time of the interview, and was gradually phasing out his bardic activities around Segu in favor of farming at Ngoin. The interview, conducted in Bamana, was held under a shade tree in front of a house on the eastern edge of Segu, and my assistant Ibrahima Diawara was the only other person in attendance.[132]

Interview I: Sadyo Camara, March 10, 1975, Segu

Question: Can you tell me about the origin of the *funéw?*
Answer: The origin of the *funéw* goes back to when the Prophet left Mecca for Medina. He arrived at Medina by camel. When he got there, the entire village came out to welcome him. But our ancestor who originated the *funéw* was called in Arabic Aba Yiruba Lazarihu. He was poor. When the Prophet arrived, all the people rushed to him, each wanting him to lodge with them. The Prophet set free his camel to see where it would go, because the place where the camel lay down, only that family would be his host.

When the camel directed itself toward our ancestor's compound, our ancestor had a goat with only one teat. In the compound there was a date palm. From that time until his death, all of the Prophet's speeches were made under that date palm. When the camel got there, it lay down in the compound of our ancestor. The townspeople were bewildered because instead of going to one of the rich noblemen's houses, the camel made its way to the home of a poor family. This was truly a choice made by God.

At that moment our ancestor possessed only one measure of grain, one kilo for the wife to prepare the day's meal. She milked the goat, and with the milk and the millet she prepared a *daika,* similar to *mukufara* of the Bamana, or *vinza.*[133] But the townspeople brought all kinds of things to prepare a special meal in honor of the Prophet. When the feast began, the Prophet asked for the food of his host, who was not present. But before that, the wife of our ancestor complained that their meal was not worthy. The husband replied that he could do nothing else, for that was all there was to be found in his house. So the food was carried out. The Prophet took a piece of bread. Then he began to eat, saying, "The camel is a creature of God, and I am the same. He chose this compound, therefore it is God's will. I will take nothing other than this." Then the Prophet stayed there with his host.

As you can see, the very basis of *funéya* comes from Quranic study. We study. The *funéw,* it is they who learn the Quran, they who are learned. But their debasement to begging is a change brought by the new generation.[134] The presence of the Prophet in the family of our ancestor was the source of great prestige for our ancestor who was a poor man. After that Yiruba Lazarihu got up to go into the neighboring villages to ask for alms, riding on a donkey that had a bell hanging from its neck. When he arrived in the villages, he rang the bell and all the villagers came out and gave gifts according to what they could afford. That is how the *funéw* originated, but it was by way of the *shurafa* who passed by Timbuktu on their way to our land that the *funéw* arrived at our present situation.[135]

It was in that way that the *shurafa* and the *funéw* both arrived at a certain [social] level, and that was because of the bonds that united them since very remote times. Upon their arrival in the land of the blacks they dispersed, some to Wagadu, and the others to Mande. The storyteller himself was among those who went to Wagadu.[136] Owing to the good relationship that the *funéw* had with the people of Wagadu, the Diawara, they ended up by intermarrying with the Diawara. They then became the special *funéw* of the Diawara. They then reproduced themselves and the *funéw* increased their numbers. Some of them went with the Kagoro,[137] that is to say the Fofana. Others joined the Magassa. We know of the presence of other *funéw* among the Diaby, the Dukuré, whom they call Almamy Tamba.

The Diaby and the Magassa all came from Wagadu. So each *funé* uses the dialect of the locality where he lives. In that way they contribute to the diversity of the *funé* language. But thanks to God, our ancestors were among those who remained with the Diawara. That is to say, Shaykh Umar. When Al-Hājj ʾUmar came, our grandfather Funé Musa followed Madu Kanjan to Wagadu.[138] Madu Kanjan, Karunga, and Tamangily were [of] the Diawara.[139]

When Al-Hājj ʾUmar came, he was followed by our grandfathers,[140] and our grandfathers said to the Diawara, "Eh! This one we are following is a man of truth. We believe that you will be destroyed by this war. But before that we have decided to demonstrate our military power to you." That is how our grandfathers became involved in war. Now, each of our grandparents was provided with the skilled tongue (speaking ability, *materiaux de langue*) of his kind, learning to use his tongue to sing the praises. For example, we learned the praises of Tiramakan. They describe the deeds of Tiramakan Traoré.[141]

Q: Can you give us some of the praises of Tiramakan?
A: We have the praises of Tiramakan, of Fakoli, of the Kulubali and others.

Q: Is it true that only the *jeliw* are the guardians of genealogy?
A: In fact, the *jeliw* know their genealogies, and the *funéw* know theirs.

Q: Are the *jeliw* considered to be more knowledgeable than the *funéw?*
A: That is so. The *jeliw* acquired their position in society from their ancestor Surakata Boum Malik. That Surakata Boum Malik on the field of battle exalted the moral and physical courage of the Prophet and his warriors to encourage them to deeds of bravery. After the victory, Surakata Boum Malik would receive the

largest share of the Prophet's booty from the war. The warriors were often dissatisfied with the privileges given to Surakata by the Prophet. After seeing this show of jealousy by the other warriors, the Prophet sent Surakata to stay in the village during the next battle to be fought. The absence of Surakata from that battle caused them to be defeated, with the loss of many important warriors. Upon their return the Prophet asked them, "What happened?" The warriors admitted that many of them had been killed. And to that the Prophet added, "It is the exalting praises of Surakata that encourage us. There, because of his absence, we were defeated by whomever was there. Therefore, he plays a very important part among us." That is the history of the *jeliw*. But the *funéw* are another thing.

Q: Were there *funéw* here before the arrival of Islam in this country?
A: No, they did not exist then. The *funéw* began with Aba Yiruba Lazarihu.

Q: What is the oldest *nyamakala* group in the land?
A: The blacksmiths were [once] the only *nyamakalaw* in the land. The groups of *jeliw* and *funéw* all came from Wagadu to spread out across the other regions of Africa. When the wars . . . when a warrior accomplished a deed, the *nyamakalaw* congratulated them by singing their praises. That is where clan names [*jamuw*] came from, a [heroic] situation such as when a warrior came to save someone from disaster.

Q: At that time were the people of Wagadu and its neighboring regions Muslims?
A: No, Islam had not yet touched those places. They were all animists.

Q: If the *jeliw* and *funéw* were Muslims at Mecca, and Wagadu was not yet in its Islamic period, were there no bards at Wagadu?
A: It was above all the *nyamakalaw* who brought Islam. That is to say that during the same period in Wagadu, the bards originated with the praising of men's brave deeds. For example, Balla Fasséké was a *horon*. But when Sunjata saved him and he began to praise Sunjata, he became a bard. That is how the bardic occupation is determined. ["Toute l'explication des griots reside la."] In a situation where you give me something and in return I praise you, I automatically become your bard.

Q: Were the bards of Wagadu not Muslims?
A: In fact, they were not Muslims. It was Shaykh Umar who brought Islam here. The propagation of Islam among us began with the arrival of Shaykh Umar.[142] At that time Islam was practiced in secret because the Muslims were not here in strength and did not dare to show their belief in that religion. For example, a Muslim stranger could not pray in the home of his host because at that time the host had an aversion to Islam. When Al-Hājj 'Umar arrived, some Bamana were converted to Islam. But when they were discovered by the other, non-Muslim Bamana, they were beheaded.

Q: When the *jeliw* and *funéw* ancestors who were Muslims from Medina arrived at Wagadu, did they conceal themselves to pray, or did they not pray at all?

A: Their hosts were powerful animist chiefs at the time. So the bards could not pray at all, or they would hide to do it. But with the expansion of Islam they began to worship freely.

Q: How is it that one encounters Camara who are *funéw,* but at the same time Camara who are of other occupations and social classes?
A: The name Camara was easily separated from the *funé* class. One meets a great many Camara who are not *funéw.* There are Camara *numuw.* In the Sarakolé [Soninké] society one meets the names Diaby, Magassa, and others, but that has no relationship with the origin of those who are called Camara, Diaby, or the others. The family names might have nothing to do with the origin of certain individuals. For example, when a child goes to live with a man's family, he will be raised there until he is offered a wife. The children who issue from that marriage can take the name of the family of their adoptive grandfather. That is one of the main differences between the name and its origin. There are many such cases here in Africa, and usually the orphan will take the name of his adopted family.

Q: Does that explain what happened with the Camara?
A: That is part of it, aside from the two kinds of Camara, those who came from Medina, and those who came from Wagadu. The difference between them is that the Camara who came from Medina were Muslims, and those who came from Wagadu were animists.

Q: Which of those among them were the Camara nobles?
A: The Camara of Wagadu were the nobles, because those who came from Medina were the *funéw.* I have already explained the origin of the *funéw* who go to villages and ask for alms with the aid of a donkey with a bell hanging from its neck. The ability to do that originated with the *funéw.*

Q: Were the Camara of Wagadu only Bamana, or were they also other people?
A: Among the Camara there are both Bamana and Sarakolé, but all the Camara come from the Kagola who were animists.[143]

Q: Did the early *funéw* live with both Bamana and Mandenka people?
A: On their arrival from Medina, they could not show a belief contrary to that of their hosts, who were powerful pagan chiefs. Then they were obliged to support the beliefs of their hosts. The Camara *funéw* historically came from Mecca. Before lodging the Prophet in the family of their ancestor, their ancestor called himself Camara. But after the Prophet stayed with that family, there arose the question of *funéya.* In the beginning he was of the Arabs. It is with the mixing [of the races] that one meets the black *funéw.*

Q: Why was a distinction made between the nobles and the *nyamakalaw?*
A: I have already explained that. That is, in the beginning I explained the difference between the social classes. But during the course of the battles, when one man came to save another, the rescued one would praise his rescuer, and in

that way become a bard. That is what determined the difference between nobles and *nyamakalaw.*

Q: Aside from that event, what established the distinction between people?

A: I have already given the genealogy of the *funéw* as best I can. Aside from that, I cannot provide any more answers to the question.

Q: I have heard that among Samory's brave soldiers there was a *funé* man. Did *funéw* sometimes go to war?

A: Actually, in those days the *funéw* were great warriors. Our grandfathers were. The great *funé* warrior of Samory was named Nangabaly. My grandfather fought with Al-Ḥājj ʾUmar and took some prisoners.

Interview II: Tayiru Banbera, February 27, 1976, Segu

Question: Before talking about the history of Segu, can you tell me anything about the *funéw?*

Answer: Well, of the three kinds of bards I've told you about, the *funéw* are one type. I already spoke about Surakata, who is the ancestor of the *jeliw.* The ancestor of the *funéw* was Fosana. Therefore, since then the descendants of Fosana have been known through time as good people. The *funéw* are basically flatterers or praisers. Everything they do involves praising. We do this or that, and the *funéw* are like us.

What they tell me of the *garankéw* is that they are descendants of Walali Ibrahima, who was also a celebrated person in the time of the Prophet. All of these people worked as praisers. But it cannot be said that they farmed or participated in war or that they did kinds of work other than follow famous men. They did no other kinds of work. They praised their hosts in the best way that they could. The *funéw* did that. Even now, when things have changed and knowledge has increased, everybody has decided to take up the hoe and farm for himself. A person wants to enroll his children in school, he wants to find them a way to make a good living. The problem with being a bard is that he remains in poverty. If you are poor, you have nothing. You serve people who have things and who take pity on you, and in that way you hope to get something.

Nowadays we are getting away from the old kind of social system, and people don't want to be called *nyamakalaw* or *jeliw* or *kuléw* or *numuw.*[144] None of this was set forth by God Himself. Since Lawalé[145] it was never written that there are *numuw, jeliw, kuléw.* All of these things were made up by mankind.

That system was a custom adopted to help organize society and to help everyone to live together in the world with entertainment and amusing diversions. But to say that since the origin of man there were three or four classes of men, no! People were not supposed to be divided into three or four classes. There are only two kinds of people. The only real distinction between people is that some are born men and others are born women. That is all. Aside from that, everybody came from the same source. Whether white or black, everybody is of the same species without distinction. God arranged for us all to be reproduced in various ways, but we are all descended from Father Adam. There is no tree of *jeliw,* no tree of *funéw,* no tree of *kuléw.* It was men who created social differences. These are customs that facilitate our work on earth.

As for the *funéw,* all I know about their specialty is that some of them are traders and others are laborers. They travel from place to place and work for anyone who will hire them. There are also the *funéw* who do absolutely nothing. They go from house to house, from village to village, begging from people, and then they sit themselves down and fold their arms. This last type of *funéw* are people of speech like we are.

The *garankéw* are also people of speech, in a way similar to what we do. Then the people among us who are not praisers are the *numuw.* They work with iron, and that is their special occupation. As for the other types of *nyamakalaw,* without lying one could not describe the details of their occupations from the time of their origin. This is all I know about their occupations in earliest times.

Those who worked were their hosts. It was the host who worked. It was the host who took care of his *nyamakala.* He built a house for him and gave him a wife. It was the host who supported the members of his family. The *nyamakala* did nothing but serve his host. The bard would recite the speeches that pleased his host, and this would mean he was *nyamakala.* He would play music for him on the *ngoni* if he was an *ngoni* player. He would sing his praises if he wanted them, whatever songs he knew.

But to speak of the condition of being a *garanké,* of being a *numu,* of being a *jeli,* to say these are things with a very specific source coming from the Quran and preserved in writing since the beginning of life like men are divided from women, is nothing but a lie. It was men themselves who began these things. You can ask anybody about that.

The *funéw* derive from the customs of people, and they do things similar to what we do. They speak in the same way we do. As I have told you, I am a *jeli.* Because of their work as go-betweens and praisers, the three groups became known as *nyamakalaw.* It was men themselves who made those distinctions between branches. Aside from that, if you study the history of men since the beginning of the world, you will not see in any document, in any book, nor in anything else, that there is such a thing as the occupation *jeliya.* You will not see anything about a branch called *numu.* You will not see anything about a branch called *kulé.*

If you look you will see that there was humanity between men. Men, when they noticed that a certain prosperity derived from one occupation, and that it produced good things, they would see that this was preferable and continue in that way. But there would always be a person to make war. As we find in history since ancient times, there has always been a person who made war.

But you must look carefully at this subject of the origin of *nyamakalaya,* you must look for the truth of the matter. It would be easy to depart from the truth in trying to discover the origin of *nyamakalaya.* You will not see it written anywhere in a document that there are *jeliw,* that there are *numuw.* You will not find that the *nyamakalaw* come from a source other than men.

All men come from two people. Our father Adam, and our mother Eve. Blacks and whites, we are all issued from these two. But because of their reproduction, there came to be different branches. Oh yes, after there came to be different races, some of them were born black and others were born white. The whites are the descendants of Adam and so are we. We are sons of Adam. You understand? Just like them, if I become a good musician, I will get a nickname. If you are a builder, you will be given a title. This title does not mean that you have departed from your own race, as those of us who are distinguished from the whites by the color of our black skin. There is no task that makes such a division among the *nyamakalaw*. It can only be said that this one does that, and the other does something else. However God wills it.

As for the *garankéw,* these are the ones who make leather goods, *tuliw.* When somebody goes to see a *mori* [marabout], the *mori* says to him, "If you put such-and-such a thing on your body, you will accomplish what you need." That man is going to give a gris-gris to the *garanké.*[146] Once the *garanké* got into the habit of making the amulets out of leather, he became identified with the occupation of leatherworker. They called them the *garankéw.* They tanned leather. As for the *jeliw,* they became people of speech. As for the *funéw,* they also ended up acquiring the power of the word. They became very eloquent. After that, the difference between the conditions of *numuw, jeliw,* and *garankéw* is that the *jeliw* speak and the *garankéw* speak too, but the true work of the *garankéw* is leatherwork.

The men who work with iron are the *numuw.* But to say that the *funéw* have some particular kind of work that they do, no! They do not perform any special tasks. But as I have already told you, they came from Fosana. Also, the *jeliw* came from Surakata ibn Maliki. The *numuw* came from Dunfaila. The *funé* ancestor was Fosana. They praise the Messenger of God. They praise our Prophet called Muhammad. They encourage with good speech. In time of war, we do the same thing. Those who remind others of their responsibilities, we say this one is a *jeli,* that one is a *funé,* or the other one is a *garanké.* But according to the book [i.e., the Quran], there is no mention of a special kind of work for the *funéw.* Do you understand what I am saying? In the course of conversation someone can explain to you that he descended from Fosana, therefore he is a *funé.* But to say now that there is an origin of the division of men into classes other than what I have told you, I do not know about it.

Q: How is it that there are some people named Camara who are *horonw* and others who are *nyamakalaw,* some Dumbia who are *horonw* and others who are *nyamakalaw,* even though there can be no marriage between the two classes?

A: Ah yes, you know the question of *jamuw* or family names is really something. It is a problem. It is not very important, but it is difficult. What you say about certain family names is true. There are family names among the *funéw* that you will also find among the *horonw.* Do you understand? There are those family names, huh! What you find among the *funéw* you can also find among the *horonw.* You understand? But the whole question of *jamu* is not very im-

portant. If I leave here suddenly to go somewhere, I could tell the people that
my name is Tayiru and that my family name is Kulubali. If they don't know me
they will always call me "Kulubali," "Kulubali," and finally I will be a Kulubali.
You understand? We see things like this happen. But as for what you want to
know, that is why there are Camara, Kulubali, and Dumbia, and people of
different classes with the same family name, with some of them *nyamakalaw* and
the others *horonw,* and why there are Camara and others who are both. There
is no particular origin of such a thing, as I told you before. You understand?

   In society when people come to know about many [new] things, they abandon
many customs. In ancient times the early people had many totems. They chose
their *tinéw* [totems, taboos] according to their desires.[147] You understand? Say, for
example, that you have had a very dangerous experience, han! If some thing, some
person, or an animal of some kind came and saved you from danger, you would
vow, "Eh! That thing has helped me. If it were not for that, I would have lost my
head. I will never again do anything bad to that." Because of that incident, the
thing would become a *tiné.* You understand? It would become something that was
protected. A man who does something for you, saves you from danger, can become
a kind of *tiné* for you no matter what his background is.

   I will say then, "So-and-so has been good to me. I will not do any harm to a
descendant [or relative] of that person. I do not want to cause any problem for
any of his kin." It is in that way that you begin to observe a certain custom
between people. A kind of barrier is created between them. The situation degen-
erates into one of those strange things. According to some, a bard cannot marry
a blacksmith, or a blacksmith cannot marry a bard, but I find this to be a false
way. All men are the same. There are the Camara blacksmiths whom I know.
There are the Camara bards [i.e., *funéw*], as we know very well. But all the *tinéw*
are customs that were established by the people of ancient times. We do not
know the exact origin of each custom. It is true that in present times we have
come to look for the origins of these customs. These are interesting subjects to
study. These customs were not established for nothing. There was a reason. But
if one does not know that reason and one talks about them anyway, a lie will
be told. You understand?

   Otherwise, to say that the Diabaté or other people. . . . Elsewhere there are
even notables whose family name is Diabaté.[148] The Diabaté, the Traoré are of
the same origin. But as they left together from a certain place, one of them began
to speak to the other, to talk, talk, talk. The first of them spoke and spoke to
the second. The elder brother talked and talked. When the elder talked and
talked, the other told him he would give him something, and he said, "*karissa,*
your way has been truly good." He said, "Nobody can refuse me anything. What
I know, if I say it, nobody can refuse me anything." And the other brother
replied, "This is the truth, nobody can refuse you anything, you are Diabaté."
This phrase "i jè bagatè" was repeated, and it became the family name of the
elder brother, Diabaté, Diabaté. That is the origin of the name Diabaté. Otherwise, Traoré is Diabaté. They were the same. But I cannot tell you why there are
Camara *horonw* and Camara *nyamakalaw.* I cannot tell you that truthfully. I

have never learned why there is a difference between the Camara. As there is a reason for the name Diabaté, there is no doubt a proper story about this, some event that explains the difference between the Camara and the Dumbia. But I do not know that story.

Notes

I am grateful to Professors Humphrey Fisher, Michael Lecker, and Nehemia Levtzion for critical comments which benefited this paper.
 1. Levtzion and Hopkins (1981); Al-ʾUmari (1337–38:261–74); Ibn Battuta (1355:282–301); Ibn Khaldun (1374–94:321–37). Ibn Battuta describes a grand "interpreter" at the court of the *mansa* who performs the secular oral and musical functions of a bard and is obviously a very successful *jeli* (1355:291–93).
 2. Sightings of bards identified as Muslims are occasionally mentioned in earlier sources, but the descriptions are not detailed enough to tell if they were *funéw*. For example, griots (called Judeus, i.e., Jews, by the Portuguese because griots were viewed by them as outcasts) are identified as Muslims in an early source on Upper Guinea (Father Guerreiro [1607–1609:243–44]). Stephan Bühnen brought this source to my attention.
 3. Tautain (1885:345). Tautain was a member of the first Gallieni mission to Segu (1879–1881).
 4. Labouret (1934:107).
 5. Arcin (1907:261).
 6. Leynaud and Cissé (1978:111).
 7. Moreau (1897); Tautain (1885:345).
 8. Delafosse (1912, III:118 n. 1); Delafosse (1955, II:204).
 9. Dieterlen (1955:40); English translation, Dieterlen (1957:125).
 10. Sidibé (1959:14).
 11. Hopkins (1971:106).
 12. Camara (1969).
 13. Zahan (1963:127).
 14. Zemp (1966:627 n. 1).
 15. Kaba (1972:6); Interviews with Jeli Manga Sissoko, August 13, 1975, Kolokani; Karonga and Yamuru Diabaté, February 3, 1976, Keyla; Kele Monzon Diabaté, October 3, 1975, Kita.
 16. N'Diaye (1970:110).
 17. Interview with Tayiru Banbera, February 27, 1976, Segu. For an excerpt from this interview see the Appendix, "Interview II."
 18. Fakama Kaloga (*garanké*), October 12, 1975, Bamako. The rest of this story (a transcript of about fifty lines) is concerned with Muhammad's own sickness and death, subjects which reflect the elderly informant's own situation at the time of recording. Many of my meetings with Fakama Kaloga were postponed because of the frequent illness of both the old *garanké* and his wife, who died during this period.
 19. Interview with Jeli Manga Sissoko (a *jeli*), August 13, 1975, Kolokani. After the *garanké* and *numu* ancestors also refuse, the *jeli* ancestor Surakata accepts the commission and sends some fellow bards to do the job for him, thus collecting the gold but avoiding the stigma attached to informing people of the death of their relatives. The bearer of such news would become identified with the deaths because it was customary for mourners to wander through the village wailing that "so-and-so" told them about it.
 20. Interview with Fanyama Diabaté (*jeli*), October 18, 1975, Bamako. Jean-Loup

Amselle encountered a Malian community where pubescent *funé* males (about the age of fifteen) are said to begin menstruating, wear a small bag between their legs to soak up the menstrual blood, and are regarded as having been emasculated (private conversation, International Conference on Mande Studies, Bamako, Mali, March 17, 1993). It seems possible that this could be related to the tradition of the *funé* ancestor's self-sacrifice on behalf of the Prophet, perhaps commemorating the legendary deed said to have proven Fosana's trustworthiness.

21. Interview with Manga Sissoko, August 13, 1975, Kolokani.

22. Laing (1825:132, 251).

23. Park (1799), published in 1907 as *The Travels of Mungo Park* (1907:213).

24. Mage (1868:226, 307–308).

25. Zeltner (1908:222).

26. Innes (1974:3–4). For this type of recitation by a *funé*, though of northern Côte d'Ivoire rather than the Gambia, see Kamara et al. (1982:38 n. 16).

27. Darbo (1972:2).

28. An example of such a taboo is the strict injunction against a *funé* sitting on the bed of a *horon*. Darbo (1972:2).

29. Conrad (1983:335–37).

30. Conrad (1985:38).

31. Ibid., 48–49.

32. Guillaume (1955:225–26).

33. Conrad (1985:48–49).

34. Al-Bakrī (1068:79, 83); for a French translation of Al-Bakrī see Cuoq (1975:99–104); for an earlier translation see that by Baron MacGuckin de Slane (Al-Bakrī [1913:328]).

35. For the enduring importance of indigenous religious belief in part of the Mande world, see Tauxier (1927) and Dieterlen (1951).

36. Levtzion (1973:200).

37. Conrad (1985:36).

38. Interview with Sadyo Camara, March 10, 1975, Segu; N'Diaye (1970:110); Interview with Fadian Soumanou, November 5, 1975, Bamako.

39. Huart (1960:108–109).

40. Fosana is often praised as being "better" than everyone else in terms of his treatment of the Prophet; e.g., in an epic narrative by the *funé* Sory Fina Kamara, "Fisana" is praised as "the greatest of all." From a market tape (n.d.) purchased and translated in Macenta, Guinea, July 1992.

41. Darbo (1972:2).

42. Conrad (1985:38–39). Surāqa ibn Mālik was of the Mudlij tribe and had a dark complexion. Professor Michael Lecker suggests that his mother might have been an Ethiopian, as was the mother of Bilal (private correspondence via Levtzion, June 2, 1993).

43. Guillaume (1955:xiii-xiv).

44. Nevertheless, it must be kept in mind that the material from Ibn Isḥāq is tradition, that his account is not always consistent with other versions of Muslim tradition, and that sometimes inaccuracies can be detected according to information now available to modern scholarship. The passages referred to here have been checked by Professor Michael Lecker of The Hebrew University of Jerusalem, who specializes in Mecca and Medina at the time of the Prophet. His comments as cited in these notes were kindly translated from the Hebrew and sent to me by Nehemia Levtzion.

45. Humblot (1918:537–40). He evidently prepared this publication while spending the first three months of 1918 in Baraweli ("Barouéli"), in what is now southern Mali, but beyond this the manuscript's provenance is obscure. Two sections of the text were evidently left out, and there is no indication as to whether the translation was from Arabic direct to French, or if it passed through Malinke on the way. Humblot's remark that the fragment was "communicated" to him might mean that the manuscript was read aloud for transcription.

This could have involved the bard in the translation process, possibly to the extent of reading and translating the fragment orally into either Malinke or French (Could the "griot" have been a literate *funé?*) while someone wrote it down. In 1975 at Janna in Bijini, Guinea-Bissau, Bakari Sidibé received this kind of contribution by a local informant. Koba Gassama, a farmer and scholar, translated into Mandinka as he read from an Arabic manuscript (Conteh et al. [1987:iii]). I cannot now provide documented examples of literate *funéw* at the time and place in question, but as followers of Muslim clerics and reciters of Quranic verses, the *funéw* have been respected for their "scholarship," e.g., the tradition noted earlier of the *funé* ancestor said to have been rewarded with the "writings of the angels."

46. However, fairly knowledgeable *nyamakala* traditionists can be unaware of things one would expect them to know. The *garanké* Lasana Tunkara was well informed about many of the *nyamakala* ancestors claimed from Arab tradition, and recounted variants of some stories from the Arabic. Nevertheless, he named Surakata (of the *jeliw*), rather than Walali Ibrahima, as the *garanké* "ancestor" (February 16, 1976, Konobugu).

47. Humblot (1918:539).

48. Diawara (1990:121–23)

49. Humblot (1918:537).

50. Brun (1910:857–58); Zeltner (1913:135–36); "Chanamba," narrated by Mamary Kouyaté, August 9–10, 1975, Kolokani.

51. For example, in one variant, "Fatamata Bintu Yarasurulai" is the wife of "Seydou Naliu" (Interview with Lasana Tunkara, February 16, 1976, Konobugu). It is just possible that this composite character was influenced by the Arab heroine Fātima d. al-Khaṭṭāb, wife of Sa'īd (i.e., "Seydou") Nufayl, both of whom were early followers of Muhammad. Fatima was wounded in a dramatic confrontation with her brother 'Umar that ended in his conversion. This was regarded as a victory because it brought an important, powerful man into the faith (Guillaume [1955:155–57]).

52. Interview with Fadian Soumanou (*jeli*), November 5, 1975, Bamako.

53. Muhammad's mother died when he was six, but in the context of Mande tradition, whether she lived or died at any particular time appears to have been a matter of storytelling expediency. Later, the informant Fadian Soumanou says Muhammad received a message from God, delivered by Jibril (the angel Gabriel), directing him to go to his mother's home in Medina.

54. Ibn Ishāq in Guillaume (1955:70–71).

55. Interview with Fadian Soumanou, November 5, 1975, Bamako.

56. Jeli Mori Kouyaté of Niagassola, Guinea, market tape, n.d.

57. Interview with Lasana Tunkara (*garanké*), February 16, 1976, Konobugu.

58. Interview with Manga Sissoko (*jeli*), August 13, 1975, Kolokani.

59. Interview with Satigi Soumarouo (*numu*), September 2, 1975, Kabaya.

60. The *nyamakalaw* consistently rank the social orders according to "patron and client" on the domestic level, while the street version is usually expressed in terms of donors and beggars or, as Satigi Soumarouo describes it, "those who gave, and those who were given to" (September 2, 1975, Kabaya). The *funéw* received a boost in this regard through their Islamic affiliation, being generally characterized as good and righteous people, especially deserving of largess.

61. Interview with Tayiru Banbera (*jeli*), February 27, 1976, Segu.

62. Interview with Satigi Soumarouo, September 2, 1975, Kabaya.

63. Excerpt from a poem by Ḥassān b. Thābit in Guillaume (1955:320).

64. Interview with Fadian Soumanou, November 5, 1975, Bamako.

65. Ibn Ishāq in Guillaume (1955:214). Another prominent blind man is Abu Quḥāfa, whom Guillaume places in the *hijra* period (ibid., 225), although according to Michael Lecker, Abu Quḥāfa was of an earlier generation. Private correspondence via Nehemia Levtzion, June 2, 1993.

66. Ibn Ishāq in Guillaume (1955:82).

67. Ibid., 79–80.

68. Interview with Sadyo Camara (*funé*), March 10, 1975, Segu. For the complete text of this interview, see the Appendix, "Interview I." In a variant of the camel story told by a *garanké*, he claims to know the camel's name: "The Prophet Muhammad had with him a camel called Fakam Misazariu, but Muhammad himself was on Buragu" (Interview with Lasana Tunkara, February 16, 1976, Konobugu).

69. Ibn Isḥāq in Guillaume (1955:228). According to Michael Lecker, the Prophet had first founded the mosque of Qaba in the upper section of Medina, which was not the same as the one usually called "the Prophet's mosque," in the lower part of Medina and close to the house of Abū Ayyūb. Private correspondence via Nehemia Levtzion, June 2, 1993.

70. This image of a camel kneeling at the door of a humble mosque is apocryphal because at the time there was no mosque there, though one was built later. Michael Lecker via Nehemia Levtzion, private correspondence, June 2, 1993.

71. Huart (1960:108–109); Watt (1960:514–15).

72. Ibn Isḥāq in Guillaume (1955:228–30).

73. Humblot (1918:539). My discussion of the Islamic connection claimed in the Teliko *tarīkh* is too cumbersome to be included here. It is available in an earlier draft at the Melville J. Herskovits Library of African Studies at Northwestern University, in their collection of papers presented at the 1991 meeting of the Canadian Association of African Studies. The relevant lines in the *tarīkh* constitute a claim to what would be a basically Arabian link between the Camara surname and the *funéw*. In the process of establishing this link, the Mande text manages to contribute to the legendary distinction of both the Camara clan and the *funéw*.

74. McNaughton (1988:130–45).

75. Darbo (1972:2). There are some popular griot legends claiming that certain bardic ancestors descended to *jeli* status from *horonya* through either personal choice or bad judgment, but no equivalent tale for the *funéw* has come to light. For legends claiming that nobles became bards through association with other *nyamakalaw*, see Zemp (1966:613–14); for variants of a story in which a younger brother becomes a bard by praising his elder sibling, see Diagne and Télémaque (1916:277); Bathily (1936:192–93); Colin (1957:65); Sidibé (1959:14–15).

76. Houseborn slaves (*wolosow*) could, through several generations, achieve free status, but no one is aware of any case histories tracing one family through all the stages of transition from *horonya* through *jonya*, and from there to *nyamakalaya*, partly because no informant wants to admit it in his own case, or to risk slandering anyone else. For the gradual movement out of servitude, see Conrad (1981:69–80); for a more comprehensive study see Bazin (1975:135–81).

77. Zeltner (1913:30); Frobenius (1925:335); Niane (1965:70).

78. Conrad (1983:335–37).

79. Conrad (1985:43).

80. Interview with Jeli Manga Sissoko, August 13, 1975, Kolokani.

81. Arcin (1911:58). Occupational titles are frequently incorporated into individuals' names, such as "Numu Fayiri" and "Jeli Baba," and it seems safe to assume that Fina Silla Makha is the same Silamaka described elsewhere as the *funé* ancestor. This Silamaka is not to be confused with Sunjata's war chief Silamaka Ba Koita of the Segu region. See Arnaud (1912:171); Adam (1903:237); Delafosse (1913:302). A later Silamaka, hero of Masina, is prominent in the Bamana Segu epic. See Seydou (1972); Kesteloot (1972, 4:4–21).

82. Massing (1985:38). There are so many variants of "Feni Kamara" that there is no knowing the original, much less certainty that it derives from *funé:* Funikama, but also Foningama, Falikaman, Foni Kaman, Feren Kaman, Fangamma, Farin Kaman, Foninkama, Foningama, Ferningaman, Farligaman, Fonikgema, Falingama, Fali Kama, Faligama, Fanikama, Foningaman (Geysbeek and Kamara [1991:46]). Geysbeek does not believe Feni Kamara was a *funé,* on the grounds that "the Kamara lineage related

to this Feni Kamara is known to have resisted Islam until the present century." Geysbeek, who collected genealogies indicating descent from Kamanjan, a legendary noble associate of Sunjata, suggests that if Feni Kamara was a *funé,* either he was a bad Muslim, or his descendants rejected Islam and suppressed any mention of his having been a Muslim (private communication, June 1, 1990).

83. Niane (1960:125) and (1965); Interview with Jeli Baba Sissoko, July 14, 1975, Bamako; Innes (1974:147); Zeltner (1913:7).

84. Anṣāri: singular of Al-Anṣār, "the helpers," men of Medina who supported Muhammad, in distinction from the Muhādjirūn or "emigrants" i.e., his followers from Mecca (Watt [1960:514]).

85. Both "Manga" and "Makha" appear as given names, but they probably derive from Soninke and Malinke titles for "chief," "king," and "emperor," with a wide variety of usages that include "Maghan," "Makhan," and "Maga," and which are related to "Mansa." Therefore both "Fina Manga" and "Sylla Makha," seen here combined into one ancestral name, can be interpreted as carrying connotations of leadership at some point in the evolution of the tradition. The first would translate as "Chief of the *funé,*" the second, usually rendered "Silamaka," as "Chief of the Sylla," which is a Soninke kin group.

86. Compare the gifts offered Mamari Kulubali, including a hundred each of horses, cows, sheep, *mithqals,* goats, and slave girls, in Conrad (1990:74–75). See also the *Ta'rīkh Ghunja,* where Jakpa offers the *'alim* Fati Morukpe horses, slaves, sheep, gowns, and trousers in lots of one hundred, in Wilks, Levtzion, and Haight (1986:158–59). For rewards occurring in increments of ten (slaves, cows, and sheep), see a Sunjata variant in Zeltner (1913:8–9).

87. For a variant in which the dry wood sprouts from the touch of a Muslim "saint," see Oral History Division, Banjul, Tape 106 A: "The History of the Baayos of Wuli," collected by Bakari K. Sidibé and Winifred Galloway, 1971 (trans. Bakari K. Sidibe), passage reproduced in Conteh et al. (1987:ii-iii).

88. Al-Bakrī (1068:80–82).

89. Levtzion (1971:34).

90. Bala Fasseké is a Muslim here, probably because the narrator was himself a Muslim, a young Soninke marabout and one of a group of possibly literate traditionists of Nioro. For more on the Nioro traditionists, see Conrad (1984:35–53).

91. Adam (1903:358–59).

92. See Joseph Miller's discussion of oral traditions as "evidence in spite of themselves," involving sources that reveal information about the past in ways of which the narrators could not have been cognizant, and which they could therefore not have fabricated (1980:4–12).

93. Conrad (1992:174–80). On the subject of "firstcomers and latecomers" see Kopytoff (1987:52–61). For more on the *blaw,* see de Moraes Farias (1989:156).

94. Monteil (1929:316). The idea that the *bla* kin groups preceded the *mansaré* ancestors is contrary to those who claim that the Traoré, Koné, and Konaté were the firstcomers (e.g., Leynaud and Cissé [1978:134 n. 13]).

95. According to Humblot, Camara women were called "Boula Damba," i.e., Damba of the *blaw* (1918:527); Monteil says "boula" women are greeted as "Damba" (1929:316, 347); N'Diaye claims that the Dabo are the second principal *jamu* of the "Finah" (1970:112). Konaré specifies that within the Sissoko kin group *blaw,* women carry the *patronyme* Damba or Sakiliba (1981:139), and Diawara says Sisoxo women among the Soninke of Jaara are Danba (1990:43).

96. Bathily (1936:192–93); Monod-Herzen (1908:52); Diagne and Télémaque (1916:277); Colin (1957:65); Sidibé (1959:14–15); Interview with Jeli Manga Sissoko, August 13, 1975, Kolokani. Tayiru Banbera refers to this legend, but does not tell it (see Appendix, "Interview II").

97. The *sènèkun* relationship (*sènèkunya, senakuya, senankuya*), also known as a

"joking relationship," is a kind of alliance, usually between clans, calling for mutual aid when needed, in the form of food, lodging, material goods, or refuge in time of war. See Pageard (1958:123–41).

98. Montrat (1935:121).

99. Dérive et al. (1976:222).

100. Dwelling as it does in the realm of folklore, it is not surprising that the story of the starving brothers is offered as the explanation of the origin of several different social groups, depending on who is telling the story, and the same is true of the "gift of the pregnant wife" theme. But it is interesting that available versions of the two legends show no overlapping in that regard; for example, the origin of the Traoré relationship with their Diabaté bards is confined to the two brothers legend, and the story of Dabo origins remains with that of the "gift of the pregnant wife." However, a more exhaustive collection of variants could turn up instances of overlapping claims.

101. This is probably putting too fine a point on the matter. Any such interpretation is entirely speculative, because what appears to be the message in the tradition as we find it may bear little or no relationship to that of the original tale, which is presumably many generations old.

102. N'Diaye (1970:111–13) (awardee *funé* ancestor, descendant Dabo); Monod-Herzen (1908:53) (pregnant wife a Dabo, descendant a branch of the *blaw*); Adam (1903:238–39) (awardee *funé* ancestor, descendant Dabo); Interview with Fanyama Diabaté, August 18–21, 1975, Bamako (pregnant wife a Dabo).

103. Kopytoff (1987:57–58).

104. Zeltner (1913:1–3).

105. Monod-Herzen (1908:53); Interview with Fanyama Diabaté, October 18–21, 1975, Bamako.

106. Zeltner (1913:8).

107. N'Diaye (1970:111–12).

108. Darbo (1972:2) (he renders the place name "Tabung," while most say "Tabo" or "Tabon"). Fran Camara is described as the king of Tabo in Niane (1975:28), and in a Zeltner variant (1913:44) he is located at "Tabou" and styled Taboung Nana Farang Kamara.

109. It is not clear if these traditionists think there were places with these names in Wagadu, or if they are saying descendants of immigrants in the post-Wagadu Soninke diaspora settled at Tabon and Sibi. Some Sunjata texts identify these places as the home of Kamanjan, noble Kamara ancestor. See maps in Cissé (1975:475) and in Poncet et al. (1980, maps 5–7). The Wagadu end of the question is complicated by Arnaud's learned informant Batchili, who refers to "the Sibi" not as a place but as a people (Arnaud [1912:167]). One bard who makes clear reference to Sibi's location within the oral tradition is the *funé* Karamogo Kamara, who specifies that a *funé* ancestor who "came from the east" settled for a time at Sibi in Mali (Kamara et al. [1982:9]).

110. The text reads:

> The *jamuw* were started at Wagadu.
> They would say,
> "This is my *jeli*,
> This is my *numu*,
> This is my *garanké*."
> These four *ngaraw* had their beginnings in Mande.

The term *ngara* is often used to describe *nyamakalaw* who are especially accomplished at their arts. Jeli Baba Sissoko's narrative was copied from a tape at the archives of the Institut des Sciences Humaines, July 14, 1975, Bamako, with permission of the director, and the assistance of Cheick Umar Mara.

111. Meillassoux (1964:186–227).

112. Interviews with Sadyo Camara, March 10, 1975, Segu; Lasa Camara, March 5, 1976, Funébugu; Jeli Manga Sissoko, August 13, 1975, Kolokani; Nanténéjé Kamissoko, July 21, 1975, Bamako; Mamady Diabaté, February 3, 1976, Keyla.

113. Delafosse (1913:302) (Finanou Niagalé Missâné); Adam (1903:237) (Fina Niakalé Missansé); Zeltner (1913:11) (Niarhalé Mbomou).

114. Delafosse (1913:302); Adam (1903:237).

115. Leynaud and Cissé (1978:103).

116. Al-Bakrī describes drums, though not bards specifically, at the court of the eleventh-century pagan king of Ghana, whose interpreters, incidentally, were Muslims (1068:80).

117. For the full text of the bard's comments, see the Appendix, "Interview II."

118. Arnaud (1912:167).

119. Conrad (1984:39–41).

120. The story concerns a bed that was made for Muhammad's grandfather in the shade of the Ka'ba, upon which only the orphaned boy Muhammad was allowed to sit (Guillaume [1955:73]).

121. Tautain (1885:346).

122. Bazin (1906:214).

123. Soleillet (1887:420, 463).

124. Dieterlen (1951:94–97). In addition to sacrifices made in periods of crisis involving the kingdom and its administrators, Dieterlen says the corpse of a sacrificed albino buried in the floor beneath an important chief's seat was thought to help secure the stability and longevity of his office.

125. Conrad (1990:182).

126. For more on this problem, see Henige (1986:177–93).

127. The reference for my tapes is Acc. No. 88-061-F, Cass 2995-3029.

128. According to Dumestre (1979:41).

129. Interview with Jeli Yoro ("Joro") Kouyaté, September 11, 1975, Yonfolila.

130. The anthropologist John Lewis recorded an epic narrated by a *funé* (private conversation in Bamako, Mali, 1975), and I collected one by Sory Fina Kamara of northern Guinea.

131. I am grateful to Moulaye Kida for his kind help, and to Institut des Sciences Humaines of Bamako for its authorization to conduct research in Segu.

132. Thanks go to Charles Bird, who first apprised me of Tayiru Banbera's existence, and provided me with a note of introduction. For more information about this bard and an extended version of his discourse in English translation, see Conrad (1990). For selected episodes of Tayiru's narrative in French translation, see Dumestre (1979 and 1980).

133. My assistants described *vinza* as Bamana food made from grains of pounded, boiled millet, to which condiments are added; *mukufara* is made the same way, only it is not cooked.

134. Sadyo's "new generation" cannot be taken as a claim to very recent change, owing to his extremely telescoped sense of chronology, which is evident in his lack of discernment between eleventh-century Wagadu and the mid-nineteenth century of Al-Hājj 'Umar.

135. *shurafa*: Bamana *sirifiya*, Ar. *shurfa* (sing. *sharif*). Muslim lineages claiming descent from the Prophet's family.

136. It is not clear who he means by "storyteller," though it is probably Fosana and/or his descendants. Wagadu is the local, non-Arabic name for ancient Ghana.

137. "Kagoro": Transcribing this as true as possible to the recorded sound, my assistants have rendered it variously as "Kakòrò" and "Kakolo," as where I have Jeli Manga Sissoko's remark that "the ancestor of the *funé*, Fosana, came from the Kakolo" (August 13, 1975, Kolokani). Also relevant is Sissoko's recitation of a vastly telescoped genealogy combining Arab and Mande names:

Fosana was the father of Silamaka.
Silamaka was the father of Biraman.
Biraman was the father of Kabiné,
Kabiné was the father of Malé.

Compare the genealogy by the *garanké* Lasana Tunkara (February 15, 1976, Konobugu), who mentions only Arab names (the translation retains the orthography used by my assistant, Ahmadu Traoré):

Those who put *funéw* into the world were named:
Ina-Alilu, Fufulu al-Alimi, and Nasuru Nabiu;
Ali al-Kufaru, Ina-Dali Chibaï, and Baïnali-Ilzala;
Yahudul-Kuluchu, Yomali-Kiamati, and Abdul-Kubaru.

For the Kagoro in their proper historical perspective, see Ardouin (1988:443–61).

138. Noteworthy in this line is the juxtaposition of Wagadu (flourished in the ninth to the eleventh centuries) with the nineteenth-century hero Al-Hājj 'Umar.

139. "Tamangily" is recognizable as Dama N'Guilli (Damïgile, N'Damangillé, etc.), a legendary ancestor of the Diawara.

140. " . . . followed by our grandfathers": He is saying that there were many *funéw* among the followers of the nineteenth-century *jihad* leader. For more on Al-Hājj 'Umar, see Robinson (1986).

141. Tiramakan is one of the most important generals of Sunjata, central figure of the Mande epic. Sadyo is saying that *funé* expertise was not confined to Islamic texts and oral discourse, that they also knew the stories of old Mande.

142. This is an apparent contradiction of the earlier claim that the *funé* ancestor was a prominent Muslim in the time of Muhammad, and it illustrates the high degree of Al-Hājj 'Umar's prestige among the *funéw*.

143. Sadyo identified the "Kagola" as *numuw* (blacksmiths).

144. *kuléw: nyamakala* specialists in woodwork.

145. Tradition recalls Lawalè or Lawalo as a son of Bilali, and one of the first Mande kings to make the pilgrimage to Mecca (see, e.g., Leynaud and Cissé 1978:108).

146. He means that to prepare the gris-gris or amulet, the *mori* will write an Arabic formula on a piece of paper and give it to a *garanké* to be sewn into a small, decorated leather case.

147. *tiné* (*tné, tené, tana*): This word has been translated variously as "totem," "taboo," and "sacred animal" (Bazin [1906:593, 610]), none of which are entirely satisfactory. The problem of definition is discussed by Delafosse (1920:87–109), and by Monod-Herzen (1908:34–53). The term often refers to an animal or plant that is regarded as the protector of a particular clan, lineage, or branch thereof (e.g., the lion is the *tiné* of the Jara clan). These beliefs are supported by legends telling how the animal, tree, etc. once saved the life of an ancestor or performed some other critical service. Henceforth, as the custom goes, the ancestor's descendants are forbidden to kill that creature or plant which is the *tiné* of their clan. For examples of these legends and tables matching families with their *tiné,* see Brun (1910:843–69) and Humblot (1918:527).

148. " . . . even notables": People named Diabaté are usually *jeliw.*

References

Adam, M. G. 1903. "Légendes historiques du pays de Nioro (Sahel)." *Revue Coloniale,*
n.s. 14 (Sept.–Oct.):232–48, 15 (Nov.–Dec.):354–72.
Al-Bakrī. 1068. *Kitāb al-masālik wa-'l-mamālik.* English trans. by J. F. P. Hopkins in

Corpus of Arabic Sources for West African History, ed. N. Levtzion and J. F. P. Hopkins. Cambridge: Cambridge University Press, 1981.

———. 1913. *Description de l'Afrique septentrionale.* French trans. by Baron MacGuckin de Slane. 1st ed., 1859. Rev. ed., Paris: P. Geuthner, 1913. Reprint, Paris: Librarie d'Amerique et d'Orient Adrien-Maisonneuve, 1965.

Al-'Umari. 1337–38. *Masālik al-absār fī mamālik al-amsār.* English trans. by J. F. P. Hopkins in *Corpus of Arabic Sources for West African History,* ed. N. Levtzion and J. F. P. Hopkins. Cambridge: Cambridge University Press, 1981.

Arcin, André. 1907. *La Guinée française.* Paris: Augustin Challamel.

———. 1911. *Histoire de la Guinée française.* Paris: A. Challamel.

Ardouin, Claude. 1988. "Une formation politique précoloniale du Sahel occidental malien: Le Baakhunu à l'époque des Kaagoro." *Cahiers d'Etudes Africaines* 28 (3–4):443–61.

Arnaud, Robert. 1912. *L'Islam et la politique musulmane française en Afrique occidentale française, suivi de la singulière légende des Soninkés.* Paris: Comité de l'Afrique française.

Bathily, Ibrahima. 1936. "Les Diawandos ou Diogorames: Traditions orales recueillies à Djenné, Corientze, Ségou et Nioro." *Education Africaine* 25:173–93.

Bazin, Hippolyte. 1906. *Dictionnaire Bambara-Française.* Paris: Imprimerie nationale. Reprint, Ridgewood, N.J.: Gregg Press, 1965.

Bazin, Jean. 1975. "Guerre et servitude à Ségou." In *L'esclavage en Afrique précoloniale,* ed. Claude Meillassoux. Paris: F. Maspero.

Brun, P. J. 1910. "Le totémisme chez quelques peuples du Soudan occidentale." *Anthropos* 5:843–69.

Camara, Sory. 1969. "Gens de la parole: Essai sur la condition et le rôle des griots dans la société Malinké." Ph.D. thesis, University of Bordeaux.

Cissé, Youssouf Tata, ed. and trans. 1975. *L'empire du Mali. Un récit de Wâ Kamissoko de Krina.* Paris: Fondation SCOA.

Colin, Roland. 1957. *Les contes noirs de l'ouest africain.* Paris: Présence Africaine.

Conrad, David C. 1981. "Slavery in Bambara Society: Segou 1712–1861." *Slavery & Abolition* 2:69–80.

———. 1983. "Maurice Delafosse and the Pre-Sunjata trône du Mandé." *Bulletin of the School of Oriental and African Studies* 46 (2):335–37.

———. 1984. "Oral Sources on Links between Great States: Sumanguru, Servile Lineage, the Jariso and Kaniaga." *History in Africa* 11:35–53.

———. 1985. "Islam in the Oral Traditions of Mali: Bilali and Suraxata." *Journal of African History* 26:33–49.

———. 1992. "Searching for History in the Sunjata Epic: The Case of Fakoli." *History in Africa* 19:147–200.

Conrad, David C., ed. and trans. 1990. *A State of Intrigue: The Epic of Bamana Segu According to Tayiru Banbera.* London: Oxford University Press for the British Academy.

Conteh, Isatou; Miguel Gomes; Bakari K. Sidibé; David E. Skinner; and Nicholas Wood, eds. and trans. 1987. *A History of the Migration and the Settlement of the Baayo Family from Timbuktu to Bijini in Guinea Bissau.* Banjul: Oral History Division, Ministry of Education, Republic of the Gambia.

Cuoq, Joseph M., ed. and trans. 1975. *Recueil des sources arabes concernant l'Afrique occidentale du VIIIe au XVIe siécle (Bilad al-Sudan).* Paris: Editions du Centre national de la recherche scientifique.

Darbo, Seni. 1972. "A Griot's Self-Portrait: The Origins and Role of the Griot in Mandinka Society as Seen from Stories Told by Gambian Griots." Paper presented at the Conference on Manding Studies, School of Oriental and African Studies, University of London.

Delafosse, Maurice. 1912. *Haut-Sénégal-Niger (Soudan Française).* 3 vols. Paris: Emile Larose. Reprint, Paris: G.-P. Maisonneuve et Larose, 1972.

——. 1913. "Traditions historiques et légendaires du Soudan occidental." *Renseignements Coloniaux et documents* (supplement to *Bulletin du Comité de l'Afrique française et du Comité du Maroc*) 8:293–306.

——. 1920. "Des soi-disant clans totémiques de l'Afrique Occidentale." *Revue d'ethnographie et des traditions populaires* 1 (2):87–109.

——. 1955. *La langue mandingue et ses dialectes (malinké, bambara, dioula).* Vol. 2: *Dictionnaire mandingue-française.* Paris: Paul Geuthner.

de Moraes Farias, P. F. 1989. "Pilgrimages to 'Pagan' Mecca in Mandenka Stories of Origin Reported from Mali and Guinea-Conakry." In *Discourse and Its Disguises: The Interpretation of African Oral Texts,* ed. Karin Barber and P. F. de Moraes Farias. Birmingham: Center for West African Studies.

Dérive, Jean; Ano N'Guessan; and G. Dumestre, eds. and trans. 1976. *Chroniques de grandes familles d'Odienné.* Abidjan: Université d'Abidjan, Institut de linguistique appliquée.

Diagne, Ahmadou Mapaté, and Hamet Sow Télémaque. 1916. "Origine des griots." *Bulletin de l'enseignement de l'Afrique Occidentale Française* 25:275–78.

Diawara, Mamadou. 1990. *La graine de la parole: Dimension sociale et politique des traditions orales du royaume de Jaara (Mali) du XVème au milieu du XIXème siècle.* Stuttgart: Franz Steiner Verlag.

Dieterlen, Germaine. 1951. *Essai sur la religion Bambara.* Paris: Presses Universitaires de France.

——. 1955. "Myth et organisation sociale au Soudan française." *Journal de la Société des Africanistes* 25 (1–2):39–76.

——. 1957. "The Mande Creation Myth." *Africa: Journal of the International African Institute* 27 (2):124–38.

Dumestre, Gérard, ed. and trans. 1979. *La geste de Ségou. Racontée par des Griots bambara.* Paris: A. Colin.

——. 1980. "L'élection de Mamari Biton Koulibali." In *Recueil de littérature Manding.* Paris: Agence de coopération culturelle et technique.

Frobenius, Leo. 1925. *Atlantis.* Vol. 5: *Dichten und Denken im Sudan.* Jena: E. Diederichs.

Geysbeek, Tim, and Jobba K. Kamara. 1991. "'Two Hippos Cannot Live in One River': Zo Musa, Foningama, and the Founding of Musadu (Guinea) in Oral Traditions of the Konyaka." *Liberian Studies Journal* 16 (1):27–78.

Guerreiro, Padre Fernão. 1607–1609. *Relação Anual das Coisas que Fizeram os Padres da Companhia de Jesus nas suas Missões.* Edited by Artur Viegas. Vol. 3. Lisbon: Imprensa Nacional, 1942.

Guillaume, A., ed. and trans. 1955. *The Life of Muhammad: A Translation of Ibn Isḥāq's Sīrat Rasūl Allāh.* Lahore, Karachi, Dacca: Pakistan Branch Oxford University Press.

Henige, David. 1986. "Putting the Horse Back before the Cart: Recent Encouraging Signs." *History in Africa* 13:177–93.

Hopkins, Nicholas S. 1971. "Maninka Social Organization." In *Papers on the Manding,* ed. Carlton T. Hodge. Bloomington: Indiana University Press.

Huart, Cl. 1960. "Abū Ayyūb Khālid B. Zayd B. Kulayb Al-Naḏjḏjārī Al-Anṣārī." In *The Encyclopaedia of Islam,* New Edition, vol. 1, pp. 108–109. Leiden: E. J. Brill; London: Luzac & Co.

Humblot, P. 1918. "Du nom propre et des appellations chez les Malinké des vallées du Niandan et du Milo (Guinée Française)." *Bulletin du Comité des Etudes Historique et Scientifique de l'Afrique Occidentale Française* 1 (3–4):519–40.

Ibn Battuta. 1355. *Tuḥfat al-nuẓẓar fī gharāʾib al-amṣār wa-ʾajāʾib al-asfār.* English trans. by J. F. P. Hopkins in *Corpus of Arabic Sources for West African History,* ed.

N. Levtzion and J. F. P. Hopkins. Cambridge: Cambridge University Press, 1981.

———. 1854–74. *Voyages d'Ibn Battuta (Tuḥfat al-nuẓẓar fī gharā'ib al-amṣar wa-'ajā'ib al-asfār)*. Arabic text and trans. by C. Defrémery and B. R. Saguinetti. 1st. ed., Paris: Imprimerie Nationale. Rev. ed. by Vincent Monteil, Paris: Editions Anthropos, 1969.

Ibn Khaldun. 1374–94. *Kitāb al-'Ibar wa-dīwān al-mubtada' wa-'l-khabar fī ayyām al-'arab wa-'l-'ajam wa-'l-barbar*. English trans. by J. F. P. Hopkins in *Corpus of Arabic Sources for West African History*, ed. N. Levtzion and J. F. P. Hopkins. Cambridge: Cambridge University Press, 1981.

Innes, Gordon. 1974. *Sunjata: Three Mandinka Versions*. London: School of Oriental and African Studies, University of London.

Kaba, Lansiné. 1972. "The Maninka-Mori of Bate, Guinea: A Preliminary Survey for Research in Ethno-history." Paper presented at the Conference on Manding Studies, School of Oriental and African Studies, University of London.

Kamara, Karamogo; Jean Dérive; Ano N'Guessan; C. Braconnier; and S. Diaby, inf., eds., and trans. 1982. *Griots de Samatiguila*. Documents linguistiques, 96. Abidjan: Université d'Abidjan, Institut de linguistique appliquée.

Kesteloot, Lilyan. 1972. *Da Monzon de Segou: Epopée bambara*. 4 vols. Paris: F. Nathan.

Konaré, Oumar. 1981. "La notion de pouvoir dans l'Afrique traditionnelle et l'aire culturelle manden en particulier." In *Le concept de pouvoir en Afrique*. Paris: Presses de l'UNESCO.

Kopytoff, Igor. 1987. "The Internal African Frontier: The Making of African Political Culture." In *The African Frontier: The Reproduction of Traditional African Societies*, ed. Igor Kopytoff. Bloomington and Indianapolis: Indiana University Press.

Labouret, Henri. 1934. *Les Mandingue et leur langue*. Paris: Librarie Larose.

Laing, Alexander Gordon. 1825. *Travels in the Timannee, Kooranko, and Soolima Countries in Western Africa*. London: John Murray.

Levtzion, Nehemia. 1971. "Patterns of Islamization in West Africa." In *Aspects of West African Islam*, ed. Daniel F. McCall and Norman R. Bennett. Boston University Papers on Africa, V. Boston: African Studies Center.

———. 1973. *Ancient Ghana and Mali*. London: Methuen & Co., Ltd.

Levtzion, N., and J. F. P. Hopkins, eds. 1981. *Corpus of Early Arabic Sources for West African History*. Translated by J. F. P. Hopkins. Cambridge: Cambridge University Press.

Leynaud, Emile, and Youssouf Cissé. 1978. *Paysans Malinké du Haut Niger (Tradition et développement rural en Afrique Soudanaise)*. Bamako: Imprimerie populaire du Mali.

Mage, Eugène. 1868. *Voyage dans le Soudan occidentale (Sénégambie-Niger) 1863–1866*. Paris: Hachette.

Massing, Andreas W. 1985. "The Mane, the Decline of Mali, and Mandinka Expansion towards the South Windward Coast." *Cahiers d'Etudes africaines* 25 (1):21–55.

McNaughton, Patrick R. 1988. *The Mande Blacksmiths: Knowledge, Power, and Art in West Africa*. Bloomington and Indianapolis: Indiana University Press.

Meillassoux, Claude. 1964. "Histoire et institutions du kafo de Bamako d'après la tradition des Niaré." *Cahiers d'Etudes Africaines* 4 (2):186–227.

Miller, Joseph. 1980. "Introduction: Listening for the African Past." In *The African Past Speaks: Essays on Oral Tradition and History*, ed. Joseph C. Miller. Folkstone, England: Dawson; Hamden, Conn.: Archon.

Monod-Herzen, Gabriel. 1908. "Essai sur le totémisme soudanais." In *Revue d'Histoire des Religions*, pp. 34–53.

Monteil, Charles. 1929. "Les Empires du Mali: Etude d'Histoire et de Sociologie

Soudanaises." *Bulletin du Comité d'Etudes historiques et scientifiques de l'Afrique Occidentale Française* 12 (3–4):291–447.

Montrat, M. 1935. "Note sur les Malinkés du Sankaran." In *Outre Mer,* pp. 107–27.

Moreau, Lieutenant J. L. M. 1897. "Notice générale sur le Soudan, 2 ème partie ethnologique." Archives Nationale du Mali, ID-19.

N'Diaye, Bokar. 1970. *Les castes au Mali.* Bamako: Editions Populaires.

Niane, Djibril Tamsir. 1960. "Le problem de Soundiata." *Notes Africaines* 88:123–26.

———. 1965. *Sundiata: An Epic of Old Mali.* Translated by G. D. Pickett. London: Longman.

———. 1975. *Recherche sur l'Empire du Mali au Moyen Age suivi de mise en place des populations de la Haute-Guinée.* Paris: Présence Africaine.

Pageard, Robert. 1958. "Notes sur les rapports de 'Senankouya' au Soudan française particulièrement dans les cercles de Segou et de Macina." *Bulletin de l'I.F.A.N.* 20, sér. B (1–2):123–41.

Park, Mungo. 1799. *Travels in the Interior Districts of Africa in 1795, 1796, and 1797.* London: W. Bulmer and Co.

———. 1907. *The Travels of Mungo Park.* Rev. ed., ed. Ronald Miller, London: Dent; New York: Dutton, 1954.

Poncet, Yveline; R. Mauny; J. Rouch; Y. Cissé; and C. Meillassoux, eds. 1980. *Atlas historique de la boucle du Niger.* Paris: Association SCOA pour la recherche scientifique en Afrique noire.

Robinson, David. 1986. *The Holy War of Umar Tal: The Western Sudan in the Mid-Nineteenth Century.* Oxford: Clarendon Press.

Seydou, Christiane. 1972. *Silâmaka et Poullôri: Récit épique raconté par Tinguidji.* Paris: A. Colin.

Sidibé, Mamby. 1959. "Les gens de caste ou nyamakala au Soudan française." *Notes Africaines* 81:13–17.

Soleillet, Paul. 1887. *Voyage à Ségou 1878–1879.* Edited by Gabriel Gravier. Paris: Challamel aïné.

Tautain, Dr. 1885. "Notes sur les castes chez les Mandingues et en particulier chez les Banmanas." *Revue d'Ethnographie* 3:343–53.

Tauxier, Louis. 1927. *La religion Bambara.* Paris: Paul Geuthner.

Watt, W. Montgomery. 1960. "Al-Ansari." In *The Encyclopaedia of Islam,* New Edition, vol. 1, pp. 514–15. Leiden: E. J. Brill; London: Luzac & Co.

Wilks, Ivor; Nehemiah Levtzion; and Bruce M. Haight. 1986. *Chronicles from Gonja: A Tradition of West African Muslim Historiography.* Cambridge and New York: Cambridge University Press.

Zahan, Dominique. 1963. *La dialectique du verbe chez les Bambara.* Paris: Mouton & Co.

Zeltner, Fr. de. 1908. "Notes sur la sociologie soudanaise." *L'Anthropologie* 19:217–33.

———. 1913. *Contes du Sénégal et du Niger.* Paris: Ernest Leroux.

Zemp, Hugo, 1966. "La légende des griots malinké." *Cahiers d'Etudes Africaines* 6 (4):611–42.

VI

SONINKE *GARANKÉW* AND BAMANA-MALINKE *JELIW*
MANDE LEATHERWORKERS, IDENTITY, AND THE DIASPORA

Barbara E. Frank

In the literature on social organization among Mande-speaking peoples of West Africa, three primary "castes," known collectively as *nyamakalaw,* are usually identified and distinguished from each other by their particular craft specializations. *Garankéw* are said to provide their skills as leatherworkers, *numuw* as blacksmiths and potters, and *jeliw* as bards, messengers, musicians, and oral historians. However, in the course of my research on leatherworking traditions in Mali, various contradictions arose between this literature and my field observations concerning the identity of leatherworkers and the relationship between ethnicity, *nyamakala* status, and craft specialization.

In this essay, I present evidence to suggest that the *garankéw* are of Soninke origin, and are not the only Mande *nyamakalaw* to specialize in leatherwork. *Jeliw,* while practicing their primary role as bards, often serve a major role as leatherworkers, an aspect of their identity that has been overlooked by scholars in the past. An awareness of such distinctions and other variations in the relationship between ethnicity, *nyamakala* status, and craft specialization is critical to understanding not only the history of the *nyamakalaw* within the Mande world, but also the diffusion of Mande social and cultural institutions among neighboring peoples. In fact, I will argue that the geographical distribution of both *garankéw* and *jeliw* as leatherworkers reflects a diaspora parallel to, if not part and parcel of, the Mande commercial and religious diasporas beginning perhaps as early as the eleventh and twelfth centuries with the decline of the empire of Ghana and continuing with the state-building activities of the Mali Empire and succeeding Mande trader, clerical, and warrior groups.

Finally, I will suggest that Mande *jeliw* and *garankéw* have created and preserved a sense of distinctive identity across time and space that transcends ethnicity. Their identity rests in part on their status as *nyamakalaw* and in part on occupational specialization, as overlapping but not contiguous categories, enabling them as individuals to respond to changing political and economic circumstances.

Mande Leatherworkers in the Literature

Discussions of *nyamakala* groups in the accounts of early European travelers provide a sense of the importance of the craft of leatherworking, its geographical extent, and the separate but parallel status of leatherworkers, blacksmiths, and bards. One of the first Europeans to use the Mande term for leatherworker was Mungo Park, the Scottish adventurer-explorer, who, in the late eighteenth century, traveled up the Gambia River and into the Sudan along the Niger River as far as Silla, east of Segu. He was especially impressed by the professional status of both leatherworkers and blacksmiths in this region. He wrote,

> As the arts of weaving, dyeing, sewing, &c. may easily be acquired, those who exercise them are not considered in Africa as following any particular profession; for almost every slave can weave, and every boy can sew. The only artists which are distinctly acknowledged as such by the Negroes, and who value themselves on exercising appropriate and peculiar trades, are the manufacturers of *leather* and of *iron*. The first of these, are called *Karrankea* (or as the word is sometimes pronounced *Gaungay*). They are to be found in almost every town, and they frequently travel through the country in the exercise of their calling.[1]

At about the same time, Thomas Winterbottom was traveling in the interior of Sierra Leone. He too was impressed by the skills of the leatherworkers, comparing their industry to what he perceived to be the indolence of most African men. He reported:

> Among the Foolas, however, and other nations beyond them, some progress has been made in forming distinct occupations or trades. One set of men, called garrankees or shoemakers, are exclusively employed in manufacturing leather, and converting it into a variety of useful articles, as sandals, quivers for arrows, bridles, saddles, &c.[2]

Although Winterbottom associates these leatherworkers with the Fula, it is significant that he uses the Mande term to identify them. Indeed, there is evidence to suggest that these leatherworkers may have been Mande craftsmen working for Fula patrons.[3] Both Park and Winterbottom seem to associate the peculiar status of these craftsmen with the specialized nature of their chosen profession, rather than with their membership in what were to become known as "castes."

In 1856, Anne Raffenel recognized three distinct "castes" among the Bamana of the state of Kaarta (northwestern Mali)—the *garankies* or *guanguis* as leatherworkers, the *dialis* as griots, and the *noumous* as blacksmiths.[4] Even though he uses the term "caste," Raffenel suggests that their status is closer to that of the guilds of medieval Europe than that of the castes of India. The same three groups are also identified by Dr. Tautain, a member of the first Gallieni mission to Segu in the late nineteenth century (1879–1881). He argued that they must be considered "castes" because of the hereditary nature of the trades. He reported that although others can and do learn the skills associated with each of these groups, they will not be considered true members of the group unless they are born into it. He wrote,

> Noumô [*numu*], Garanké or Diali [*jeli*] born, Noumô, Garanké or Diali you remain until your last day, even if you never exercise the profession designated by one of these names, and you will be the father, grandfather, great-grandfather, etc. . . . of children who perhaps will never be blacksmiths, leatherworkers, nor musicians, nevertheless each will remain Diali, Noumô, Garanké. Moreover, in general, the name alone, the name of the family or the clan, is sufficient to identify the caste.[5]

In these and other early accounts, we begin to see the emergence of a rather limited view of Mande society which tended to underestimate the complexity of social identity in the region. It was during the colonial period that European notions of Mande social structure as a tiered tripartite system became codified. According to this rigidly perceived hierarchical framework, the *horonw* or "nobility," including farmers, traders, clerics, and warriors, formed the top level, and slaves (*jonw*) occupied the lowest level. The *nyamakalaw* made up the intermediate position. Conveniently, the "caste" stratum could be subdivided into three dominant identities (*jeli, garanké,* and *numu*), each associated exclusively with a single occupation. Occasionally added to the list are the *funéw* or *finaw,* whose occupational status as oral practitioners overlaps with that of the *jeliw.*[6]

Most of the more recent literature on the social structure of different Mande-speaking peoples largely accepts this pattern, regardless of the specific ethnic focus of the study. The *garankéw* are thus consistently identified as "the" leatherworking group among the Soninke, Bamana, and Malinke.[7] However, although they are presented as equivalent in status to the *jeliw* and *numuw,* there is a great deal of variation in the amount and nature of information concerning the *garankéw* within these different ethnic contexts. This unevenness is especially apparent in discussions of the roles played by each *nyamakala* group in oral traditions.

For example, in her article on Mande myth and social organization, based primarily on research in Bamako and Kangaba in the 1950s, Germaine Dieterlen reported that the *garankéw,* along with the *dyelu* (*jeliw*), *numuw,* and *finaw* (*funéw*), are said to be among the forty-four clans to have "come out" of Mande. However, the myths of origin and other oral traditions she presented do not mention *garankéw* (or *funéw*), while *numuw* and especially *jeliw* figure prominently. In addition, according to Dieterlen, *numuw* and *jeliw* are represented in the meanings attributed to the designs and figures molded and painted on the surface of the ritual sanctuary in Kangaba, but not *garankéw.*[8] Similarly, Nicholas Hopkins later identified *numuw, jeliw, garankéw,* and *finaw* as the four principal *nyamakala* groups among the Maninka (or Malinke) of Kita and the surrounding region. However, he cited one of his informants as saying that the ideal village consists of several "noble" lineages, with just one *numu* and one *jeli* lineage. Neither the *garankéw* nor the *finaw* seem to fit into the traditional symbiotic relationship he described.[9]

The data on the *garankéw* are equally ambiguous in the literature on Bamana social organization, in contrast to the sometimes extended discussions concerning the status and various roles of *jeliw* and *numuw*.[10] Dominique Zahan, for example, distinguishing between Bamana *nyamakalaw* and those of foreign origin, identified the *garankéw* as a "caste of tanners and leatherworkers" who, along with the *numuw, dyeliw,* and *kulew,* form an integral part of Bamana society, but admitted that they are not well understood "from an ethnological point of view."[11]

In contrast, *garankéw* figure prominently in Soninke oral traditions. In the publication of the results of their research in 1965 among the Soninke in the region of Dyahunu (cercle of Yelimane) in northwestern Mali, Eric Pollet and Grace Winter provide some of the oral traditions surrounding special relationships between certain *garanké* clans and certain noble families, relationships said to date back to the time of Wagadu.[12] In fact, two of the leatherworker clans present in the region at the time of their research (whom they identify as the Samabone branch of the Dyawara [Jawara] and the Kore branch of the Simaka), along with at least two blacksmith families, were counted among the 144 clans said to have dispersed from Wagadu and to have arrived in the region at the end of the twelfth century.

Although not always in a favorable light, *garankéw* appear in a wide variety of Soninke traditions. One such tradition was recorded by Frantz de Zeltner around the turn of the century. According to the tradition, a member of the Simaga *garanké* clan came upon a member of the noble Soninke Kaga family stranded in the countryside in the heat of day without water. The *garanké* offered him a vessel full of water, but no sooner had the man taken a drink than he fell dead. Since that time, Zeltner reported, if a member of one of these families offers a drink to a member of the other, he must place the vessel on the ground rather than hand it directly; the procedure is the same for returning the vessel.[13] According to Zeltner's informants, leatherworkers are the totem of the Soninke Turé family. If one of the latter needs to have a cover made for an amulet, he commissions the work from a *garanké,* but has someone else wear the amulet for a period of time before wearing it himself.[14] In another Soninke tradition, the destruction of a town was credited to be the result of the deception of a *garanké.* As the story goes, a leatherworker of the Dembaga family had been sent on a mission by the chief of one of the capital cities to another town. En route he apparently took a nap and managed to tear his clothing. Upon his return, the chief asked who had done this to him. The *garanké* replied that he had been beaten by the people of the other town. Without verification of the leatherworker's story, the chief called on his people to take revenge against the other town.[15]

Other roles played by *garankéw* in Soninke oral traditions are equally visible, but somewhat less injurious. In the legends collected by Adam in the Nioro region concerning the founding of the Diawara (Jawara) kingdom, it was a leatherworker by the name of Diawara who was the first to meet the legendary founder Dama N'Guilli and his comrades upon their arrival in the Mande region, by tradition becoming their host.[16] When Sundiata, the ruler of Mali, discovered that Dama had no given name, he requested him to take that of his host Diawara, as was the custom. Because of the important role they played in the Dama N'Guilli legend, Diawara leatherworkers have always occupied an important position among the noble Diawara; the latter are even sometimes referred to as the slaves of the *garanké* Diawara.[17] Upon their arrival in the region that was destined to become the Diawara kingdom, once again it is a leatherworker that Dama N'Guilli and his companions encounter who informs them of where they are and who presents them to the ruler of the country.[18] Thus, whether they are rendered as untrustworthy and perhaps dangerous individuals, or as hosts and intermediaries, it is significant that among the Soninke these roles went to *garankéw,* not to blacksmiths or bards.

Soninke *garankéw* and Bamana-Malinke *jeliw*

One of the goals of my research, as I had defined it in my original proposal for fieldwork, was to attempt to fill in some of the gaps in our understanding of Bamana *garankéw*. However, during my research in Mali I was unable to locate a leatherworker who identified himself as both *garanké* and Bamana. *Garankéw*—even those working in predominantly Bamana areas—consistently claimed Soninke origins. Furthermore, I discovered that the *garankéw* are not the only Mande *nyamakalaw* to provide their services as leatherworkers. In the absence of *garankéw,* and often in competition with them, I discovered that Bamana and Malinke *jeliw* do tanning and leatherwork in addition to their roles as bards.

The *garankéw* I interviewed were careful to distinguish between their birthright as *garankéw* and the occupational specialization that is but one part of that heritage. One of my informants explained, "Anyone can learn to be a *garanké,* even if you are not of *garanké* origin. In Jenne, anyone can do it, even Bambara do it, even *jeli.* But *garanké* is our race [*siya*], not just a profession."[19]

They are quite adamant about the distinction between themselves as a particular social category and other leatherworkers, especially *jeliw.* For example, when asked whether *garankéw* could be included among the *nyamakalaw,* one of my informants said, "If you were our neighbor, we would lower ourselves, and cut a shoe, and go and give it to you, and you would take something out and give it to us, but we don't beg, [and] we don't dance."[20] He then indicated that if by *nyamakalaw* we did not mean *jeliw,* then *garankéw* could be included. Another asserted that *garankéw* are the "true" *nyamakalaw,* while *jeliw* are nothing more than beggars.[21] *Garankéw* explain that others took up leatherworking in the past because it was lucrative; there was much work and a profit to be made.

On the other hand, Bamana and Malinke leatherworkers consistently identified themselves as *jeliw* and did not view their occupation as leatherworkers as an exception to the rule, let alone a usurpation of *garanké* specialization. For example, Abdoulaye Diabaté, a Bamana leatherworker I interviewed in Segu, stated that prior to his coming to the city from a village in southeastern Mali, he did not know of *garankéw* since there were none in his home country. He told us that they were *jeliw,* and that his father, grandfather, and great-grandfather before him had always done leatherwork.[22] In fact, *Jeliba,* in addition to being an honorific title for masters of oral history throughout the Mande world, is also a common term of address for leatherworkers in Segu, whether or not they are Bamana. For example, a Fula leatherworker who identified himself as a *sakké* said that even he was called *Jeliba,* and that people in Segu do not distinguish between *jeliw, garankéw,* and *sakké.*[23] Although the general population may use these terms interchangeably, preferring to view differences among these identities as insignificant, that is not the case for the leatherworkers themselves. *Jeli* leatherworkers are explicit about the distinction between their identity and that of the *garankéw,* saying that the latter are not *nyamakalaw,* that only *jeliw* are true *nyamakalaw.*[24]

In reexamining the literature after my return from the field, I discovered that there are references to bards as leatherworkers that I, and perhaps others, had either overlooked or considered an exception to the rule. In 1898, for example, Georges Tellier described the *jeliw* of Kita by what are now accepted as standard roles—as bards, praise singers, genealogists, messengers, and so forth. He added, however, that

> some of them are *karangués,* those who understand all the work of the currier, the tanner, the saddle-maker, the shoe-maker, etc., in a word, the manufacture of all leather objects. . . . Certain songs, certain dances, and the making of certain musical instruments, even the profession of the *karangué* is theirs exclusively.[25]

Thus while Tellier recognizes the term *karangué* as referring to the profession of leatherworking, perhaps drawing from earlier written accounts, it appears that in Kita these services were provided by *jeliw.* By the time of my own visit there in 1983, several *garanké* families were well established in the community. Most of them traced their origins to the Soninke region of Nioro or Kayes. I found them working side by side with *jeli* leatherworkers as well as one or more Tukulor leatherworkers from Senegal.

Louis Tauxier provides additional evidence of the role of *jeliw* as leatherworkers in the Mande heartland. In 1908, he described the importance of the craft of the leatherworker in Guinea as second only to that of the blacksmith, cautioning that the word *cordonnier* (French for shoemaker) is really too narrow for all the items made by these leatherworkers. Although he does not discuss their identity, he does provide the names of several of his leatherworker informants, including Dieli Mori Kourouma, Manké Kamara, and Fanfodé Doumbouya. Since the practice of using *nyamakala* identity as part of a proper name is rather common, it seems likely that Dieli Mori Kourouma was a *jeli*. In addition, Kamara, Kourouma, and Doumbouya (or Doumbia) are sometimes identified as Mande bard clan names.[26]

In a later publication, Tauxier contrasted the position of leatherworkers among the Mossi of Yatenga with that of Mande leatherworkers. He said that *dieli* was the only term known for leatherworkers among the Malinke and Wasulunke, while the Bamana use the term *garanké*. He added, "Dieli accurately means griot, but, since among the Malinke and Wasulunke, only griots exercise the profession of leather-worker, there is no other name for them."[27] More recently, Jean-Loup Amselle reported that the bards of Wasulu earn a significant part of their livelihood from leatherwork.[28] Although Dominique Zahan identifies the *garankéw* as a Bamana caste of leatherworkers, he also mentions in a footnote that Bamana *jeliw* often do leatherwork in addition to their own profession as bards.[29]

There are also references in the literature to Mande bards doing leatherwork for non-Mande patrons outside the core Mande region, too easily dismissed as the result of isolated responses to a lack of demand for their oral skills. In his research among the Dan of western Côte d'Ivoire, Hugo Zemp found that in addition to Dan musicians, there were also bards of Malinke origin, some itinerant, others attached to the courts of chiefs. He noted that while it is usually assumed that Mande bards are professional musicians, earning their livelihood from their musical skills and oral artistry,

> this is not the case for the *yoebo* [the Dan word for *jeli*] among the Dan . . . whose revenues come primarily from their occupation as leatherworkers. . . . They do not sing or drum any more frequently than the Dan musicians who are farmers. . . . The *yoemi* [plural] among the Dan exercise above all the second profession of leatherworkers.[30]

Like my informants in Mali, these Malinke bards perceive themselves as quite separate from the *garankéw*. According to Zemp,

> The *yeli* guard their distance from the *garankéw*, who are, among the Mande peoples, the true leatherworkers, and they consider them with contempt: [quoting one of his informants, who said] "If the *garankéw* request a gift from someone and he refuses them, they piss on him or dirty his household with their excrement. But we, we don't do that, we sing!"[31]

Apparently many of these Malinke bard families no longer work as musicians, but are settled, earning part of their income from farming on land requested from their Dan hosts, and part from leatherwork.[32]

Among the artisan groups of the Senufo of northern Côte d'Ivoire, there are several that are clearly of Mande origin, including the *numuw* (blacksmiths and woodworkers) and the *kulew* (woodcarvers and calabash workers). Leatherworkers in this region are called Tyeli (Dieli, Tyele) or Jelebele (Tyelibele). Their origins are a topic of debate; although Bohumil Holas and Yves Person have identified them as being of Mande origin, Gilbert Bochet, Anita Glaze, and others have proposed a Senufo heritage.[33]

Glaze, for example, suggested that they may be a Senufo group that acquired artisan status at a relatively recent time after having taken up the trade of leatherworking from economic necessity. She argues:

> There is no evidence that the Senufo *Tyelibele* have any relationship with the caste-linked groups called the "Dieli" and reported widely in Manding cultures throughout the Western Sudan. . . . In all the Manding cultures where the Dieli are reported, the occupation of leatherworking is specific to a quite different group, the "Garanke."[34]

If the respective roles and occupational specialization of the *garankéw* and *jeliw* within the Mande society have been misrepresented in the literature, as argued above, then the evidence concerning Tyeli origins needs to be reevaluated.[35]

However, as Launay's contribution to this volume reveals, the identity of these leatherworkers is only further confused by questions concerning their original language.[36] According to Glaze and Richter, they speak a language which appears to be unique, neither a Senari dialect of the Senufo language, nor Gur-related, nor Mande.[37] According to Person, however, the language spoken by these leatherworkers is related to an archaic form of the Mande language spoken not only by several other groups of the Bonduku region, but also by the Vai and Kono of Sierra Leone. He suggests that the language was carried to these regions, first south and then west, during the fifteenth, sixteenth, and seventeenth centuries from the Upper Niger region (Dyalonké), and that this early Mande influence was superseded during the seventeenth and eighteenth centuries by a new wave of Mande speakers, primarily Jula.[38]

According to the recent research of Kathryn Green, *jeli* leatherworkers in the predominantly Senufo region of Kong identify themselves and are identified by others as Mande. Her informants clearly viewed this as common knowledge. In addition, the members of one of the *jeli* clans, now known as Watara, say that they were once Diabagaté (equivalent to the Mande *jeli* name of Diabaté or Jabaté). Their oral traditions state that they were invited by the Watara warriors to accompany them from the Mande heartland to Kong, to be their bards and to provide their services as leatherworkers.[39]

The broad distribution of *jeliw* as leatherworkers throughout and beyond the Mande region suggests that this is neither an isolated nor a particularly recent phenomenon. While *jeli* leatherworkers are found primarily south and east of the core Mande area, *garankéw* dominate the craft across the Northern Sudanic region west of the Niger River, throughout Senegambia, Guinea, and into Sierra Leone and Liberia.[40] In addition to the widespread use of the Mande term *garanké* (or *karanke*) for leatherworkers throughout this region, there are several other factors linking the identity of these leatherworkers to a Soninke heritage.

One possible connection between the *garankéw* of this region and a Soninke heritage is that in Guinea and to some extent in Sierra Leone, the wives of these leatherworkers are the principal indigo-dyers, traditionally a specialization of Soninke women in the Sudanic region.[41]

More important is the close association of the *garankéw* with other groups of Soninke origin and the predominance of common Soninke patronyms among these leatherworkers. In Guinea, *garankéw* are closely linked to the Jakhanké, specialized groups of Muslim clerics and traders of Soninke origin, dispersed throughout the Senegambia region and into Guinea, who have maintained a sense of distinctive identity.[42] Like the Jakhanké, these leatherworkers are perceived to be particularly devout Muslims and are often identified as being of Jakhanké or Soninke origin.[43] In a study of one of the suburbs of Conakry (Dixinn-Port), for example, Claude Rivière reported that a colony of Diakanké (Jakhanké) lived in a quarter officially called Dar-ès-Salam, a name attributed recently to replace *Garankéla* or "Place of the *Garanké.*" According to informants, the founders of the colony arrived in 1905 and requested land on which to settle and presumably practice the trade of leatherworking. They were followed by several Sarakole (Soninke) leatherworker families. At the time of the study (the 1960s), the primary occupation of these people continued to be leatherwork, although some had become clerks, chauffeurs, and mechanics.[44] Furthermore, many of these leatherworkers had family names recognizable as Soninke *garanké* patronyms, including Djoura (Diawara or Jawara), Diakité (Jakité), Kaloga, and Tounkara (Tungara).[45]

Leatherworkers in Sierra Leone are also known by the Mande term *karanké* (or *garanké*) and bear Soninke patronyms. However, there is a perception in Sierra Leone today that the *garankéw* are of Fula, not Mande, origin. According to Joseph Opala, Temne paramount chiefs report that they send for "Fula" leatherworkers from Guinea to commission the elaborate regalia of chieftaincy.[46] Although my sample was limited, every one of the approximately fifteen or so leatherworkers with whom I spoke in 1988 identified himself as Mandingo or Soninke. In fact, those with whom I was able to conduct more extended interviews all traced their family histories back to Guinea, where their fathers or grandfathers had worked for Fula patrons, suggesting a possible explanation for people thinking of them as Fula.[47] Several referred to the Soninke region of Jafunu in northwestern Mali as their ancestral homeland. Like their counterparts in Guinea as well as Mali, many of their family names, such as Diawara (Jawara), Kalon (or Kaloga), Sylla, and Tounkara (Tungara), are recognizable as Soninke *garanké* patronyms.

A Historical Sketch: The Diaspora

The present geographical distribution of these two Mande leatherworking groups suggests a diaspora of *garankéw* and *jeliw* extending beyond the core

Mande region into areas where these craftsmen have settled among non-Mande patrons—a diaspora, I would suggest, that is neither recent nor random. Furthermore, I argue that these leatherworkers may have played a significant role equivalent to that of their commercial and religious counterparts in the diffusion of Mande social and cultural institutions in West Africa.

Most discussions of the earliest phases of the Mande diaspora have focused on the dispersal of Soninke trading and clerical clans as part of the expansion of trade networks during the heyday of Ghana—a dispersal accelerated by the decline of the empire, the so-called "fall of Wagadu" described in oral traditions. The commercial networks of Ghana came under the control of the empire of Mali during the thirteenth and fourteenth centuries, when a process referred to as the "Mandingization" of Soninke trading and clerical clans resulted in the emergence of new identities, including the Marka of the Middle Niger region, the Jakhanké (or Diahanké) in the west, and ultimately the Dyula to the south.[48] Although they lost their original language and adopted Malinke dialects, these clans kept Soninke patronyms and have maintained a sense of distinctive heritage in part through the preservation of oral traditions. These Muslim traders and clerics established themselves as strangers in communities outside the core Mande area. They were followed by the more aggressive expansion of Mande warrior groups.[49]

While the movements of traders, clerics, and warriors have received a great deal of attention, those of craftsmen remain poorly understood. George Brooks has recently suggested that Mande smiths may have accompanied, or even preceded, traders and clerics into the forest regions as entrepreneurs developing new markets for their products and in search of fresh supplies of timber for charcoal.[50] The smiths might have been well received by some local farmers in need of tools for agricultural production, and they would have been especially important as a source of weapons for the military designs of Mande warrior groups. In addition to their expertise in ironworking, the smiths would have been able to offer their spiritual resources and knowledge of the occult, perhaps in competition with that of the clerics.[51]

While data may not be available to prove conclusively that leatherworkers were part of the earliest movements of Mande peoples, there are various reasons why leatherworkers, like blacksmiths, might have followed or accompanied any or all of these three groups—traders, clerics, and warriors. First of all, the traders' expanding network of markets would have been an attractive incentive for the migration of leatherworkers. Unlike most other artisans, who produce items in their compounds or workshops and bring the finished product to the market to sell, leatherworkers arrive with their tools and some supplies, setting up a workshop on the spot. They tend to work directly on commission from clients, and therefore would have been more likely to travel with traders than to stay put and supply the latter with goods in quantity. The development of new trade routes and associated markets would have provided these craftsmen with a setting for soliciting the patronage of new clients.

Secondly, as the ones who are entrusted with enclosing amulets in leather casings, the leatherworkers would have found their skills in demand in communities where Muslim clerics provided amulets for both Muslim and non-Muslim clients.[52] They would also very likely have been commissioned by the clerics themselves to make covers or slipcases for the Quran and other precious manuscripts.

Finally, leatherworkers would have been essential to the state-building activities of Mande warriors in the production and repair of equipment for warfare, including sword and knife sheaths, saddles and other horse trappings, boots, quivers, shot pouches, and powderhorns. They would also have taken part in the production of regalia for established chiefs, including crowns, staffs, and flywhisks, a task they continue to fulfill for certain paramount chiefs in Sierra Leone.[53]

Although establishing a chronology for the dispersal of Mande leatherworkers may never be possible, much remains to be done concerning the history of particular clans as well as their impact on the societies among whom they settled and found a livelihood. And while the historical framework sketched above remains speculative, I believe the notion of a diaspora, beginning as early as the eleventh or twelfth century, makes sense in light of the dominance of *garanké* and *jeli* leatherworkers throughout and well beyond the Mande region.[54] Perhaps more important, however, is the extent to which these leatherworkers seem to have created and preserved a sense of their heritage even when far removed from their ancestral homelands.

Notions of Difference

In defining the movements of Mande leatherworkers as a diaspora, I am aware of the implications of the term vis-à-vis a sense of common or shared identity held by its members across great distances. In a discussion of the diaspora of *juula* traders in the Senegambian region, Philip Curtin suggested that these Mande groups were part of a much larger cross-cultural commercial network, and that they may have "had more in common culturally with other *juula* hundreds of miles away than they did with non-*juula* secular nobility or peasantry of their own region."[55] I suggest that a similar sense of distinctiveness based on identity, occupation, and Mande heritage can be found among Mande leatherworkers, including both *garankéw* and *jeliw*.

This is a conclusion drawn almost exclusively from my own interviews and interactions with leatherworkers in Mali and Sierra Leone. A persistent problem in interpreting the literature on *nyamakala* identity in general has been that it seems that much of the information was obtained from members of the non-*nyamakala* majority. I think most would agree that the pitfalls of viewing the identity of a minority class through the lenses of the majority cannot be underestimated. Yet this is precisely the perspective that has skewed our understanding of social identity throughout the Mande world. This is perhaps most apparent in discussions of the hierarchical nature of Mande society and the position of the *nyamakalaw* within that system. But it is equally misleading to rely on such a perspective when the issue is origins, identity, and ethnicity.

An example from Sierra Leone will suffice to illustrate the point. The context was an interview with a leatherworker in the northern town of Kabala. I wanted to know how he would identify himself to us (as noted above, there is a perception in Sierra Leone that the *garankéw* are Fula). He provided his name when asked and immediately added that he was a *garanké*. Although I already recognized his family name (Sylla) as a common Mande patronym, I asked my interpreter to pose a follow-up query about my informant's ethnicity. His question came out something like "You're a Fula, aren't you?" While this was hardly the subtle, open-ended approach I had tried to convey to my interpreter, the response was unequivocal: "No, I am Mandingo!" In the course of further questioning, he traced his family back through Guinea to the Soninke region of Jafunu. Had I not interviewed this and other leatherworkers in Sierra Leone myself, and instead relied solely on the literature, I might have concluded that Fula leatherworkers dominate the trade in this region. My task would then have been to speculate on how the Mande term (*karanké*) came to be used for Fula leatherworkers.

My informant's response to the question of ethnicity also provides a chance to examine the relative nature of ethnic labels. The permeability of ethnic groups and the flexibility of ethnic categories is hardly a new topic. Most recently, Amselle has argued that ethnic labels in the African context are at best meaningless, at worst the legacy of a colonial construction designed to control and oppress.[56] Thus, ethnicity might more accurately be viewed as one of a number of negotiable aspects of one's identity. Identifying himself as Mandingo in the context of our interview (i.e., after having been accused of being Fula) was sufficient for my informant to distinguish himself as Mande from a quite separate ethnic category, the Fula, as well as from other Sierra Leonean ethnicities such as Limba or Temne. It was only during the course of the interview that the leatherworker more precisely defined the origins of his family as Soninke.

Studying the origins of different Mande identities is important not solely as an academic exercise in reconstructing history, but for understanding how individuals choose to play that heritage in the contemporary arena. My sense is that *nyamakala* identity has long been grounded in more than simply occupational specialization as leatherworkers, bards, or blacksmiths. It has transcended ethnicity in a way that allowed *garankéw* and *jeliw* to maintain a separateness from their client majorities. *Nyamakala* identity seems to have been both stronger and less negotiable than ethnicity. It is this sense of difference that has informed *garanké* and *jeli* identity whatever the particular ethnic context. What the future holds for these identities in an increasingly industrial and pluralistic world is hard to predict. The demand for their skills as leatherworkers has certainly diminished, and they no longer claim a monopoly on knowledge of specialized technology. Indeed, their heritage as *garankéw* or *jeliw* may perhaps be the only element of their identity available to future generations to distinguish themselves from others, if they so choose.

Notes

This chapter is drawn from my research on Mande leatherworking traditions, made possible by a Fulbright-Hays Dissertation Research Fellowship (1982–84) for fieldwork in Mali, where I was granted affiliation with the Institut des Sciences Humaines. Further research in Mali and Sierra Leone during the summer of 1988 was made possible by a grant from the University of Tulsa. I am grateful to all those who assisted my research in the field, especially Kassim Koné, and to the numerous individuals who generously shared their time and knowledge. I would also like to thank Charles Bird, David Conrad, Kathryn Green, Barbara Hoffman, Adria LaViolette, Thomas Martin, and Patrick McNaughton for their comments on various previous drafts.

1. Park (1799:282). To my knowledge this is the first use of the Mande term in the literature. In one version of the seventeenth-century Arabic manuscript the *Ta'rikh el-fettach,* edited by Houdas and Delafosse, the term *Kourounkoi* is identified as the Songhay term meaning "masters of the skin," and applied to a caste of leatherworkers (Ibn al-Mukhtar [c. 1665:21, 46, 112]). However, in a critical analysis of conflicting information in the different versions of this manuscript, Nehemia Levtzion has argued that references to the various occupational groups were a nineteenth-century fabrication designed to legitimate Shehu Ahmadu's policy toward these groups (1971:571–93). The Mande term for bard appears in the fourteenth-century Arabic account of Ibn Battuta's visit to the empire of Mali; he refers to poets who perform at the court following the performance of Dugha, the king's principal interpreter: "They are called *jula,* of which the singular is *jali*" (Ibn Battuta [1355:293 and 416 n. 39]).

2. Winterbottom (1803, I:91).

3. There is a popular perception in Sierra Leone that the *garankéw* (or *karanke*) there are of Fula, not Mande, origin. However, the leatherworkers identify themselves as Mande (Mandingo). This contradiction probably stems from the fact that they came to the country from regions in Guinea dominated by Fula. In addition, Winterbottom tended to confuse Fulas and Mandingos, and he frequently refers to "Africans" when Temne might have been more precise, since he spent most of this time in the Temne region (Joseph A. Opala, personal communication, 1984).

4. Raffenel (1856, II:384–85).

5. "Noumô, Garanké ou Diali vous êtes né, Noumô, Garanké ou Diali vous resterez jusqu'à votre dernier jour, même si vous n'exercez jamais la profession désignée sous un de ces noms et vous serez père, grand'père, bisaïeul, etc. . . . d'enfants qui, peut-être, ne seront jamais ni forgerons, ni cordonniers, ni musiciens, mais dont chacun restera Diali, Noumô, Garanké. D'ailleurs, en général, le nom seul, nom de famille ou de tribu, suffirait à faire reconnaître la caste." Tautain (1885:346).

6. The *finaw* or *funéw* are variously described as entertainers and mimes, as a kind of bard's bard closely associated with Islamic traditions. For more information on the *funéw,* see David Conrad's contribution to this volume.

7. For Mande peoples in general, see Labouret (1934:106); Sidibé (1959:13–17); N'Diayé (1970:83–87); and Launay (1972). For the Soninke, see Zeltner (1908:217–33); Saint-Père (1925:19–21, 48–51); and Pollet and Winter (1971:206–37). For the Bamana, see Pâques (1954:63–64) and Zahan (1963:126–32). For the Malinke, see Camara (1976:77) and Hopkins (1971:106).

8. Dieterlen (1955:39–76) and (1959:119–38).

9. Hopkins also cited another informant concerning the importance of the presence of *numuw* and *jeliw* at public meetings (1971:106–108). In a later publication, Hopkins identifies the leatherworkers of Kita as being mostly Soninke from the region of Nioro (1972:70, see also 25–26). In 1983–84, most of the leatherworkers in Kita were Soninke from Nioro, Kayes, and Yelimane. Claude Meillassoux mentions the *garankéw* as one of

the Soninke castes in Bamako, but he does not include them among either the Bamana or the Maninka (Malinke) (1968:43, 48).

10. In his initial discussion of Bamana castes, Delafosse includes *Somono* (fishermen), *Noumou* (blacksmiths), *Lorho* (jewelers working in brass), *Koulè* (woodworkers), *Diêli*, *Founè* or *Founérhè* (religious bards and magicians), and *Donso* or *Lonzo* (hunters), but not *garanké*, although he does mention them later in a footnote listing different castes in the area. Delafosse (1912, I:139 and III:118 n. 1). Apparently following Delafosse, Pâques includes *garankéw* in her list of Bamana artisans but does not add much information, except that the men do both tanning and leatherworking (1954:63, 66).

11. Zahan (1963:127–28, 131–32).

12. Pollet and Winter (1971:187–265, esp. 223–24).

13. Zeltner (1908:218).

14. Ibid., 218–19.

15. Pollet and Winter (1971:65).

16. Adam (1903:234–35).

17. Ibid., 235.

18. Ibid., 238.

19. Interview with Boubou Soumanou, February 25, 1983, Bamako.

20. Interview with Amadou Laye Sylla, March 26, 1983, Bamako. In a personal communication (1989), Barbara Hoffman cautioned against taking such statements too literally, because this kind of public posturing about other groups is quite common. Such comments are often framed in terms of social categories in general, but rarely if ever in reference to particular families or individuals. Hoffman's research revealed a good deal of mutual respect and cooperation between such groups.

21. Interview with Tamba Soumanou, June 8, 1983, Garankébougou.

22. Interview with Abdoulaye Diabaté, June 22, 1983, Segou.

23. Interview with Shekou Amadou Gakou, April 6, 1983, Segou. *Sakké* is the Fulfulde term for the Fula caste of leatherworkers and saddlemakers. On another occasion, someone else told me of a saddlemaker in Segou, whom he referred to as "Jeliba." In addition, my interpreter addressed Adama Gana, a Dogon leatherworker in Sevare, as "Jeliba." When I asked if he was a *garanké*, he said yes, that he was a *jeli-garanké*, and then that he was actually a *jeli*, but that he practiced *garankéya*. Interview with Adama Gana, July 17, 1983, Sevare. According to Thomas Hale, Djibo Badie, the most prominent bard in Niamey, is better known as "Jeliba" (1984:207–20, 217 n. 26).

24. Interviews with Jejon Kouyaté, May 18, 1983, Somba; Nyene Kouyaté and Lassana Kouyaté, May 18, 1983, Kolokani; Niandu Tarawele and Madu Diabaté, January 10, 1984, Sinsani; Abdoulaye Diabaté, June 22, 1983, Ousman Danté, June 22, 1983, and Boubacar Danté, June 21, 1983, Segou. See note 20 above.

25. ". . . enfin, quelques-uns sont *karangués*, ce qui comprend tout le travail du corroyeur, du tanneur, du sellier, du cordonnier, etc., et un mot la fabrication de tout objet en cuir. . . . Certains chants, certaines danses, la confection de certains instruments, de meme que le métier de *karangué*, sont leur apanage exclusif." Tellier (1898:83).

26. Tauxier (1908:38–40). Sidibé identifies Koroma and Doumbia as typical bard names, although he notes that they are also noble and blacksmith patronyms (1959:13). Camara identifies Kourouma as a patronym for noble *numu* as well as *jeli* clans, and Kamara as a noble *numu* and *funé* patronym (1976:103). Jean-Loup Amselle identifies Dumbiya as a typical griot-leatherworker name among the Wasulunke (1972:10). Several of Hugo Zemp's Malinke griot informants among the Dan of west-central Côte d'Ivoire were of the Doumaya clan (1964:370–82 and 1966:622–42). According to N'Diayé, Kamara (or Camara) is a "finah" name (1970:112).

27. "En bambara cordonnier se dit *garanké* et *dieli* chez les Malinkes et les Ouassoulounkes (*Dieli* veut dire exactement griot, mais, commes chez les Malinkes et les Ouassoulounkes, il n'y a pas les griots qui exercent la métier de cordonnier, il n'y a pas d'autre nom pour designer ceux-ci)." Tauxier (1917:213).

28. Amselle (1972:10). This was also confirmed for me by Gerald Cashion, who conducted research on Mande hunters in the Wasulu region (personal communication, 1984).

29. Zahan's use of the word *actuellement* suggests that he thinks this may be a recent trend (1963:147 n. 1).

30. "Ce n'est pas le cas pour les *yeobo* chez les Dan (pas plus que pour la plupart des *yeli* en pays malinké), dont les resources proviennent pour la plus grand part de leur travail de cordonnier . . . ils ne chantent et ne tambourinent pas plus souvent que les musiciens dan qui sont agriculteurs . . . le *yeomi* chez les Dan exerce surtout son second métier de cordonnier." Zemp (1964:378).

31. "Mais les *yeli* gardent leurs distances des *garanké,* qui sont chez les peuples mandé les véritables travailleurs de la peau, et ils les consièrent avec mépris: 'Si les *garanké* demandent à quelqu'un un cadeau et qu'il leur est refusé, ils pissent sur lui ou salissent sa maison avec leur excréments. Mais nous, nous ne faisons pas cela, nous chantons!'" Zemp (1964:379).

32. Ibid.

33. See Robert Launay's contribution to this volume and Holas (1966:70–71); Person (1964:328); Bochet (1959:61–101); Glaze (1981:40–42); see also Richter (1980:15).

34. Glaze (1981:228 n. 33, see also 40–42).

35. For a thorough reevaluation of the information, see Launay's contribution to this volume. Part of Glaze's conclusion is based on similarities between elements of the Tyeli Poro and those of other Senufo Poro initiation societies (1981:40–42, and 228 n. 33). See also Bochet (1959:61–101).

36. According to Launay (in this volume), part of the problem of classifying the language lies in the extensive use of loanwords. He reported that Father Pierre Boutin, a linguist who has studied the languages of the region, including "Dieli," still considers its origin an open question.

37. Glaze (1981:41); Richter (1980:15).

38. Person (1964:328). Launay (in this volume) suggests that if the Dieli can be identified as Mande (through further study of their language and oral traditions, etc.), they would probably have preceded other Mande immigrants to the area, including traders and clerics.

39. According to Kathryn Green, in addition to the Watara/Diabagaté clan, the other bard-leatherworker clans in Kong are the Baro, said to be from Sikasso, and the Kouyaté (a typical Mande *jeli* patronym).

40. Other leatherworking groups in this region include the Tukulor *sakke* (Wane [1969:54]) and the related Fulani *sakke,* as well as the noncasted Arma of Jenne and Timbuctu and Maure women (see especially Gardi [1985]).

41. Barry (1943–44); Rivière (1969:607, 611); Marty (1921:434). Henri Labouret (1934:106) went so far as to suggest that the name *garanké* (*gèr-ik'e, gara-nk'é,* M. *kara-nkè*) may be derived from the Mande word for indigo (*gala* or *gara*).

42. On the Jakhanké, see Curtin (1971 and 1972); Sanneh (1976:49–72) and (1979). According to Peter Weil, two of the leatherworker lineages in the Senegambian state of Wuli are identified with the early history of the state, although their association with Muslim clerical and trading lineages is unclear. The patronym of one of these lineages is Silla (Sylla), a common Soninke family name recognized as either *garanké* or noble. The patronym of the other lineage is Fati, a family name, to my knowledge, not found among the Soninke in Mali (personal communication, 1988).

43. Durand (1932:62–64); and two articles by Rivière, (1967:446–47) and (1969:610–11).

44. Rivière (1967:446–47).

45. Ibid.; Rivière (1969:610).

46. Personal communication, 1988.

47. Interviews with Sini Mansaray, July 4, 1988; Mohamed Sylla, July 8, 1988; and Mohamed Tounkara, July 12, 1988, Makenie.

48. Sanneh (1976:49–72); Sanneh (1979); Curtin (1971, 1972); Brooks (1986); Perinbam (1980); Person (1972); Person (1963:125–56).

49. Brooks (1986).
50. Ibid.
51. However, Adria LaViolette (personal communication, 1992) suggested to me that negative attitudes toward smiths may have cost them acceptance in certain communities. The archaeological record reveals that ironworking did not spread evenly in African prehistory. It is possible that some communities chose to do without iron technology because of fear or distrust of the powers wielded by blacksmiths.
52. The importance of amulets in non-Muslim communities is evident in the descriptions of early European travelers, who were impressed by the strength of belief in their efficacy. In the 1620s Richard Jobson observed,

> The Gregories [*grisgris,* i.e., amulets] bee things of great esteeme amongst them, for the most part they are made of leather of severall fashions, wonderous neatly, they are hollow and within them is placed, and sowed up close, certaine writings, or spels which they receive from their Mary-buckes [marabouts, i.e., Muslim clerics], whereof they conceive such a religious respect, that they do confidently beleeve no hurt can betide them, whilst these Gregories are about them, and it seems to encrease their superstition. . . . (1623:63)

In a later passage, Jobson referred to the leatherworker as

> one that doth make all their Gregories, wherein truely is a great deale of art shewen, they being made and fashioned of leather into all shapes, both round and square, and triangle, after that neate manner as might be allowed for workemanship, even amongst our curious handicrafts. . . . (1623:154)

53. Prussin (1986).
54. *Garankéw* and *jeliw* are not the only leatherworkers in the region, but they do outnumber the others. See note 40 for references to some of the other leatherworking groups.
55. Curtin (1972:14).
56. Amselle (1985:11–48).

References

Adam, M. G. 1903. "Légendes historiques du pays de Nioro (Sahel)." *Revue Coloniale,* n.s. 14 (Sept.–Oct.):232–48, 15 (Nov.–Dec.):354–72.
Amselle, Jean-Loup. 1972. "Histoire et structure social du Wasulu avant Samori." Paper presented at the Conference on Manding Studies, School of Oriental and African Studies, University of London.
―――. 1985. "Ethnies et espaces: Pour une anthropologie topologique." In *Au coeur de l'ethnie: Ethnies, tribalisme, et état en Afrique,* ed. Jean-Loup Amselle and Elikia M'Bokolo. Paris: Le Découverte.
Barry, Ibrahima. 1943–44. "Deux industries locales: Tannage et Teinturerie du Fouta Djallon à Pita [Guinea]." Devoir de Vacances, Ecole William Ponty, Sébikotane, Senegal. Cahiers du William Ponty, I.F.A.N. Bibliothéque (Documentation), Dakar.
Bochet, Gilbert. 1959. "Les poro des Diéli." *Bulletin de l'I.F.A.N.* 21, sér. B (1–2):61–101.
Brooks, George E. 1986. "A Provisional Historical Schema for Western Africa Based on Seven Climate Periods (ca. 9000 B.C. to the 19th Century)." *Cahiers d'Etudes Africaines* 26 (1–2):43–62.
Camara, Sory. 1976. *Gens de la parole. Essai sur la condition et le rôle des griots dans la société Malinké.* Paris and the Hague: Mouton.
Curtin, Philip D. 1971. "Pre-Colonial Trading Networks and Traders: The Diakhanke."

In *The Development of Indigenous Trade and Markets in West Africa,* ed. Claude
Meillassoux. Oxford: Oxford University Press.

———. 1972. "The Western Juula in the Eighteenth Century." Paper presented at the
Conference on Manding Studies, School of Oriental and African Studies, University of London.

Delafosse, Maurice. 1912. *Haut-Sènègal-Niger (Soudan Français).* 3 vols. Paris: Emile
Larose. Reprint, Paris: G.-P. Maisonneuve et Larose, 1972.

Dieterlen, Germaine. 1955. "Mythe et organisation sociale au Soudan Français." *Journal
de la Société des Africanistes* 25 (1–2):39–76.

———. 1959. "Mythe et organisation sociale en Afrique Occidentale (suite)." *Journal de
la Société des Africanistes* 29 (1):119–38.

Durand, Oswald. 1932. "Les Industries locales au Fouta." *Bulletin du Comité d'Etudes
historiques et scientifiques de l'Afrique Occidentale Française* 15:42–71.

Gardi, Bernhard. 1985. *Ein Markt wie Mopti. Handwerkerkasten und traditionelle Techniken in Mali.* Basler Beiträge zur Ethnologie, 25. Basel: Ethnologisches Seminar
der Universität und Museum für Völkerkunde.

Glaze, Anita. 1981. *Art and Death in a Senufo Village.* Bloomington: Indiana University
Press.

Hale, Thomas A. 1984. "Kings, Scribes, and Bards: A Look at Signs of Survival for
Keepers of the Oral Tradition among the Songhay-Speaking Peoples of Niger."
Artes Populares 10/11:207–20.

Holas, B. 1966. *Les Sénoufo (y compris les Minianka).* 2nd ed., rev. Paris: Presses
Universitaires de France.

Hopkins, Nicholas S. 1971. "Mandinka Social Organization." In *Papers on the Manding,*
ed. Carleton T. Hodge. Bloomington: Indiana University Press.

———. 1972. *Popular Government in an African Town.* Chicago: University of Chicago
Press.

Ibn al-Mukhtar. c. 1665. *Tarikh el-fettach.* Arabic text and French translation by O.
Houdas and M. Delafosse. 1st ed., Paris: E. Leroux, 1913. Reprint, Paris:
Adrien-Maisonneuve, 1964.

Ibn Battuta. 1355. *Tuhfat al-nuzzar fi ghara'ib al-amsar wa-'aja'ib al-asfar.* English translation by J. F. P. Hopkins in *Corpus of Early Arabic Sources for West African
History,* ed. N. Levtzion and J. F. P. Hopkins. Cambridge: Cambridge University Press, 1981.

Jobson, Richard. 1623. *The Golden Trade, or A Discovery of the River Gambra, and the
Golden Trade of the Aethiopians.* Reprint, edited by Charles G. Kingsley,
Teignmouth, England: E. E. Speight and R. H. Walpole, 1904.

Labouret, Henri. 1934. *Les Manding et Leur Langue.* Paris: Librarie Larose.

Launay, Robert. 1972. "Manding Clans and Castes." Paper presented at the Conference
on Manding Studies, School of Oriental and African Studies, University of
London.

Levtzion, Nehemia. 1971. "A Seventeenth-Century Chronicle by Ibn Al-Mukhtar: A
Critical Study of Ta'rikh al-Fattash." *Bulletin of the School of Oriental and
African Studies* 34 (3):571–93.

Marty, Paul. 1921. *L'Islam in Guinée. Fouta Diallon.* Paris: Editions Ernest Leroux.

Meillassoux, Claude. 1968. *Urbanization of an African Community.* Seattle: University of
Washington Press.

N'Diayé, Bokar. 1970. *Les Castes au Mali.* Bamako: Editions Populaires.

Pâques, Viviana. 1954. *Les Bambara.* Paris: Universitaires de France.

Park, Mungo. 1799. *Travels in the Interior Districts of Africa.* London: W. Bulmer and
Co.

Perinbam, B. Marie. 1980. "The Julas in Western Sudanese History: Long Distance
Traders and Developers of Resources." In *West African Culture Dynamics:*

Archaeological and Historical Perspectives, ed. B. K. Swartz, Jr. and Raymond
  E. Dummett. The Hague: Mouton Publishers.
Person, Yves. 1963. "Les ancêtres de Samori." *Cahiers d'Etudes Africaines* 4 (1):125–56.
———. 1964. "En quête d'une chronologie ivoirienne." In *The Historian in Tropical
  Africa,* ed. J. Vansina, R. Mauny, and L. V. Thomas. London: Oxford Univer-
  sity Press for the International African Institute.
———. 1972. "The Dyula and the Manding World." Paper presented at the Conference
  on Manding Studies, School of Oriental and African Studies, University of
  London.
Pollet, Eric, and Grace Winter. 1971. *La Société Soninké (Dyahunu, Mali).* Brussels:
  Editions de l'Institut de Sociologie, Université Libre de Bruxelles.
Prussin, Labelle. 1986. *Hatumere: Islamic Design in West Africa.* Berkeley: University of
  California Press.
Raffenel, Anne. 1856. *Nouveau Voyage dans le Pays des Nègres.* 2 vols. Paris: Imprimerie
  et Librairie Centrales des Chemins de Fer.
Richter, Delores. 1980. *Art, Economics and Change: The Kulebele of Northern Ivory Coast.*
  La Jolla, Calif.: Psych/Graphic Publishers.
Rivière, Claude. 1967. "Dixinn-Port. Enquête sur un quartier de Conakry (République
  de Guinée)." *Bulletin de l'I.F.A.N.* 29, sér. B (1–2):446–47.
———. 1969. "Guinée: La difficile émergence d'un artisanat casté." *Cahiers d'Etudes
  Africaines* 9 (4):600–25.
Saint-Père, J.-H. 1925. *Les Sarakollé du Guidimakha.* Paris: Emile Larose.
Sanneh, Lamin 0. 1976. "The Origins of Clericalism in West African Islam." *Journal of
  African History* 17 (1):49–72.
———. 1979. *The Jakhanke: The History of an Islamic Clerical People of the Senegambia.*
  London: International African Institute.
Sidibé, Mamby. 1959. "Les gens de caste ou nyamakala au Soudan Français." *Notes
  Africaines* 81:13–17.
Tautain, Dr. 1885. "Notes sur les castes chez les Mandingues et en particulier chez les
  Banmanas." *Revue d'Ethnographie* 3:343–52.
Tauxier, Louis. 1908. *Le Noir de Guinée.* Paris: Bureaux de la Science Sociale.
———. 1917. *Le Noir du Yatenga.* Paris: Emile Larose, Librarie-Editeur.
Tellier, G. 1898. *Autour de Kita. Etude Soudanaise.* Paris: Henri Charles-Lavauzelle.
Wane, Yaya. 1969. *Les Toucouleurs du Fouta Tooro, stratification sociale et structure
  familiale.* Dakar: IFAN.
Winterbottom, Thomas. 1803. *An Account of the Native Africans in the Neighborhood of
  Sierra Leone.* 2 vols. London: C. Whittingham. 2nd ed., New York: Frank Cass
  & Co. Ltd., 1969.
Zahan, Dominique. 1963. *La Dialectique du verbe chez les Bambara.* Paris: Mouton &
  Co.
Zeltner, Fr. de. 1908. "Notes sur la Sociologie Soudanaise." *L'Anthropologie* 19:217–33.
Zemp, Hugo. 1964. "Musiciens autochtones et griots malinké chez les Dan de Côte
  d'Ivoire." *Cahiers d'Etudes Africaines* 4 (3):370–82.
———. 1966. "La légende des griots malinké." *Cahiers d'Etudes Africaines* 6 (4):611–42.

III

The Power of Agency
and Identity

VII

THE DIELI OF KORHOGO
IDENTITY AND IDENTIFICATION

Robert Launay

The majority of the indigenous population of the region around Korhogo, in northern Ivory Coast, consists of native speakers of one dialect or another of Siena-re. Native Manding speakers constitute a very sizable minority. Indeed, language serves as one of the primary markers of ethnic identity, distinguishing not only the Siena-re speaking "Senufo" from the Manding-speaking "Dyula," but also different Senufo peoples—Tiembara, Nafara, Kufulo, Fodonon, etc.— from one another. The two categories "Senufo" and "Dyula" are almost—but not quite—exhaustive. Most of the groups usually labeled "castes" in the scholarly literature on West Africa are native Siena-re speakers. A few such groups, notably the Numu and the Milaga blacksmiths, are native Manding speakers. The notable exception is a group called the Dieli,[1] traditionally leatherworkers, whose language is comprehensible neither to native Siena-re speakers, at least locally, nor to Manding speakers.

Not surprisingly, the anomalous status of the Dieli has led to discrepancies in the way they are identified in the scholarly literature. By and large, they have nevertheless been classified as Senufo. For example, Holas concludes that "il semble qu'ils appartiennent en realité au rameau senoufo."[2] The tentative way in which this conclusion is phrased is itself revealing. The fact that the Dieli language is incomprehensible to other Siena-re speakers in the region does not, indeed, rule out the possibility that it is a dialect of Siena-re. Although most dialects of Siena-re spoken in the region are closely related, and form part of the Central Siena-re cluster, there are significant enclaves of Fodonon speakers in the region, whose dialect belongs to the southern Siena-re cluster. While the various dialects of Central Siena-re are more or less mutually comprehensible, native Central Siena-re speakers cannot understand Fodonon, whereas native Fodonon speakers are uniformly bilingual, speaking the local Central Siena-re dialect as well as their own language. Glaze explicitly makes the analogy between the Dieli and the Fodonon in order to argue that "the Tyeli are a distant branch of the Senufo language family, separated linguistically from the Central Senari cluster at a remote time in the past."[3]

Indeed, both Glaze and Bochet[4] argue that the parallels between Dieli and Fodonon run deeper than analogy. Specifically, they argue that there are intrinsic resemblances between elements of the Dieli and the Fodonon Poro ritual complexes, as opposed to the Poro society practices of various Central Siena-re speakers. Bochet, in particular, stresses that he considers both the Dieli and the Fodonon as representatives of an "archaic" Senufo population. As a matter of fact, Dyula oral traditions do cast the Fodonon as the "original" inhabitants of the region[5] as well as identifying the Dieli as the "original" occupants of the site of Korhogo village and consequently (relatively) early arrivals to the region, if not autochthones. The notion that both the Fodonon and the Dieli are remnants of an earlier, "archaic" Senufo population might explain their anomalous presence as enclaved linguistic minorities. However, claims that one or another group is autochthonous are not without ideological ramifications, either in African or in "Africanist" discourse. Claims to political or other prerogatives are frequently expressed in terms of arguments about who arrived before or after whom in any particular location.[6] Consequently, statements by African informants about the relative antiquity of the Fodonon or Dieli, while they are not necessarily false, can certainly not be taken simply at face value. In a very different vein, statements by Western Africanists that a particular population is "archaic" and "autochthonous" often carry the implication of "primitiveness" in a more general developmental sense. From this perspective, the Poro societies of the Fodonon and the Dieli can be represented as privileged, pristine examples. In any case, resemblances between the ritual practices of Dieli and Fodonon Poro societies cannot in and of themselves be taken as evidence of a common historical origin, much less of a common "archaic" status. Such an argument implies that Poro societies are, if not static, at least highly culturally conservative institutions, embodiments of the most time-honored traditions. On the contrary, one can just as cogently argue that such societies are highly dynamic, borrowing readily and continuously from one another and in a perpetual state of change. Resemblances between the Poro complexes of Dieli and Fodonon are quite as plausibly due to borrowing as they are to a hypothetical common origin for both groups.

Ultimately, the argument that the Dieli are an enclaved remnant of an "archaic" Senufo population rests on the identification of the Dieli language as a dialect of Siena-re. However, Person contends that the Dieli language is actually "une forme meridionale du Malinke," along with Vai and Kono of Sierra Leone, to the west, and Ligbi and Hwela in the region of Bondoukou, to the east.[7]

This would suggest that the Dieli might rather, like the Ligbi, be labeled "proto-Dyula," remnants of an earlier migration from the central Mande heartlands preceding the arrival of the Dyula. Finally, Richter has asserted that the Dieli language is related neither to Siena-re nor to Mande.[8] For the most part, however, scholars have identified the Dieli as either "Senufo" or "Mande," as archaic remnants of an earlier Senufo population or as pioneers of Mande immigration.

It is certainly ironic that, although the debate hinges in principle on whether the Dieli language is related to Siena-re or to Manding, none of the scholars concerned is a trained linguist, nor has any linguistic evidence been cited in this literature substantiating any of the peremptory identifications which have been proffered with an air of authority. Pierre Boutin, who *is* a trained linguist familiar with the region, has, on the basis of word lists which he has personally collected as well as on lists collected much earlier by Louis Tauxier, expressed some skepticism about all of these assertions.[9] It would seem that the evidence collected as yet does not point conclusively in one direction as opposed to the other.

In the absence of firm and sound conclusions about the identity of the Dieli language, there still remains a considerable amount of "circumstantial" evidence about the Dieli which can allow scholars to speculate (for better or for worse) about their origins.[10] Whereas, as we have seen, certain scholars have argued that elements of the Poro complex of the Dieli resemble those of the Fodonon, it seems even more certain that the techniques of their craft, leatherworking, derive from farther north, quite plausibly from the Mande heartlands. Those scholars, such as Glaze, who argue in favor of a Senufo origin for the Dieli do not dispute the idea that leatherworking is a "foreign" import to the region. Presumably, the Dieli, if they were in fact "archaic" Senufo, borrowed leatherworking from Mande artisans; or else, if they were "proto-Dyula" immigrants, they borrowed elements of their Poro complex from their newfound Fodonon neighbors.[11] Culturally, it would seem, the Dieli are as ambivalent as they are linguistically, neither fish nor fowl, neither unambiguously "Senufo" nor "Mande."

There remains one last clue to their identity, a clue every bit as elusive, perhaps, as all the others: their very name, Dieli. The name is homonymous—or one might say identical—with that of the well-known "caste" of Mande bards, the *jeli.*[12] Might the Dieli of Korhogo actually be descendants of the Mande *jeli?* Or is the resemblance between these two category labels simply one of those unfortunate linguistic coincidences that seem to breed so much idle speculation? Admittedly, both the Korhogo Dieli and the Mande *jeli* are among those West African populations often labeled as "castes." On the other hand, the Mande *jeli* are usually associated in the scholarly literature with the occupations of music and praise singing, stereotypically depicted as walking libraries or as professional sycophants, depending on one's particular biases. The *garanké,* and not the *jeli,* are typically identified as the Mande "caste" of leatherworkers. Indeed, it is on these grounds that Glaze explicitly rules out any possible connection between the Korhogo Dieli and the Mande *jeli.*[13] However, Barbara Frank has demonstrated conclusively that the Mande *jeli* are, on the contrary, very frequently involved in the activity of leatherworking, and are by no means confined to the occupation of bards.[14] In other words, once one identifies both the Mande *jeli* and the Korhogo Dieli as "castes" involved in the manufacture of leather goods, the coincidences at once appear more striking. Of course, this hardly demonstrates that the Korhogo Dieli and the Mande *jeli* are in fact identical, but at least it establishes that such a proposition, however speculative, is not absurd. In other words, the Dieli of Korhogo are conceivably descendants of

Mande *jeli* immigrants who would have preceded the more massive influx of
Dyula into the region. Indeed, there is another example of such an early migration of so-called "casted" individuals into the southern hinterlands of the Mande
world: the Numu of the Bondoukou region along the border of Ghana and
Ivory Coast, who, along with the Hwela and Ligbi, have been labeled as "proto-
Dyula."[15] In the absence of a clear and convincing identification of the Dieli
language, one may still consider the evidence which might tend either to support
or to refute such a hypothesis.

First of all, all Dieli are known by Manding patronyms: Koné or Coulibaly.
These patronyms, among the most common in the Korhogo region, are hardly
specific to the Dieli. On the other hand, they are not patronyms usually
associated with Mande *jeli,* such as Kouyaté, Diabaté, Cissoko, or
Kamissoko.[16] In any case, one cannot place too much weight on patronyms
as evidence. Patronymic labels can and do change in the region. Such changes
are invariably justified on the grounds that one name is "really" equivalent to
another. In particular, Senufo patronyms have roughly standardized Mande
equivalents; for example, the Senufo patronym Soro is "translated" as
Coulibaly in Manding. The use of Mande patronyms by Senufo, at least in
certain contexts, is unquestionably not a recent phenomenon,[17] though the
process has become so widespread that it has aroused the consternation of
certain Senufo intellectuals.[18] However, this notion of patronymic equivalents
is by no means restricted to the adoption of Mande surnames by Senufo
groups and individuals. Senufo patronyms may also have putative Mande
equivalents. I have been told, for example, that Tondosama are "really"
Wattara, Kangoté are "really" Kamara, Samagassi are "really" Suwaré, or at
any rate that the two names are in some sense equivalent. Most typically,
patronyms which are relatively rare or unusual are provided more widely
recognized (if not more prestigious) equivalents.[19] Equivalencies which are
recognized in one location may be flatly denied in another, and one must be
very cautious in evaluating what, if any, historical truth they may reflect. They
demonstrate, however, that patronymic identities are far from inflexible, and
even suggest a mechanism by which, in the long run, certain identities might
disappear altogether, replaced by their putative equivalents. Conceivably, the
Dieli could have adopted the patronyms of Koné and Coulibaly after the
arrival of the Dyula in the region. If so, the process has not been a recent
phenomenon, or else it would not be so complete. On the other hand, such a
process could explain how Mande *jeli* might have lost their typical patronyms
after emigrating to the Korhogo region.

A more striking feature of the Korhogo Dieli is the degree to which they,
alone among non-Manding-speaking groups, have assimilated to the Dyula.
Nowadays, the Dieli are not entirely unique in this respect. On the contrary,
large numbers of Senufo, particularly in towns such as Korhogo, have converted
to Islam and taken up occupations, such as trade, once monopolized by the
Dyula. The Dyula themselves sometimes say of such individuals, "a kera jula
ye," "They have become Dyula." This, however, is a relatively recent phenome-

non, whereas the assimilation of many—by no means all—Dieli to the Dyula dates at least as far back as the nineteenth century.

Let me provide an example from the village of Kadioha, the seat of a small precolonial chiefdom. Both Dyula and Senufo oral traditions concur that the first occupants of the site were Senufo, and that the Dyula arrived initially as an immigrant minority. However, when the chiefdom was established under Dyula overrule, all Senufo in the village moved (or were pushed) out to found the nearby village of Pundya (the original name of the site of Kadioha), and Kadioha assumed the identity of an all-Dyula village. I was told that the *jinns* (spirits) living on the hill overlooking the village, being good Muslims, hold the pagan Senufo in abhorrence, and that Senufo cannot even spend the night safely in the village. Yet one quarter of the village, Koko, is recognized as peopled by individuals of Dieli origin. Both the inhabitants of the village and, presumably, the neighboring *jinns* consider these people to be Dyula, for all intents and purposes, and there are no barriers to intermarriage between such individuals and the other Dyula of the village.

The situation is somewhat more complex in Koko, the oldest quarter of the town of Korhogo. The Dieli are acknowledged as the "first" occupants of the site. When Korhogo later became the capital of a Senufo chiefdom, the chiefs moved a short distance away "across the stream." Various ethnic, linguistic, and occupational minorities clustered in Koko quarter alongside the Dieli: the Dyula, in large numbers, but also encapsulated Fodonon speakers as well as members of various Senufo-speaking "castes": sculptors (*kulebele*), blacksmiths (*fonombele*), and brass casters (*kpeembele*); but also the Milaga, a Manding-speaking "caste" of blacksmiths. Each of these groups lived in a distinct quarter, so that Koko was spatially divided and subdivided into social units. The Dieli, as firstcomers, enjoyed (and still enjoy) the office of chief of Koko.

Aside from the large "indigenous" Dieli neighborhood, Koko also contains a smaller group of later immigrants of acknowledged Dieli origin. Significantly, this group did not move into Koko's Dieli neighborhood, but settled instead in the Dyula quarter. In this case, initiation society practices are revealing; who initiates together with or separately from whom is, like language, an important symbol of social identity. Koko's complex social mosaic meant that it had a multitude of distinct initiation societies (*poro* for Senufo, *lo* for Dyula), each with its separate grove. The Tiembara, the politically and numerically dominant Senufo group in the chiefdom, had (and still have) an initiation society grove in Koko, as well as a grove "across the stream" in the chief's quarter. Fodonon speakers, as a socially as well as linguistically distinct minority, had a separate grove, as did each of the Senufo-speaking "castes." The Dieli "founders" of Koko, needless to say, had their own grove. Those Dyula clan wards who engaged in initiation society activity all shared one grove, and finally the Milaga, the Manding-speaking blacksmiths, had their grove. Just as the "immigrant" Dieli chose (or were obliged) to live apart from the "indigenous" Dieli, so they initiated separately. Conceivably, the "indigenous" Dieli kept their immigrant fellows at arm's length deliberately, in order to ensure their exclusive claim to firstcomer status. One way or the other, it is revealing that the immigrants ended by sharing an initiation grove with the Milaga—in other words, a Mande "caste." Such decisions about where the Dieli lived and with whom they initiated their adolescents provide some evidence about how they classified themselves and were classified by others. The Dyula clearly considered the Dieli to be more "like" themselves than any Senufo group. Like the Milaga, they were, as a "caste," socially distinct in certain respects. (In the Korhogo region, such "caste status" did not necessarily include barriers to intermarriage; marriages could be contracted between Dyula and Dieli, just as, in the Bondoukou region, they were contracted between Dyula and Numu.)[20] One way or the other, whether or not the Dieli were historically "proto-Dyula," they were often accepted as "quasi-Dyula" by the nineteenth century.

Obviously, the rate of Dieli assimilation to the Dyula varied, both nowadays and in the past, according to local circumstances. In villages with both Dieli and Senufo inhabitants but no Dyula quarter, the Dieli have, if anything, tended to assimilate to the Senufo. However, most Dieli communities are in fact situated near Dyula communities, and in all such cases that have come to my attention, they have been integrated far more fully into the Dyula community than have any Senufo, even pious Muslims. Some of these groups—those of Kadioha, for example—no longer are referred to, or refer to themselves, as Dieli, but have been fully assimilated to "Dyula" status by now; their Dieli origins, though they may be remembered, are no longer socially salient. In other cases, such as the "indigenous" Dieli of Koko, while cultural assimilation to the Dyula is nearly complete, there are advantages in maintaining a distinct social identity. In the first place, this serves to maintain the prerogatives of "firstcomer" status, such as the office of chief in Koko. Secondly, an ambiguous identity, between "Senufo" and "Dyula," carries political advantages; the Dieli are obvious compromise candidates in any circumstances where there is a risk of ethnic polarization. All in all, the fact that the Dieli have *collectively* assimilated to Dyula status more completely than any Senufo group in the region suggests, although it does not prove, a common Mande origin.

Even if one identifies the Dieli as a "caste" of Mande origin, it is important to note that both they and their Dyula neighbors distinguish quite clearly between the Dieli "indigenous" to the region and members of the Mande *jeli* "caste," locally known as *jeliba.* These *jeliba,* it should be pointed out, are performing "griots," and so the word denotes not only a social identity but also a profession. In fact, no professional bards of any sort—Senufo, Manding, or Dieli—are indigenous to the Korhogo region. Nowadays, professional praise singers—Mande *jeli* as well as Hausa musicians—are among the many immigrant "foreigners" living in the town of Korhogo. They are sometimes invited to perform at weddings, funerals, or other such events in Koko, and occasionally attend without an invitation, though nevertheless expecting proper remuneration for their praises. Itinerant musicians also tour the region from time to time, also expecting to be paid for their usually unsolicited services; moreover, there is no reason to believe that itinerant performers are necessarily a recent phenomenon.

In short, *jeliba,* professional bards, are quite familiar, although "foreign," to the region, and—it must be said—have a less than savory reputation. In the absence of any enduring social ties between such *jeliba* and their occasional patrons in the Korhogo region, bards are stereotyped as quintessential "spongers" who sing praises only for money, using the implied threat of public ridicule to extort as much as they can from their victims. Not surprisingly, the indigenous Dieli deny any connection whatsoever, past or present, with these *jeliba,* and, consequently, with Mande *jeli* as a "caste." In many respects, this is quite true; at present, the Dieli "leatherworkers" of Korhogo are socially entirely distinct from Mande *jeli.* However, the Dieli have a vested interest in denying any past connection as well. Even assuming that the Dieli of Korhogo were originally Mande *jeli,* one would suspect that the Korhogo Dieli would either conveniently forget their origins or else keep them a closely guarded secret.

To summarize the circumstantial evidence, their craft of leatherworking and their patronyms both point in the direction of a Mande, if not a *jeli,* origin. Of course, crafts can be learned and patronyms borrowed, in the virtual absence of any migration at all. On the other hand, the putative resemblances between the Dieli and the Fodonon Poro complexes point, it has been argued, to a Senufo origin. However, ritual practices can be borrowed just as readily as crafts and patronyms. Moreover, we know very little in detail about the now-defunct Dyula *lo* initiation societies. As a result, Dieli practices have been compared only to those of the Fodonon and of their "Central Senufo" neighbors. The possibility that the putatively "archaic" features of their initiation societies might also have been shared by their Dyula neighbors has never been raised, much less ruled out. Were this to be the case—though, admittedly, we will probably never have enough evidence to judge one way or the other—the argument for the Senufo origins of the Dieli would be seriously weakened.

Aside from these cultural affinities of the Dieli with either their Mande or their Senufo neighbors, one can also consider their social identity as constituting a kind of evidence. However, the Dyula readiness to accept the Dieli as "close cousins" of a sort is arguably less a question of common origins than of the success which the Dieli have had in deliberately maintaining an anomalous social identity to their own advantage. It is certainly no accident that scholars who have studied the Senufo tend to label the Dieli "Senufo," whereas those who have studied the Mande tend to label them "Mande"!

It would seem, at this point, that the evidence is contradictory, and can be used to support—or to refute—anyone's favorite speculative hypothesis. However, these different hypotheses suggest alternate scenarios for how the Dieli came to be the leatherworking "caste" in the region. Glaze provides the following example:

> I propose that the Tyeli are a distant branch of the Senufo language family, separated linguistically from the Central Senari cluster at a remote time in the past, and that in more recent history the Tyeli found themselves under pressure by the movements of increasing numbers of Senari peoples into their settlement

area and, out of economic necessity, were forced into learning the leatherworking trade from itinerant members of an artisan group from outside the Senufo
culture sphere.[21]

In short, the Dieli are, she argues, an encapsulated autochthonous minority who
have collectively adopted a new craft while retaining their "archaic" language
and ritual. The problem with such a scenario is that, sociologically speaking, it
is highly implausible. In the first place, there is little intrinsic reason why the
immigration of Central Siena-re speakers would necessarily place economic
pressures on autochthones. Admittedly, population densities in the immediate
vicinity of Korhogo are high, but much of the region is relatively sparsely
populated. Under such circumstances, autochthonous minorities are most often
culturally and linguistically assimilated to the incoming majority, with certain
families or villages perhaps retaining a tradition of having arrived earlier than
others. In cases where they have not—the Fodonon are a good example—such
enclaved linguistic minorities of real or putative autochthones have virtually
always remained agriculturalists. It is difficult to imagine that a previously
constituted ethnic "group," particularly one of agriculturalists, would collectively adopt a new craft. Individuals, of course, can change their identities in
such a manner, but to imagine that this would occur at a collective level in this
way seems quite fantastic.

It is far more likely that the Dieli are descendants of immigrant craftsmen, as
may well be the case for Siena-re speaking "castes."[22] If so, the link between the
Mande *jeli* and the Korhogo Dieli is likely to be more than a question of
coincidental homonymy. A scenario suggesting how Mande *jeli* came to be
Korhogo's leatherworking "caste," while it would be just as speculative as
Glaze's, would be sociologically far more plausible. In this respect, Zemp's
findings concerning Mande *jeli* among the Dan of western Ivory Coast are highly
suggestive.[23] *Jeli* arrived in that area in the late nineteenth century, attaching
themselves as clients to prominent local leaders. From time to time, their patrons
had (and still have) recourse to their services as musicians. Such orchestras, even
occasionally used, were clearly an item of prestige, if only as an exotic luxury
and as a form of conspicuous consumption. Even as musicians, the *jeli* hardly
supplanted local Dan orchestras, as music was not associated with "caste" status
among the Dan. Significantly, Mande *jeli* among the Dan made their living
largely through leatherworking; their "bardic" activities were only a sideline.

One need only assume that a similar process took place among the Senufo
several centuries earlier in order to explain the presence of Dieli leatherworkers
around Korhogo. Well before Mande settlement in the Senufo area, Mande
traders were settled in Begho, in northwestern Ghana, one of the major sources
of the gold trade. The Senufo were certainly in contact with Mande trade
networks, if only peripherally and perhaps indirectly. Like other "acephalous"
or loosely centralized peoples in the vicinity of major trade routes, they would
have constituted a market—if only a comparatively minor one—for prestige
goods manufactured or conveyed by the Mande. Indeed, individuals of "caste"

status may well have been able to travel throughout such peripheral areas much more easily than ordinary individuals. Frequently, joking relationships are said to exist between certain "castes" and entire local populations. Such relationships could be used by "casted" individuals to ensure themselves a safe conduct through the territory, as was the case, for example, of the Kooroko among the Fula of the Wassulu region.[24] Even in the absence of such joking relationships, "casted" persons were usually more welcome in peripheral areas than others, partly because they had valuable goods, skills, or services to offer, and partly because their very status meant that they were not a political threat to local leaders. In this way, itinerant Mande *jeli* could have attached themselves as clients to local Senufo notables, much as they did among the Dan. However, among the Senufo, as among the Dan, having one's own bard might have been a symbol of prestige, but it would have remained a relatively dispensable one, an added but ultimately superfluous luxury. Music is not a "casted" profession either among the Senufo or among the Dan; one did not need professionals to sing one's praises. Like their Mande *jeli* counterparts among the Dan, these hypothetical *jeli* clients of Senufo chiefs would have found leatherworking more lucrative than music. Indeed, leather goods—horsehair whisks, for example— were arguably more effective symbols of power and prestige than client musicians or even orchestras. Later Mande immigrants—the Dyula—were to adopt a similar strategy, specializing in weaving cloths which their Senufo neighbors acquired and used as symbols of power and prestige.[25] One way or the other, immigrant Mande *jeli* would have found a monopoly on the manufacture of scarce and highly valuable leather goods far more profitable than any bardic or musical activities. In the long run, these immigrant leatherworkers would have every interest in dissociating themselves from their bardic cousins, both because of the unsavory reputation of itinerant bards, who would have continued to visit the region from time to time, and as a means of preserving their local monopoly on leatherworking from any later *jeli* arrivals.

This scenario suggesting a Mande *jeli* origin for the Dieli of Korhogo certainly does not imply that there ever was any massive *jeli* immigration into the Senufo area. The valuable—and lucrative—skills the *jeli* possessed might well have attracted other individuals, whether autochthones or foreigners, to attempt to assimilate to the *jeli,* learning their language and their craft. The "foreign" origin of the Dieli, it must be stressed, refers to their social identity, and not necessarily to all the individuals who assume this identity.

Of course, this scenario—like any other—is purely speculative. There is no evidence to disprove it, but, as we have seen, the evidence is ambiguous at best, and can be interpreted to support almost any case. More important, there are well-documented historical parallels—the Kooroko among the Fula of Wassulu, the *jeli* among the Dan, the *numu* among the "proto-Dyula" of the Bondoukou area—whereas alternate scenarios, particularly those which argue that the Dieli are "archaic" Senufo, call to mind no historical analogues whatsoever in the region.

When all is said and done, the most remarkable mystery about the Dieli of Korhogo is not their "origins," but rather the fascination that this relatively small population has exerted over the scholars, myself included, who have conducted research in the area. Why should we all throw caution to the winds, engage in the kind of speculation of which, in our more sober moods, we heartily disapprove (and with good reason), all in order to dispute an issue which, in perspective, is only one of the innumerable minutiae of West African ethnohistory? Why should it matter to us, much less to anyone else, whether the Dieli are "really" Senufo or "really" Mande, and why should each of us attempt (highly suspiciously) to claim the Dieli as relatives of the peoples we have studied? The answer is quite simple. The Dieli are an anomaly. They are not quite "Senufo," they are not quite "Dyula," either socially or linguistically. As an anomaly, they call into question the salience, if not the validity, of our own categories, or, to be more blunt, our pigeonholes. One need only label them "archaic Senufo" or "proto-Dyula" for the anomaly to disappear and the pigeonholes to be vindicated.

As long as scholars restrict themselves to debating their origins, the anomalous status of the Dieli is in any case reduced to a historical accident of one sort or another, whether immigration or encapsulation. But this anomaly is precisely anything but an accident; rather, it is the product of deliberate social action on the part of the Dieli themselves. The Dieli language, which has until now survived as distinct (though it is rapidly on its way to oblivion), is a symbol of this effort. One can easily point to other groups—the *kulebele*, for instance, or certain Dyula of avowedly Hausa origin—who maintain traditions of immigration but who have lost their languages of origin. Precisely because of their ambivalent identity, the Dieli have been able to assimilate more easily to their neighbors, particularly Dyula, than other groups; but they have also, when it has been to their advantage, managed to remain distinct as a social category, in order to preserve their economic monopoly on leatherworking, but also such prerogatives as firstcomer status in Korhogo's Koko quarter.

Ultimately, the Dieli example raises questions about another category which scholars use to label them, perhaps all too conveniently: "caste." In a West African context, the term has been used to distinguish certain kinds of social groups or categories from others. In Korhogo, for example, the Dieli would be labeled a "caste" whereas the Dyula would not. It follows, at least in principle, that "castes" possess features which distinguish them from other kinds of groups or categories. Prototypically, they are hereditary, endogamous minorities associated with particular occupations as well as particular ranks (generally low) in the social hierarchy. The Dieli, alas, do not fit into this pigeonhole much more neatly than into any others. They are not endogamous, but intermarry readily with the Dyula. As chiefs of Koko quarter, they were acknowledged as political superiors, at least symbolically, by other residents of the quarter, Senufo and Dyula, "caste" and "noble" alike—hardly a position consistent with "low," much less "despised," rank.

Undoubtedly, the problem lies less with the Dieli than with the implications of the concept of "caste" itself, assimilating as it does social identity, rank, and occupation in a static rather than in a dynamic relationship. If, indeed, the relationships between identity, occupation, rank, and patterns of intermarriage are seen as variable and mutable, subject to the manipulation of groups and individuals in specific historical contexts, then the distinction between "castes" and other kinds of social identities ceases to be a very useful explanatory device.

For example, it is increasingly apparent that the relationship between "caste" and occupation is not a simple one. In a single region, more than one "caste" may practice a single craft, and/or a single "caste" may practice more than one craft. The Mande *jeli* are a case in point, practicing music and leatherworking, but not always with a monopoly on either activity. In the Korhogo area, there existed both Mande-speaking and Siena-re speaking blacksmiths, and the Senufo smiths (*fonombele*) were also sculptors, alongside the *kulebele* carvers.[26] In the first place, one must not forget the rather obvious point that the activities of specialists, of whatever kind, depended, broadly speaking, on local demand for specific goods or services. It was clearly in the interest of specialist groups to be able to practice a number of occupations, on one hand, and to attempt to monopolize specific techniques, on the other.

The establishment of hereditary monopolies or quasi-monopolies, however, was hardly limited to those groups usually labeled "castes." For example, in the Korhogo area, weaving was a hereditary monopoly of the Dyula, as an ethnic category. Other activities such as fishing, long-distance trade, and Islamic scholarship were also monopolies, sometimes of ethnic groups as a whole, sometimes of specific local kin groups. For the most part, such monopolies involved knowledge of particular technical skills, and the maintenance of such monopolies depended in large measure on the degree to which the groups involved could control the transmission of specialized technical knowledge. However, aside from purely technical skills, the maintenance and sometimes the manipulation of key social relationships was equally essential—relationships between specialists and their patrons or customers, but also within supralocal networks of specialists themselves.

At one level, then, "castes" in West Africa are simply examples of hereditary monopolies of one sort or another. The features which presumably distinguish them from other cases, such as ethnic monopolies, are endogamy and a special hierarchical position. The problem is that it is difficult to pin down the nature of their position in the hierarchy. Clearly, to argue that members of "castes" are despised, or even of inferior rank (inferior to whom?), is at best simplistic, at worst demonstrably false. What emerges most clearly is that they are, in some fundamental sense, "different." This difference can be expressed symbolically in spatial terms—where they live in separate quarters, if not separate communities—but also precisely in terms of rules of endogamy, where such rules exist. Here again, "caste" and "ethnicity" emerge as different labels for very similar processes, involving the social differentiation of various groups and the symbolic marking of identity and difference.

Indeed, Richter has gone so far as to substitute the notion of "ethnic group" for categories of individuals usually known as "castes" among the Senufo.[27] The problem, however, is deeper than a simple question of terminology, of whether scholars ought to call such groups "castes," or "ethnic groups," or "artisan groups," or, by using African labels, to dodge the issue altogether. One way or another, this labeling process tends to suggest that the identities are in some sense fixed, and that the proper label in the proper language will tell us the properties of these identities.

The Dieli of Korhogo, precisely because of their apparent refusal to conform to this pigeonholing process, suggest an alternate way of looking at the problem. The temptation has been to "identify" the Dieli in terms of their origin—Senufo or Mande, *jeli* or whatever. The implication is that the origin of the Dieli tells us who they "are," in some fundamental sense. Yet it should be obvious that Dieli identity is not a static feature of the social landscape, but on the contrary a dynamic entity which is constantly being redefined, if not manipulated, by various groups and individuals for a variety of ends. In this regard, it is perhaps less important to know whether the Dieli ever "were" Mande *jeli* than to know that, nowadays, they insist, and with success, in maintaining a sharp distinction between themselves and their "homonyms."

The Dieli example suggests that it may be fruitful to consider "caste" in West Africa not as a category but as a process. From this perspective, questions about whether African labels such as *nyamakala* or *fijembele* ought or ought not to be glossed as "caste," or about whether specific groups (the Bozo, for example) ought to be labeled "castes" or "ethnic groups," are beside the point. Rather, the *process* of "caste" involves the creation and maintenance of hereditary occupational monopolies or quasi-monopolies. From a purely economic standpoint, such monopolies were potentially lucrative; otherwise, there was clearly no point in maintaining them. For this reason, rules concerning the suitability of engaging in particular occupations were generally exclusionary; the question was not so much who *could* be a blacksmith, but rather who *couldn't*. To put it another way, "blacksmiths" could (and frequently did) farm for a living, but "farmers" could never forge.

In order to exclude outsiders, it was necessary in the first place to control the transmission of technical knowledge. However, at an even more basic level, the exclusion of outsiders depended on the maintenance of distinctions between "insiders" and "outsiders." Such distinctions tend to be expressed in terms of a relatively restricted symbolic vocabulary. Categorical identity labels are perhaps the most universal and essential element: a group is "different" because its members refer to themselves, and are referred to by others, by a "different" name. However, these names need to be imbued with other symbols of difference, lest particular categories emerge as different "in name only." Language, as we have seen, is another marker. The fact, for instance, that until recently Dieli were brought up to speak their own "native" language, incomprehensible to anyone else, must be seen as a rather remarkable accomplishment; all Dieli had to become "native" speakers of Dyula or Senufo as well, and frequently of both. Patronyms, as we have seen above, constitute another identity symbol, hereditary in principle but mutable under certain conditions. The spatial layout of settlements is also used to reflect such distinctions, particularly where a no man's land or a stream separates different quarters; in general, whom one lives next to, or apart from, symbolically conveys social "closeness" or "distance." The regulation of marriage, through rules of endogamy or at least rules about who may marry whom, convey similar messages in yet another idiom. Religion serves similar purposes in a variety of ways, distinguishing "Muslims" from "pagans," but also, for example, through initiation society ritual: who is initiated with whom, who is excluded, who leads, etc. In general, those categories of people who hold hereditary occupational monopolies define themselves, and are defined, as "different" from their neighbors in fundamental ways. This "difference," in local terms, is often combined with a more highly developed supralocal identity. "Different" from their immediate neighbors, such groups and individuals are "identical" to others who may live relatively far away, but who form part of a relatively dense regional network. Particularly where monopolies involve goods which are openly and easily bought and sold in the marketplace, a monopoly which is too localized is no monopoly at all. The maintenance of these regional and often supraregional ties—through the use of strategic marriages, for example—was often as essential as the management of symbolic boundaries within local communities.

In short, these symbolic differences which serve as markers of specific identities also function as exclusionary devices, to the advantage, it would seem, of specialists who want to retain local and regional monopolies of one sort or another. However, the symbolism of difference is a double-edged sword. Specialists who exclude may also be excluded, rendered ineligible by their "different" nature from political office, for example. The "difference" also accounts for the contrary attitudes their neighbors hold about them, ranging from contempt to awe to distrust. As the Dieli example shows, this process of creating and maintaining hereditary monopolies through the manipulation of symbolic markers of difference does not operate in a vacuum. Certain occupations which are either impossible or unprofitable to monopolize in some locales are subject to monopolies in others. Around Korhogo, for example, there was no monopoly whatsoever on music-making, whereas weaving—an "open" profession in many parts of the Mande-speaking world—was an ethnic monopoly. Obviously, there were regional as well as local differences in the degree of occupational, ethnic, or other forms of symbolically expressed differentiation.

One way or the other, the outcome was, in many parts of the Western Sudan, that local populations tended to be heterogeneous. Under such circumstances, the symbols used to define identities could be combined in different ways to convey more complex—and more ambiguous—messages. In situations where there are a plurality of identity categories, of labels corresponding to different "groups," each category cannot simply be "different." Identity markers suggest various dimensions, implying that different groups are nonetheless relatively alike or relatively different. Groups who share a "native" language, who intermarry, who choose to live near one another, who participate jointly in initiation societies, who are Muslim, etc., are symbolically "similar," if not "identical." It might seem that, using these criteria, one could determine unambiguously which groups are more alike than others. The Dieli example reveals the pitfalls of such an assumption; using these criteria, scholars still disagree about whether the Dieli are more like the "Senufo" or more like the "Dyula." The problem is that the symbols often send conflicting messages, sometimes suggesting that two groups are "similar," sometimes that the same two groups are "different." The message conveyed at any one time depends on which symbols specific groups or individuals wish to stress on any given occasion, and which symbols they choose to ignore. The Dieli have been particularly successful at manipulating such symbols to their advantage. Rural Dieli who live in proximity to Senufo, but not to Dyula, continue to stress aspects of Dieli "culture"—notably initiation societies—which are similar to "Senufo" symbols. Dieli who immigrated in the nineteenth century to communities dominated by the Dyula shed all or most of their "distinctive" characteristics, adopting a relatively straightforward "Dyula" identity. The Dieli of Koko quarter in Korhogo have retained certain visible signs of their distinct identity, in order to retain their prerogatives as "firstcomers"; in some contexts, they assume a "quasi-Dyula" identity, though individuals may even claim "quasi-Senufo" status at times, for instance for political reasons.

The Dieli are undoubtedly an extreme example, which no doubt accounts for why they have both fascinated and plagued scholars who have tried to pigeonhole them. Few groups are as successful in maintaining a shifting, protean identity to their own advantage. After all, the identities of groups and individuals are not products entirely of their own making, but rather the results of interaction with other groups and individuals who reciprocally constrain each other's degrees of freedom. Nonetheless, it may be fruitful to look upon the Dieli not as an anomaly defying precise classification, but rather as a paradigm, a clear example of processes which are, after all, quite typical of societies in the Western Sudan.

The Dieli paradigm, if we follow its implications, may lead us to reexamine current orthodoxies concerning "caste" in the Western Sudan. Scholars who have objected to using the term "caste" in a West African context[28] have pointed to the absence of a "caste system." Whereas in India everyone belongs to one caste or another, in West Africa "caste" has been used only for groups such as the Dieli or the *jeli*. The contrast with India has been counterproductive in other respects as well. West Africanist scholars have tended to use Dumont's model of the "caste system" in India[29] as a frame of reference, interpreting "caste" to mean the pervasive use of the idiom of purity and pollution in order to imbue society (and the world at large) with hierarchy at all levels. The comparison, alas, does not tend to be very instructive. On one hand, one can point out that notions of hierarchy, purity, and pollution are by no means absent from West Africa, and that on this basis it is possible to draw parallels with the Indian cases. However, there are few (if any) societies in the world without any notions whatsoever of purity, pollution, and hierarchy; such parallels, drawn indiscriminately, lead logically to the conclusion that caste is a well-nigh universal human phenomenon, which is quite the contrary of what Dumont was trying to argue in the first place! On the other hand, a more restrained comparison can conclude only that hierarchy, purity, and pollution are not nearly so pervasive in West Africa as in India, and that—to no one's surprise—Dumont's model of Indian society and ideology cannot be mechanically transposed to another continent.

Unfortunately, this preoccupation with purity and pollution has obscured precisely those aspects of Dumont's argument which might well be relevant to the Western Sudan. "Caste" and the "caste system," he argues, reside not in the identity of discrete groups—"castes"—but rather in terms of a pervasive ideology of social relations. There is indeed a pervasive ideology of differentiation in the Western Sudan, though by and large the idioms of purity and pollution, while they are hardly absent, do not loom so very large. Rather, groups and individuals are differentiated in large measure by their possession of or control over "powers" of various sorts. Such powers are the product both of hereditary "gifts" (in the sense of natural aptitudes—including, for example, a "gift" for witchcraft!) and of acquired "knowledge."[30] This knowledge is, in particular, the knowledge of how to control extrahuman forces of one sort or another. It includes the knowledge connected with initiation societies, but also various forms of technical knowledge, from metalworking to Arabic literacy. In principle, different hereditary groups control different powers, whereas different members of the same group are more or less skilled or knowledgeable in exercising these specific controls. Control over "powers" is thus a question both of degree and of kind. To the extent that it is a matter of degree, the issue of hierarchy is perfectly salient, but when it is a question of kind, the notion of hierarchy can at best be applied ambiguously.

In short, "other" groups are to some extent different "in nature" from one's own, and consequently control different powers. The same logic, it must be stressed, can be applied to groups and categories of different orders: "ethnic" groups, kin groups, even segments of local kin groups. Differences are hereditary, but at the level of groups rather than of individuals. This is an ideology of hereditary specialization. *Every* group is, at least potentially, a specialist group; every group has quasi-monopolistic access to "powers" of one sort or another, be they political, ritual, or technical.

This, I would suggest, is the ideological underpinning of the "caste system" of the Western Sudan. Hereditary occupational monopolies in general, and "caste" groups in particular, are logical products of such a way of categorizing and dividing up the social universe. They represent the ways in which this ideology is expressed in the techno-economic domain, though the same ideology is expressed equally well in the domains of politics or ritual.

One must be careful, however, in avoiding the conclusion that this ideology in any sense "creates" the kinds of monopolies that are typically associated with "castes." Rather, the ideology provides a paradigm for the form which such monopolies typically take, as well as a ready-made justification for their existence. These monopolies must be created and re-created by specific groups and individuals in their interactions with "others," however defined, in specific local and regional contexts. Seen in this light, it makes relatively little difference who the Dieli once were; it is how they came to be that matters.

Notes

1. The Dieli (or Jeli) are also referred to in the literature as Tieli (or Tieli); pl. Tielibele. These variant spellings mirror the respective labels for the group in Manding and in Siena-re.

2. Holas (1966:15).

3. Glaze (1981:41).

4. Bochet (1959).

5. Launay (1982:14).

6. For a discussion of the implications of "firstcomer" status in Africa, see Kopytoff (1987:52–61).

7. Person (1964:328). Curiously enough, Person nevertheless refers to them as "la caste Senoufo des Tieli" (ibid.).

8. Richter (1980:15).

9. Pierre Boutin, personal communication.

10. In any case, it is important to point out that linguistics cannot resolve all the questions and ambiguities; the origins of the Dieli as a people cannot simply be assimilated to the origins of Dieli as a language. Of course, the precise identification of the Dieli language, even if it raises problems of historical interpretation, would necessarily constitute important evidence.

11. In fact, I see no reason to rule out the possibility that the Fodonon borrowed ritual elements from the Dieli, if indeed the Dieli are of Mande origin. Such a possibility seems absurd only as long as one insists that the Poro as an institution is in some sense "essentially" Senufo.

12. I use the spelling "Dieli" to refer to the leatherworkers of Korhogo and jeli to refer to Mande bards to avoid unnecessary confusion, although these names are pronounced identically.

13. Glaze (1981:228).

14. See chapter by Frank in this volume and Frank (1988).

15. Tauxier (1921:393–96); Goody (1964:195).

16. However, N'Diayé (1970:87) does list Koné as one of the patronyms of Mande jeli.

17. The use of Mande patronyms by Senufo was noted by Binger (1892, I:214) in 1887.

18. See, for example, Tuho (1984).

19. The Senufo use of Mande patronyms ultimately obeys the same logic; Senufo patronyms are specific to the region, whereas Mande patronyms are widely recognized throughout much of West Africa.

20. Tauxier (1921:394).

21. Glaze (1981:41).

22. Richter (1980:15) argues for a Malian origin for kulebele and fonombele. The kpeembele also have traditions of formerly speaking a distinct language, like the Dieli.

23. Zemp (1964).

24. Amselle (1977:37–49).

25. Launay (1978).

26. Glaze (1981:14).

27. Richter (1980:12–13).

28. I am no exception, and have argued similarly in the past (Launay 1972).
29. Dumont (1966).
30. In the case of individuals, and of nonhereditary groups, such powers may be acquired through "election," by spirits, for example. This is particularly true for societies of hunters and of diviners.

References

Amselle, Jean-Loup. 1977. *Les Negociants de la Savane. Histoire et organisation sociale des Kooroko (Mali).* Paris: Editions Anthropos.

Binger, Louis-Gustave. 1892. *Du Niger au Golfe de Guinée par le pays de Kong and le Mossi.* 2 vols. Paris: Librairie Hachette.

Bochet, Gilbert. 1959. "Les poro des Diéli." *Bulletin de l'I.F.A.N.* 21, sér. B (1–2):61–101.

Dumont, Louis. 1966. *Homo Hierarchicus.* Paris: Editions Gallimard.

Frank, Barbara E. 1988. "Mande Leatherworking: A Study of Style, Technology and Identity." Ph.D. dissertation, Indiana University.

Glaze, Anita. 1981. *Art and Death in a Senufo Village.* Bloomington: Indiana University Press.

Goody, Jack. 1964. "The Mande in the Akan Hinterland." In *The Historian in Tropical Africa,* ed. J. Vansina, R. Mauny, and L. V. Thomas. London: Oxford University Press for the International African Institute.

Holas, B. 1966. *Les Sénoufo (y compris les Minianka).* 2nd ed., rev. Paris: Presses Universitaires de France.

Kopytoff, Igor. 1987. "The Internal African Frontier: the Making of African Political Culture." In *The African Frontier: The Reproduction of Traditional African Societies,* ed. Igor Kopytoff. Bloomington and Indianapolis: Indiana University Press.

Launay, Robert. 1972. "Manding Clans and Castes." Paper presented at the Conference on Manding Studies, School of Oriental and African Studies, University of London.

———. 1978. "Transactional Spheres and Intersocietal Exchange in Ivory Coast." *Cahiers d'Etudes Africaines* 18:561–73.

———. 1982. *Traders without Trade.* Cambridge: Cambridge University Press.

N'Diayé, Bokar. 1970. *Les Castes au Mali.* Bamako: Editions Populaires.

Person, Yves. 1964. "En quête d'une chronologie ivoirienne." In *The Historian in Tropical Africa,* ed. J. Vansina, R. Mauny, and L. V. Thomas. London: Oxford University Press for the International African Institute.

Richter, Delores. 1980. *Art, Economics and Change: The Kulebele of Northern Ivory Coast.* La Jolla, Calif.: Psych/Graphic Publishers.

Tauxier, Louis. 1921. *Le Noir de Bondoukou.* Paris: Leroux.

Tuho, Charles-Valy. 1984. *J'ai Change de nom . . . Pourquoi.* Abidjan: Nouvelles Editions Africaines.

Zemp, Hugo. 1964. "Musiciens autochtones et griots malinké chez les Dan de Côte d'Ivoire." *Cahiers d'Etudes Africaines* 4 (3):370–82.

VIII

WOMEN CRAFT SPECIALISTS IN JENNE
THE MANIPULATION OF
MANDE SOCIAL CATEGORIES

Adria La Violette

The active role of Mande women in re-creating and manipulating aspects of the social order has been long overlooked, as men and male-dominated institutions have stayed at the center of most Mande historical and sociocultural studies. This paper focuses on women who are potters in the vicinity of Jenne, Mali—an area lying close to the northeastern periphery of Mande cultural influence. I argue that the women I interviewed and observed during fourteen months of ethnoarchaeological research in 1981 and 1983[1] exercised more social flexibility than did male specialists under study. By virtue of this, the women commonly crossed cultural boundaries through marriage and other social and economic alliances, broadening their own universe of contacts and assisting family members to form relationships across boundaries that men alone cannot so readily cross. This is a dimension of social integration that has been overlooked, both in the realm of artisan interrelations and in the embedding of artisan groups into the nonspecialist population.

Potters and the *nyamakalaw*

In the literature on Mande social structure, the *nyamakalaw* are identified as those Mande specialists who make up the so-called professional clans, described consistently as bards, blacksmiths, leatherworkers, and sometimes woodworkers. Since the late precolonial period, *nyamakalaw* have been portrayed as the middle stratum in the tripartite social hierarchy of the Mande, sitting above the slaves (*jonw*) and below the free, common persons, or nobles (*horonw*). Potters, if mentioned at all, do not figure significantly in discussions of the *nyamakalaw* except as the wives and mothers of blacksmiths,[2] although they would number at least as many as the smiths, and possibly as many as several of the *nyamakala* categories combined. Whether their virtual omission is a consequence of male dominance within the populations under study,[3] or of the fact that we, the documenters, have looked exclusively to the men to define the social structure, is unclear; very probably it is both of these.

While I find that male artisans have been examined in great detail as multidimensional social actors who also happen to contribute material culture to the Mande world, most studies involving ceramics concentrate on the minutiae of the production process to the virtual exclusion of the women at work, as if the pots make themselves.[4] This leaves us with a considerable descriptive literature on pottery and the hands that make it, but little about the women attached to those hands, or analysis of social relations and cultural behavior.[5] In the absence of other information, we not only accept the omnipresence of the rigidly tiered Mande social system as it was recorded by French officials in the nineteenth century, but have continued to seek it out and reproduce it even now, as if the observers had no hand at all in creating it, and as if the Mande themselves did not and could not change it over the past century. The present study certainly does not attempt to address all of this. Against this background, however, what we have assumed is that virtually all Mande-associated potters come from within *nyamakala* families, particularly those from which blacksmiths, or *numuw* (pl., sing. *numu*), also come. What I found in Jenne differs significantly from this literature and our general understanding of Mande society.

In Jenne the phenomenon of fluidity among the *nyamakalaw,* as acted out by women and also, at times, by men, occurs in a historical context in which factors such as the differential conversion to Islam of ethnic groups associated with the *nyamakalaw;* the rise of the Muslim Somono as a distinct group in Jenne, outside of their own core area near Segu; extreme cultural plurality; and the strongly felt presence of two other, non-Mande social systems—Fulani and Songhai—all play a part. The potential influence of these forces is touched on below. While not underestimating the impact of any of these contributing factors—on the contrary—I argue that until Mande women are studied as social actors in their own right, rather than as passive participants in an inherited system, or in a cultural system viewed as being shaped predominantly by men, the full impact of women on Mande social structure, even in the more homogeneous core Mande area, cannot be understood.

The Jenne Context

I studied potters in 1981 and 1983, in the course of an ethnoarchaeological project on the socioeconomic organization and technology of craft specialists in Jenne and its environs, a study that also included male artisans—principally blacksmiths and masons, and to a lesser extent goldsmiths, boat builders, weavers, and leatherworkers.[6] These artisans range over all socioeconomic strata and ethnic and linguistic affiliations. Some are *nyamakalaw,* some are artisans associated with Fulani specialist groups, and some are specialists within largely nonspecialist strata. Potters can be found in all categories. Most crafts have some kind of organizational structure, usually closely allied with kinship ties.

Jenne is on the periphery of the Mande cultural sphere. It is an aggressively pluralistic town, sitting atop a settlement hierarchy in an agricultural and pastoral hinterland populated by nearly two hundred ethnically heterogeneous villages.[7] The area politically serviced by Jenne, the *cercle* of Jenne, has a population of about 120,000,[8] and this area corresponds roughly to the area of economic and social influence I am calling the hinterland. In the smallest villages there are at least two languages spoken, multiple and sometimes shared subsistence strategies and ideologies, partially exclusive material cultures, and often at least two religions.

Both the hinterland and the town of Jenne are inhabited by Marka and Bozo, Songhai, Fulani and RimaiBe, Bamana, Somono, Bobo, and smaller groups, living together in village quarters and even compounds. Jenne's population numbered roughly 10,000 during the study periods.[9] Several additional groups are present in Jenne and not in the countryside, including Arma and Jennenke. Although a description and analysis of the historical interrelationships among these groups is well beyond the task at hand, the actively reproduced pluralism in and around Jenne, with its mitigated tensions, is critical to any study of component populations here. Every interest group seeks to retain identity at many levels, yet to live peacefully and prosperously within the articulated system.[10] Potters are no exception to this process, as we can see in their almost institutionalized way of remaining internally vital (as specialists) and externally connected, while upholding the appearance and concept of strict boundaries.

Historically, Jenne is considered a Soninke settlement. Jenne today, however, is not a town dominated by Mande groups, having had Songhai and Fulani, in particular, in positions of power for centuries. Songhai, urban dwellers and agriculturalists whose core area is the Niger Bend, and Fulani pastoralists, most of whom now conduct transhumance out of permanent villages, do share with the Mande a "traditional" social structure that incorporates specialist artisans and performers into their ranks. The specialists among the Fulani appear to be of mixed Mande and Fulani origins, or in some cases Fulani only, but they remain socially separate from those associated with Mande and Songhai, not actively recognizing affinity with any Mande specialists.

The Somono themselves need to be brought in at this point, for they form the context for the expression of *numu* identity in Jenne and in much of the hinterland. The Somono are mostly fishers and farmers who originated from recruited and captive groups of farmers and boatmen—probably Bamana, Marka or Soninke, Bobo, and Bozo—from the late seventeenth and early eighteenth centuries, to perform fishing and transporting services for the Bamana empire in Segu, several hundred kilometers southwest of Jenne.[11]

In their own core area, the Somono are categorized by some as a professional or occupational group[12] rather than an ethnic group. Although at the time of their origins they were highly absorptive and therefore culturally heterogeneous,

I would argue that several centuries later in Jenne, one of their northernmost extensions, they function similarly to those identified in the literature as "ethnic groups." This makes them comparable to Songhai, Fulani, Bozo, and others: a self-conscious, populous cultural entity with a shared history, in this case spanning all economic and social classes, with predictable linguistic and religious affiliations and subsistence strategies, practicing a degree of endogamy. They do allow for boundary crossing through marriage more than some, but not all, other ethnic groups in the area—I recorded many examples of intermarriage between Songhai and other ethnic groups, for example. All Somono are Muslim. A Somono cleric in Jenne described being Somono to me as "something like the Marka"—and from our discussions and the context in which he said this, I interpreted that to be historically relatively recent, absorptive, and Muslim.

It is with the Somono that the Mande *nyamakalaw* around Jenne live the most closely. And the Somono themselves often share villages with Bozo and Marka—both Mande groups. Bamana, who are the most numerous Mande in the core area, are present in low numbers in Jenne, and are scattered over the hinterland but also in relatively low numbers. Village Bamana, both men and women, come in to Jenne and act as domestic labor for urban dwellers. They tend to live with Fulani and RimaiBe more often than with other Mande groups.[13] Significantly, they are among the few who are not Muslims in this heavily Islamicized area. I will not say categorically that there are no *nyamakalaw* living with the Bamana in the hinterland, but in Jenne and in numerous villages I surveyed, this was not the case. I would suggest that the *nyamakalaw,* including the potters, aligned themselves with the Somono in this region rather than with the Bamana because the Somono are strongly Muslim, and were able to do so because the Somono have a history of heterogeneity and are still fundamentally absorptive. Being aligned with the majority religion would be a clear asset for forming other bonds, and for economic survival in a setting with competing craft specialists from within Songhai and Fulani society. This alliance between the *nyamakalaw* and Somono is actively maintained partly through the exchange of marriage partners between them.

The Jenne Potters: Somono/*numuw* and Fulani *nyenyoBe*

The potters in Jenne fall into two self-defined groups with distinct (although not exclusive) ethnic, linguistic, and social affinities. The larger group of potters is affiliated with the Mande blacksmith, or *numu,* families in Jenne and also with the Somono. These potters do not form a linguistically homogeneous group, yet they can be differentiated easily from the other potters in the area. Those from the villages speak Bozo, a Mande-related language, while those born in Jenne speak Jenne's most urban language (virtually unspoken in the hinterland), Songhai, which is not Mande in classification. Some of the women are of *numu* origins—preferring that identification to any of the possible ethnic ones—and others claimed *numu* origins but referred to themselves as Somono. Still others are Somono women who have married into *numu* families. I refer to these potters collectively as Somono/*numuw,* for either identification alone masks the mixing that has gone on between them.

The second, smaller group is made up of potters who fall into the category I will call *nyenyo* (Fulfulde, pl. *nyenyoBe*). The *nyenyoBe* are specialists associated with the Fulani, who serve as praise singers or bards and are often also craft producers. In Jenne, they are also referred to as *griots* (French, pl. used when people are speaking French) or as *jeliBe,* in a Fulfulde pluralization of the Mande term *jeli.* Many of the *nyenyoBe,* in addition to having access to the specialist professional roles associated with bard status, participate in craft production to diversify their economic bases, particularly when they are not producing any of their own food. It is extremely rare that *nyenyoBe* in Jenne raise crops or livestock, while in the majority of Somono/*numu* cases, several kinds of food production are being pursued.

The two potter groups have little to do with one another in this area despite their shared interests; by no means do they think of themselves as a single group of craft producers. The social malleability I am proposing for women, and potters in particular, does not mean that issues of class, ethnic, specialist, and other identities are perceived as less important to potters, or to women in general, than they are to men. Individual potters make their various overlapping identities—regional, ethnic, specialist, clan, family—known to the public. Each woman expresses membership in non-mutually exclusive groups partly through the manipulation of material and behavioral symbols, including pottery technology, residence patterns, product distribution and marketing practices, and their additional moneymaking activities.

The Somono/*numu* potters in Jenne are related to blacksmiths through either blood or marriage, and are generally distinguishable from griot potters by language, pottery-making techniques, kinship affiliations, and product marketing and distributional practices. These potters always act as individual artisans and businesswomen, working alone or with the help of their young daughters. The proportion of most potters' lifetimes spent in the production and distribution of pottery is considerably higher than most women are willing or able to spend on other part-time economic activities. It has been said of potters in Cameroon that "the hallmark of the successful potter is to have stopped potting,"[14] and indeed, many women are discouraged by the exhausting labor and low profits of their craft, but despite its drawbacks, it need not require any capital apart from the woman's labor. Once a woman has undergone a long apprenticeship, pottery making is a guarantee of low-capital-investment income that few other women have, providing the woman a degree of economic freedom within her marriage. It also makes a potter an advantageous choice for a wife in an economy as gravely distressed as Jenne's. But *numu* women continue to pursue pottery making also because it forms part of their identity within *numu* families, that is, those families in which a high proportion of the men are blacksmiths and the women are potters. There is pressure in such families for women to undergo apprenticeship as part of their cultural inheritance, and to have potting as an economic option if necessary. Newlywed Somono women who become part of a largely *numu* family often apprentice to their affinal female kin as part of their socialization.

One of the corollaries of being *nyamakala* in the core Mande area is that endogamy must prevail, but in practice, not surprisingly, this is not always so.[15] And one of the most striking things about the *nyamakalaw* in Jenne is that while endogamy is recognized as the normative pattern, it appears that women move into and out of *numu* families more often than the literature would imply. If, in fact, women in the core area are exchanged between groups that supposedly do not intermarry, then it merely supports the premise that we must observe more closely what is happening, even if it means deconstructing models about Mande society which we have taken to be virtually immutable.

My study was dotted with many examples of boundary crossing between Somono and *numuw,* so that they became quite unremarkable in the Jenne setting. I will not claim that there is a new set of rules, replacing the one about *nyamakala* endogamy, but instead that there is a wide range of options for them. Somono women from families with no *nyamakala* ties marry *numuw,* and when they do, they often opt to become potters. While the blacksmiths themselves are not a very absorptive group—for it is under only rare conditions that a non-*numu* boy would be apprenticed to a blacksmith (under circumstances surrounding adoption, for example)—the families of Jenne-area blacksmiths are much more permeable than expected based on the available lore, even given the fact that universally, social rules are so rarely adhered to as strictly as people claim.[16] *Numu* status generally travels to children through their fathers. A potter may choose to maintain identity as a Somono while married to a smith, yet her children by him will be *numu,* notably the boys. She can in effect become *numu* by claiming to be, and/or by potting, but does not need to do either one to be part of such a family. On the other hand, *numu* potters with classic full *numu* parentage often marry blacksmiths, but also marry Somono fishers and farmers.

It is possible to become a potter without having a relationship to *numuw,* although I encountered this only a few times in village settings, not in Jenne. For example, I interviewed a Somono mother and adult daughter who came into Jenne to sell pots. The mother had learned to pot from a Somono/*numu* potter in her village, and had taught her daughter to pot as well. They were both married to Somono farmer/fishers and in no way thought of themselves as *numuw.*

All of this points to a woman potter's ability to bring together *nyamakala* and non-*nyamakala* families—and to shape her own social identity. At the same time, I emphasize that the *numuw* in this area are a recognized, separate social entity in the Mande sense: that it is a very strong identity for both men and women involved. Not all such crossings of boundaries that I describe are necessarily condoned. Certain Somono men, for example, have risen to considerable power and status in Jenne through Muslim scholarship. They did not consider a hypothetical match between their daughters and *numuw* to be well advised, even though one *numu* in Jenne has become a powerful marabout, or Islamic scholar and holy man. *Numu* work is physically hard and dirty, and *numuw* still carry an aura which would be seen as undesirable for an upper-class Somono woman to associate with. The same men claimed they would consider marriage with *numu* women, however, although none of them had so married.

A final example of crossing that is quite illustrative of the way this can be applied practically, is that of three *numu* women who married a blacksmith, he an Arma—a specialist associated with the Songhai of non-Mande, North African ancestry—whose family had been in Jenne for several generations, apparently without marrying non-Arma. The women, two of whom were active potters, are from prominent Somono/*numu* families. These marriages—the first into the most prominent *numu* family in Jenne—tied the Arma smith into three large families and vastly extended his network. The women remained Somono/*numu*. The sons from these marriages call themselves Arma and are trained blacksmiths, but have gone on to separate themselves from the *numuw* by specializing in two fields: carpentry on the one hand, a common Arma pursuit, and a kind of clean, high-tech blacksmithing on the other. They operate out of one big shop, the largest shop involving smithing in Jenne. The pull for these sons to be *numu* was not there, despite their mothers' kin affiliations. However, the second of the three wives had had a first marriage, to a *numu,* and had several sons. These sons, who are *numuw,* share the work of the Arma sons, in the same shop. The marriage between a *numu* woman and an Arma man thus had the result of bringing these two different classes of artisans together, each man retaining his birth affiliation, but building a bridge across a distinct cultural boundary, an opportunity that would not have presented itself otherwise.

The *nyenyo* Potters

The *nyenyo* potters in Jenne and its vicinity are the wives and daughters of a number of different *nyenyo* artisans, most commonly goldsmiths, woodcarvers, woolweavers, and leatherworkers. They invariably speak Fulfulde, and they are Muslim. The external boundaries of the Fulani *nyenyo* population, male and female, are very clear in Jenne and in the villages, endogamy being upheld much more strictly than among the Jenne Somono/*numuw.* Many young girls apprentice as potters, but as *nyenyoBe* they have a range of other professional choices available to them, including the work of bards, marriage arrangement, female circumcision, and gum and lip tattooing. Being a potter in this context does not appear to be a key element of a woman's social identity the way it can be for the Somono/*numu* potters, for the essence of her prominence as *nyenyo* lies in her birthright to perform these other, noncraft activities. Pottery making is more supplemental, practiced by a low proportion of *nyenyo* women in this area, and abandoned by anyone who can make sufficient income through the other specializations, which are sometimes very lucrative. The three *nyenyo* potters active in Jenne in 1983 were in economically weak positions: one widowed, one divorced, and one married to a leatherworker (as opposed to a goldsmith, for example, who could make much more money).

Neither *nyenyo* men nor women have the condoned opportunity to marry outside the bounds of their specialist groups in Jenne. Although this is reported to occur in other parts of the Fulani world—between specialist groups serving different ethnic groups[17]—I saw no practice of intermarriage in my admittedly small sample, nor did I hear of an example of this upon repeated questioning of these three potters and other village informants. Nor was there indication of regular, professional interaction between *nyenyoBe* and *numuw,* except for one case of apprenticeship between male artisans (a *nyenyo* goldsmith apprenticing to a *numu* blacksmith who had become a goldsmith—exceptions triggering other exceptions).

Although *nyenyoBe* did not, in my experience, marry outside *nyenyo* families, they did act, within the *nyenyo* population, in a similar way to the Somono/*numu* potters in their own context. Within the *nyenyo* population there are a number of categories defined by the craft specialization of the male head of the family, forming what I see as a matrix that has both vertical and horizontal status values. For example, some craft specializations have comparable statuses (horizontal), but in today's economy, one might have a much higher potential income than others (vertical status differentiation). Goldsmiths, for instance, are by far the wealthiest of the *nyenyoBe* in Jenne, because of the international gold market they are tied into, but share with most other *nyenyoBe* the opportunity to perform praise singing and other activities for clients, in exchange for money and goods unrelated to their craft activities. Exceptionally good praise singers and bards, male and female, can grow very wealthy, whatever their low-paying craft activity might be. *Nyenyo* women marry out of one category and into another, thereby weaving together various parts of the praise-singing matrix, and also helping to distribute resources among families. The *nyenyo* population is normally represented to us as a structure, formed of a series of parallel categories, some of which have become more powerful than others. But where do the women fit into these categories? They appear to move back and forth between them, as an unacknowledged cohesive force.

Pottery Technologies and Marketing Strategies Compared

The cultural and social dichotomy between Somono/*numu* and Fulani *nyenyo* potters is symbolized and reinforced by their respective pottery technologies, the nature of their wares, and the practices of getting the pottery to their customers.[18]

The differences begin in the workplace. Somono/*numu* potters use a small ceramic turntable, set on a smoothed and oiled spot on their workplace floor. The turntable is a bowl called a *dessen* (in Songhai) with a heavy, rounded base that holds sand or crushed pottery in which a saucer is placed. It is on this saucer that the object is formed. The clay is prepared in the same way by all the women using crushed pottery as temper, but the Somono/*numuw* prepare clay to be wet, and make pots using variations on the coiling method.[19] Coiling gives them great flexibility in what they make, and it is they who provide the majority of the pottery used in this area, including all of the oddly shaped architectural pottery. Their products are relatively heavy and thick-walled, and bear bold, strong designs.

The *nyenyo* potters employ no turntable, and prepare a dry mixture of tempered clay that is paddled into shape through variations on the hammer and anvil method. Relatively small pots are shaped on the inside of a shallow wooden bowl, in which the dry clay glides easily, aided by finely ground pottery as a lubricant. Large pots are usually begun by molding a thick pancake of clay over the upturned round base of an existing pot; the clay is then removed, and the sides are worked up with paddle and anvil. The base of the new pot rests in a depression in the floor, partially filled with sand or finely crushed pottery, and the potter will support the pot with her knees as she turns it and works on the sides. These procedures result in a range of round-bottomed, thin-walled pottery favored for water containers and certain cooking needs, but less durable and slightly less sought after. The painted and applied decorations are fine linear and dot patterns with a generally delicate appearance.

Exceptions to one technique/one group of potters exist. For example, two Somono/*numu* potters began their large pots not with wet clay on the *dessen* as expected, but with a relatively dry clay mixture on overturned pots in the manner the *nyenyoBe* used and which is thought of, in Jenne, as their method exclusively. The finished product does not reveal this practice—the pots are indistinguishable from all other Somono/*numu* pots—so it is not evident to customers that this has been done. But both of these women learned to pot near the city of Mopti, Mali's commercial center 150 kilometers northeast of Jenne, in villages where most of the pottery was made by *nyenyo* potters. Each of the two women thought she was the only one making pot bases using the *nyenyo* method, and none of the other Somono/*numu* potters believed any one of them would make pottery in a fashion associated with *nyenyoBe*. With the exception of these women, the other Somono/*numu* potters pointedly identified their coiling technology as superior, and identified it with their own personal, cultural inheritance. And the finished ceramics of the two groups are immediately distinguishable from each other based on the type and shape of the object, the thickness of the walls, and the form of decoration.

Differences exist in the marketing strategies practiced by Jenne and area Somono/*numu* and *nyenyo* potters, and affect the distribution of their pottery. All potters sell pots in their own and other nearby village markets year-round, although production itself is somewhat seasonal. During the months when the Inland Niger Delta is laced with connecting waterways, the Somono/*numuw* tip the scales dramatically: they transport boatload after boatload of their pottery—hundreds of pots and pieces of architectural pottery at a time, types which they know will sell in the villages and have stockpiled during the year—and take them to dispersed villages to exchange for grain. This exchange for village grain, not village cash, is their motivation, for pots are worth more in grain than they could charge villagers in cash, and buying grain in Jenne with cash is prohibitively expensive. Not all of these potters choose to do this: it is disruptive to households with children and hard to organize, and is decided upon only when family fields have not yielded abundantly. These traveling warehouses of pottery, well received wherever they land but particularly at villages where few or no potters reside, have enormous impact on the consumer behavior in the hinterland, and result in the overwhelming dominance of Somono/*numu* pottery. The *nyenyo* potters conduct no mass marketing behavior by way of the water network. Because *nyenyoBe* in general have access to gifts and payments of grain through their other activities, and merely by virtue of being in the service of client families, when they do move out of their villages to access the grain it is rarely in exchange for pottery.

In the regional Monday market in Jenne, which attracts thousands of villagers every week, the individual groups of potters plus their out-of-town visitors sit in separate clusters, each out of earshot of the other, but close enough to observe what is going on in the other groups. By doing this they make a clear public statement of their affiliation, but manage to keep abreast of everyone's social contacts and success at selling. Other potters, Somono/*numuw* or *nyenyoBe* coming in from villages and without personal friends or family members selling in Jenne, group in another part of the market entirely, on one edge, out of sight of the former groups. This makes it clear, from both sides, that there is an "in" group and an "out" group in Jenne, and that family and social networks are all-important.

In sum, I suggest that there is a Mande core prototype in the self-identification and the social structure surrounding Somono/*numu* potters in Jenne, but that it takes on an especially flexible form there. While crossing boundaries is part of Mande social reality even in the core area, a greater acceptance of crossing in Jenne may be influenced partly by the heterogeneity of the Jenne area, and liberal Somono attitudes about intermarriage. The motivation behind this movement may be a mechanism whereby women act to integrate families for the strengthening of social and economic ties, and the same might be occurring within the *nyenyoBe*. I cannot say how strongly the Somono identify with Mande concepts of social divisions, but it is clear that intermarriage with *nyamakalaw* is ideologically acceptable. Within my study, intermarriage occurred not only between *nyamakalaw* and Somono, but between *nyamakalaw* and Arma.

The apparent estrangement of the Bamana from the Jenne *nyamakalaw* raises compelling questions. Although this is conjecture, the *nyamakalaw* alignment with the Somono may have been influenced by a desire to be associated with the majority Muslim population, and the most receptive group may have been the Somono. Finding themselves out of the core area where Bamana are dominant, the *nyamakalaw* aligned themselves with a Muslim group who were gaining economic and social strength and who could accommodate them comfortably.

It is a necessary development that possessing considerable scholarship on Mande culture, we are acknowledging the flow between ideology and practice, and are beginning to deconstruct concepts that scholars have struggled for decades to essentialize—the concepts of "caste" and "ethnic group" come to mind immediately. Our commitment to classification has often obscured the fact that people actively shape their cultures and material cultures,[20] and that we are looking not at frozen tableaux but ongoing processes of re-identification, the manipulation of symbols, and the production of new ideologies. The case of these two potter groups in Jenne, I hope, although it has dwelt on only a few of their actions, has suggested that focusing on women can affect how we define and interpret such a structure within the Mande world. How women identify themselves and symbolize their socioeconomic positions, with and apart from their male counterparts, opens up another avenue through which to examine Mande identification within and outside the core Mande area.

Notes

1. The fieldwork upon which this chapter is based was conducted under the auspices of the Institut des Sciences Humaines in Bamako, Mali, and its director, Dr. Klèna Sanogo. Funding was provided by the Wenner-Gren Foundation for Anthropological Research (Grant-in-Aid #4257), Sigma Xi, and the Graduate School of Washington University. I would like to express my deepest appreciation to the numerous informants, potters and others, who kindly and generously permitted me to conduct this research. I would also like to thank Barbara Frank for her comments and suggestions on earlier versions of this essay.

2. See, for example, N'Diayé (1970:66–75).

3. See Grosz-Ngaté (1988).

4. Gallay (1970); Raimbault (1980); Gallay and Huysecom (1989). Cf. Drost (1968), whose survey includes this area; Gardi (1981, 1985).

5. David and Hennig (1972) and Krause (1985) are exceptions, but outside the Mande area.

6. LaViolette (1987).

7. Gallais (1967, I:22ff.); LaViolette (1987:Appendix A).

8. 1976 National Census, quoted in Imperato (1986:48–49).

9. 1976 National Census, on file in the Office of the Commandant du Cercle, Jenne.

1O. See Roderick J. McIntosh (1993).

11. Roberts (1987:68ff.).

12. Ibid., 69.

13. LaViolette (1987:Appendix A).

14. David and Hennig (1972:24).

15. McNaughton (1988:3ff.).

16. Gallais (1967, I:294ff.) deals with rules of intermarriage between *numuw* and Bamana *horonw*, thus acknowledging that it does take place; my study would suggest that in Jenne, even these rules have been very liberalized.

17. See, for example, Riesman (1977:19ff.).

18. LaViolette (1987:222–66).

19. See Drost (1967) for a detailed survey of such techniques in Africa.

20. See Hodder (1982).

References

David, N., and H. Hennig. 1972. *The Ethnography of Pottery: A Fulani Case Seen in Archaeological Perspective.* McCaleb Module in Anthropology, Module 21. Reading, Mass.: Addison-Wesley.

Drost, D. 1967. *Töpferei in Afrika: Technologie.* No. 15, Veröffentlichungen des Museums für Völkerkunde zu Leipzig. Berlin: Akademie-Verlag.

———. 1968. *Töpferei in Afrika: Okonomie und Soziologie.* Jahrbuch des Museums für Völkerkunde zu Leipzig, Band XXV, pp. 131–70. Berlin: Akademie-Verlag.

Gallais, Jean. 1967. *Le Delta Intérieur du Niger; Etude de géographie regionale.* Memoires de l'Institut Fondamental d'Afrique Noire, no. 79. 2 vols. Dakar: I.F.A.N.

Gallay, Alain. 1970. "La poterie en pays Sarakole (Mali, Afrique Occidentale): Etude de technologie traditionnelle." *Journal de la Société des Africanistes* 50 (1):7–84.

Gallay, Alain, and Eric Huysecom. 1989. *Ethnoarchéologie africaine: Un programme d'étude de la céramique récente du Delta Interieur du Niger.* Document du Departement d'Anthropologie et d'Ecologie, 14. Geneva: Université de Genève.

Gardi, Bernhard. 1981. "Der Nabel der Gesellschaft: Griots und Handwerker in Westafrika." *Ethnologica Helvetica* 5:1–24.

———. 1985. *Ein Markt wie Mopti. Handwerkerkasten und traditionelle Techniken in Mali.* Basler Beiträge zur Ethnologie, 25. Basel: Ethnologisches Seminar der Universität und Museum für Völkerkunde.

Grosz-Ngaté, Maria. 1988. "Hidden Meanings: Explorations into a Bamanan Construction of Gender." *Ethnology* 28 (2):167–83.

Hodder, Ian. 1982. *Symbols in Action.* Cambridge: Cambridge University Press.

Imperato, Pascal James. 1986. *Historical Dictionary of Mali.* 2nd ed. Metuchen, N.J.: Scarecrow Press.

Krause, R. A. 1985. *The Clay Sleeps: An Ethnoarchaeological Study of Three African Potters.* University: University of Alabama Press.

LaViolette, Adria. 1987. "An Archaeological Ethnography of Blacksmiths, Potters, and Masons in Jenne, Mali (West Africa)." Ph.D. dissertation, Washington University.

McIntosh, Roderick J. 1993. "The Pulse Model: Genesis and Accommodation of Specialization in the Middle Niger." *Journal of African History.* 32 (2):181–220.

McNaughton, Patrick R. 1988. *The Mande Blacksmiths. Knowledge, Power, and Art in West Africa.* Bloomington: Indiana University Press.

N'Diayé, Bokar. 1970. *Les Castes au Mali.* Bamako: Editions Populaires.

Raimbault, Michel. 1980. "La poterie traditionnelle au service de l'archéologie: les ateliers de Kalabougou (cercle de Ségou, Mali)." *Bulletin de l'I.F.A.N.* 42, sér. B (3):441–74.

Riesman, Paul. 1977. *Freedom in Fulani Social Life.* Translated by Martha Fuller. Chicago: University of Chicago Press.

Roberts, Richard. 1987. *Warriors, Merchants, and Slaves: The State and the Economy in the Middle Niger Valley, 1700–1914.* Stanford: Stanford University Press.

IX

JALIYA IN THE MODERN WORLD
A TRIBUTE TO BANZUMANA SISSOKO
AND MASSA MAKAN DIABATÉ

Cheick Mahamadou Chérif Keita

The advent of colonization in the nineteenth century marked a decisive point in the encounter of Mandenka society with the West. With the defeat of Samory Touré, the last in the long line of great precolonial rulers, the French set out to transform the structure of Mandenka society by blurring the traditional distinctions established between the *horonw* (nobles), the *jonw* (slaves or descendants of former slaves), and the *nyamakalaw*.[1] By dispossessing the *horonw* from the power they had exercised since the days of the empire and by placing the state apparatus beyond the reach of the masses, the colonialists planted the seeds of disintegration and self-doubt, if not self-denial, in one of Africa's most elaborately structured and proudest societies. The radical changes which resulted from this encounter have forced the different components of Mandenka society to reassess the value of traditions several centuries old in the light of the new challenges of nation building and economic development. In this essay, I have chosen to highlight some of the present problems and future prospects of the griot caste by concentrating on the lives of two of its most distinguished members in the Republic of Mali, the late Banzumana Sissoko and the late Massa Makan Diabaté. By looking at the ways in which these two figures practiced their art, one may acquire an understanding of the value and enduring significance of *jaliya,* or the state of being a griot, in our modern world.

With the deaths of Banzumana Sissoko and Massa Makan Diabaté, respectively in December 1987 and January 1988, Mali lost two of the most eloquent advocates of its national unity. Working in two different languages, Bamanankan for Sissoko and French for Diabaté, and in two different media of expression, the former with the spoken word and the latter with the written word, these two poets exemplify the deep belief of the Mandenka people in the perenniality of Old Mande. This belief is expressed and translated in the following aphorism: "Le Mande vacille, mais il ne s'écroulera jamais" (Mande may stumble but it will never fall down). Among traditional griots, no one has touched the hearts of Malians, whether they be Maninka, Bamana, Soninke, or Sonrhai, more than Jeli Banzumana. He has been identified with the nation as a whole since the break-up of the Mali Federation in the early 1960s, when his patriotic songs gave his fellow Sudanese the courage to rise up and march on Senegal. It is known that whenever Banzumana's music is played on the National Radio uninterrupted for several hours, Malian people suspect that some major change is taking place in the destiny of the country. Such was the case in 1968, when the military toppled the government of Modibo Keita, and on many other occasions.

On the other hand, Massa Makan Diabaté was the most prolific of all Malian writers to date, with thirteen major works in less than twenty years. Many people consider him the founder of modern Malian literature, but to those who told him this, he always answered that one never creates a literature, one only continues a tradition. In a 1983 interview, he said the following:

> Mais lorsqu'on me considère comme le fondateur de la littérature malienne, alors là, je dois en toute honnêteté dire qu'on ne crée pas une littérature; on la prolonge en y apportant sa petite contribution.

> But when people consider me the founder of Malian literature, I must say in all honesty that one does not create a literature; one continues a tradition by adding one's small contribution to it.[2]

One factor which accounts for the great popularity these two artists have enjoyed with the citizens of Mali and of other countries formerly contained in the Mali Empire is their concern for the integrity of their art. In effect, today, among Malian intellectuals, there is a profound sentiment of wariness toward the griot and his speech, which symbolizes in the eyes of many a collusion with the political and economic powers-that-be. Very often griots display an opportunistic attitude toward their art, which is a direct reflection of the profiteering which has pervaded the administrative structures inherited from colonization. One may argue that there has always been a temptation on the part of the griot to be an accomplice of the governing class. Thus Claude Meillassoux says:

> My contention is that they [the *nyamakalaw*] are an instrument of the dominant class, and not a class in themselves. This is quite obvious for the *jeli,* or praise-singers. They act as a conservative stimulant in society; they encourage *horon* people to live up to their code of values, they drive them to war or restrain their wrath, and they are guardians of the ideology of social inequality.[3]

Since the publication in 1976 of *Gens da la parole,* the insightful study of the griots by Sory Camara, one can consider the preceding assertion an oversimplification of the role and purpose of the griot in Mandenka society. Camara analyzes from the point of view of history and psychology the mechanisms of the traditional division of his society into three castes. Thus, his analysis shows that the dynamics produced by the fierce competition between the *horon* and the *jon* necessitates the strict impartiality of the *nyamakala* caste. Camara's analysis is borne out by the Malian ethnologist Youssouf Cissé, who contends that one cannot be the censor of the power and a participant in the exercise of power at the same time. Cissé's contention contradicts Meillassoux's analysis of the role of the griot in traditional Mandenka society. The assertion by Meillassoux that griots are the instruments of power is symptomatic of the distortions introduced in precolonial society by colonialism. Massa Makan Diabaté and Banzumana Sissoko showed a clear and unequivocal concern for the image of the griot by making references to the symbolism of gold in the traditional society. In a 1983 interview, Diabaté said the following:

> Les Griots des soleils des indépendences ont troqué l'or contre du cuivre. Ce ne sont plus que des animateurs publics qui déploient les broderies de leur éloquence pour quelques pièces de monnaie.

> The griots of the suns of independence have traded gold for copper. They are but simple entertainers who display their flowery eloquence in order to gain small change.[4]

In the last years of his life, Diabaté seems to have deeply grieved over the lack of integrity among the members of his caste. It is thus no wonder that his last novel, *L'Assemblée des Djinns,* was devoted to the griot caste and its insatiable thirst for power. One of Diabaté's characters sums up his perception of the griot in modern Mali thus:

> Les griots sont morts avec l'arrivée des Blancs, quand nos rois au lieu de s'unir contre un danger commun se sont entre-déchirés. Les griots des soleils d'aujourd'hui ne sont que des animateurs publics qui chantent n'importe qui. Ce sont des *Samba danse* comme on en voit dans des cages qui se trémoussent pour quelques friandises. . . . Chef des griots! . . . Mais il n'y a plus de griots.

> Griots have died with the arrival of the whites, when instead of uniting against a common threat, our kings were at each other's throats. The griots of today are but public entertainers who will sing the praises of anybody. They are chimpanzees who can be seen dancing in their cages in the marketplace for a few candies. . . . Chief of the griots! . . . But there are no more griots.[5]

In *L'Assemblée des Djinns,* Massa Makan Diabaté castigates the griot caste for its lack of vision, a shortcoming illustrated in the inability of the different clans to agree on a common leader for the caste. In order to prove that the griots are losing their fundamental mediatory character in Mandenka society, he shows them in isolation from all the other components of society. Whereas in the past the word of the griot was credited with building families, clans, and empires, here his speech is vain, vulgar, and destructive. All in all, this novel is a pessimistic assessment of the state of the caste and of its future. This sentiment is expressed very clearly in the following statement:

Si les griots sont en rupture de ban avec leur fonction première, c'est peut-être parce qu'ils n'ont plus prise sur les aspirations du peuple malien, et ceci présage, défavorablement, de l'avenir de la culture malienne.

If the griots have broken with their original role, it may be because they no longer have any influence on the aspirations of the Malian people, and this does not bode well for the future of Malian culture.[6]

In the practice of his art, Sissoko also placed the highest premium on moral integrity, a value which is celebrated in the oral traditions through the expression *sanun suman jeli* (the griot with the purity of gold). If the word of the griot were not pure and exempt from fraud, it is unlikely that the Mandenka would have likened it to gold, their most revered metal. In fact, the Malinke concept of purity is expressed by the word *saniya* or *sanuya,* the state of being like gold. From the late 1950s, when Banzumana Sissoko became known on the national scene, to his death in 1987, the entire Mandenka nation was witness to his categorical refusal to curry favor with any politician or rich patron. It is interesting that in his immensely rich repertoire of both traditional and original songs, not a single one contains praises for a living person. This fact seems extraordinary when considered in the context of the generalized political clientelism of our modern nations. In Mali today, society has lost its ability to effectively spell out and enforce the criteria of heroism; as a result, the immediate and short-term interests of the praise singers and their *jatigiw* (patrons) are placed above those of society as a whole. Today it takes a great deal of personal integrity and sacrifice to resist the temptation of the easy money and instant stardom which opportunistic praise singing guarantees. In integrity, Sissoko has very few equals. When asked in a 1979 interview why he never sang the praises of the living, he answered:

Ces héros morts ont plus fait pour moi que les dirigeants contemporains. On ne chante que les méritants. Les Da Monzon et Soundiata détenaient un pouvoir que la communauté leur avait confié. Ils sont donc morts sans être destitués parce qu'ils s'entendaient bien avec le peuple au contact duquel ils vivaient. Aujourd'hui, la moindre parcelle de pouvoir gonfle la tête de nos dirigeants qui deviennent des oppresseurs. Eux comme leurs successeurs.

These dead heroes have done more for me than contemporary leaders. One sings only for those who deserve it. Da Monzon and Soundiata held a power that the community had vested in them. They died without ever being toppled because they got along with the people among whom they lived. Today the slightest authority swells the heads of our leaders and turns them into oppressors. They as well as their successors.[7]

When uttering such an acerbic criticism of modern African political systems, Sissoko had the strong conviction that he was putting into words the deepest sentiment of his people.

The integrity that Sissoko and Diabaté displayed in the practice of their art was a direct reflection of the pride they took in being griots. Contrary to the belief common in our time that the *nyamakala* is a person of low status, they always drew an egalitarian picture of Mandenka society, in which the *nyamakala* proudly fulfills his function of referee of social competition, of cathartic object for the *horonw* and the *jonw,* and of living memory for the society as a whole. This caste pride is clearly illustrated in one of Banzumana's original compositions, entitled "Sarafo" (The Bravest of the Brave). Since space precludes a detailed analysis of the music and the lyrics, I will confine myself here to the main themes of the song.

In the first four stanzas, Sissoko reasserts the importance for the griot of choosing the right patron, one who deserves praise. This excludes the upstart and those whose souls lack nobility. Sissoko chose to invoke a person named Sanu for several reasons: one, that person is "the bravest of the brave"; second, his name means "gold," the metal associated with purity, as we have seen. The person he chose to invoke here is the epitome of heroism because he has received unanimous social recognition and because he will never know the humiliation of losing it; this idea is an indirect but pointed criticism of modern heroes (politicians and merchants), who are often extolled one day and trampled underfoot the next. In the succeeding stanzas, Sissoko praises himself—a practice common among the griots—for having chosen the right *jatigi.* He calls on the different members of the *nyamakala* caste to come honor him and help him praise the *sarafo,* "the hero of heroes." These passages are marked by the frequent repetition of the word *naani* and several alliterations such as those found in *darapo* and *sarafo.* The verses in these three stanzas are kept short in order to develop the contrast between the different meanings of the same word and to reinforce the effect of rhymes and the rhythm:

> i yo jaliw yo
> a ye darapo naani ne ye
> a ye darapo naani
> baroro jaliw yo
> aw ka sarafo naani.

> *Jali,* I call on you
> To bring the flag for me
> Bring the flag
> Eloquent *jali,* I ask you
> To call on the bravest of the brave.[8]

In the lines just cited, the *jali* is placed on a pedestal because the flag is brought for him in recognition of the role he plays in society. This idea of privilege is reinforced even further in the next three stanzas, which center on the question of an appropriate reward for the role played by the griot. Here, Sissoko expresses his scorn for the base material objects for which other members of his caste are often ready to compromise the integrity of their conscience. He turns down the gifts of a horse, a slave, and a cow, which are perishable objects of possession.

He prefers gold, since for the Mandenka it is the very symbol of purity and integrity. "Sanu" is repeated three times in each of the stanzas in order to express the commitment of the singer to the purity of this tradition. The concluding stanzas carry this idea even further, since the merchant class is called upon to honor the griot by raising the flag for him. In this section of the song, Sissoko indirectly pays tribute to the dynamism of the Mandenka people in trade by naming all the areas where their activities took them: the Ivory Coast, Ouagadougou (Burkina Faso), Dakar (Senegal), and Bamba Niaré, the other name of Bamako, the capital of Mali. Since the Middle Ages it has been known that the *jula* played a major role in creating a sense of cultural and religious integration in West Africa through trade and the population movements that accompanied it. In the last stanza, Sissoko returns to his patron, Sanu, the son of Bugu, and indicates that the latter is a *jali,* thereby reasserting one last time the social importance of his caste.

When the works of these two griots are considered, the persistence of one major theme is striking: the beauty and the glory of Mali and the Mandenka people. On separate occasions, both griots said that only the masses deserved their loyalty, and that they consciously stayed away from *la politique politicienne* and its opportunism. Thus, in a 1979 interview, Sissoko said the following:

> Mais dans les luttes des partis africains, je n'ai pas voulu m'engager fermement d'un côté ou de l'autre. J'aime le vainqueur, de ce fait, je n'aime personne avant l'issue de la bataille. Ce qui m'intéressait le plus, c'était le peuple et sa culture.

> In the rivalries between African parties, I refused to take a firm stand on one side or the other. I like the winner; therefore, I like nobody before the end of the battle. What interested me primarily was the people and their culture.[9]

As for Massa Makan Diabaté, when asked why he did not deal with the political problems of his country and Africa in his writings, he answered, "Il y a déjà trop de spécialistes pour ce faire" (There are already too many specialists who are doing that).

What Massa Diabaté and Banzumana Sissoko proved in their work is that the art of the griot should be concerned with values which involve the community and the nation. In this respect, both tried to define the Malian identity as it was shaped by several centuries of heroism and nationhood. Thus Banzumana placed his talent in the service of the modern nation of Mali because he saw it as the heir of the medieval empire. He composed a song which was later to become the national anthem of the new republic. Much of his effort was geared toward creating links between the new state and the medieval empire in the minds of his fellow Malians. In the atmosphere of strong nationalism created by the struggle for independence, love of country and the belief in self-sacrifice were themes that resonated deeply in the hearts of all Malians, northerners as well as southerners. In his epic songs of Soundiata, Da Monzon, and Maki Tall, Banzumana exhorts the people to compete not only among themselves in meeting the challenge of nation building, but also with their forebears in the truest and most constructive spirit of *fadenya*,[10] the main source of social competition and progress among the Mandenka. His moral authority, coupled with the restrictions placed by the socialist government on opportunistic praise singing and the ostentatious gifts that come with it, helped to generate among the griots of Mali a relatively conscientious approach to the manipulation of the country's historical heritage.

This participation of the griots in the efforts at national mobilization lasted until the end of the 1960s, when the economic setbacks of the socialist regime brought about a military government and a different conception of the griots' role. In fact, the 1970s saw the rise of several aspiring griots who derived their success from taking advantage of the credulity and the vanity of certain members of the military leadership and the merchant classes. In this new atmosphere, it has been easy for the young griot to do without the long and rigorous training formerly required in the *tarikh* and other disciplines and to rely solely on a beautiful voice, charming looks, and at best a mediocre knowledge of genealogies. In this new environment the griot is perceived as a social parasite and a mercenary. This image has alienated many educated young people from any identification with the caste of their parents; they do not wish to be perceived as *jali,* nor do they wish to play his role. In this respect, Massa Makan Diabaté was an exception among Malian writers and intellectuals, many of whom are of griot ancestry. He always proclaimed himself to be a griot. Having studied the history of Mandenka society from the traditional as well as the modern point of view, he declared with conviction that:

> Avant la colonisation, il n'y avait pas de préjugés envers les hommes de caste. Ca n'existait pas. Chacun était fier de ce qu'il était. Une fois ce bouleversement introduit par la colonisation, le noble s'est senti frustré du rôle qu'il jouait autrefois, et il a eu un comportement quelquefois amer, aussi bien contre la colonisation, ce qui était tout fait normal, mais aussi contre les hommes de caste qui avaient pris la direction politique qui lui revenait de droit dans la société traditionnelle.

> Before colonization, there was no prejudice toward the people of caste. It did not exist. Everybody was proud of what he was. Once colonization overturned this order, the nobility felt shorn of the role they played formerly, and sometimes displayed bitterness toward the colonizer, which was normal, but also against the people of caste who had taken the political leadership which was his in the traditional society.[11]

Unlike most writers who come to the oral traditions as outsiders, that is, after having studied the classics of French and world literature, Massa Makan Diabaté was initiated into the art of the griot by his uncle, the late Kele Monson Diabaté, one of the greatest storytellers in modern Mali. The nephew sought to replicate the uncle's eloquence using the French language, and he was so successful that his translations of the old Mande epics are considered among the best examples of modern African rhetoric in French. Regarding his relationship to the French language, Diabaté several times compared it to adultery. Diabaté explains the meaning of this simile in the dedication of his last novel:

> To the memory of my aunt, Marie Diabaté Witiadés, who taught me French using the stick. Therefore, I refused to marry this language, my favorite among all, but instead chose to give her little bastards.[12]

From the very beginning of his career, Diabaté chose to pay tribute to his ancestors by writing down their words and translating them into French. He produced two award-winning plays, *Une Si Belle Leçon de patience* and *La Mort d'Ahmadou,* and epic poems such as *Janjon et autres chants populaires du Mali* and *Kala Jata.* Diabaté's respect for the oral tradition led him to commission a record entitled *Première Anthologie de la musique malienne,* a collection of songs performed by L'Ensemble instrumental du Mali. In the mid-seventies, he began his career as a novelist with a trilogy about his birthplace of Kita, one of the centers of old Mali. When asked if this change of genre did not constitute a break with the oral tradition, he answered no, because as he put it, "j'adopte le même ton; je conte" (I adopt the same tone; I narrate). Being a Malinke myself, I believe that Diabaté's works reflect the soul of the Malinke like no other work—that is, with love and respect for their strength as well as their weakness. In describing the most salient characteristics of the Mandenka, Diabaté states:

> Le Manding se définit lui-même comme un homme sans finesse et il le dit bien en disant: *"nalomaya de be mandenya diya"* c'est-à-dire "c'est la bêtise qui rend l'état malinké agréable"; le malinké, par essence, est bête et il le dit. Mais il compense cette bêtise par une persévérance et un courage à toute épreuve, à telle enseigne que ce qui est chanté dans l'épopée, c'est d'abord le courage: mais aussi la fidélité à ses engagements, la fidélité à sa lignée.

> The Mandenka defines himself as a witless man, and he says it well when he says: "Nalomaya de be mandenya diya," which means "It is witlessness which makes being a Malinke fun"; the Malinke is essentially witless, and he says so. But he compensates for his lack of wit with an unfaltering perseverance and courage, so much so that what is exalted in the epic is courage first; but also loyalty to one's pledges, loyalty to one's ancestry.[13]

Traditionally, the griots have distinguished themselves as social psychologists. As such, not only do they excel in detecting the most secret motives behind human behavior, but they also excel in using them in their mediatory role and in their art. Dominique Zahan uses this connection between the griot and the emotions to develop a particular etymology of the word *nyamakala.* Without entering this debate, one can say that the ability to inspire a wide range of feelings gives the griot caste an incredible power over their countrymen. Thus, in his art of the novel, Massa Makan Diabaté uses traditional institutions such as the *fadenya,* the dynamic principle of a polygamist society, the *fraternité de case,* the bond which ties together a group of men who have been circumcised at the same time. He shows his characters struggling with modern governments and their designs, which in most cases conflict with the imprint the Mali Empire and its glorious past have left on the mind of the Mandenka. In his trilogy, he shows the people of his native Kita banding together to resist the regime of President Bagabaga-Daba (Termite-with-a-big-mouth), the man who claims to be the father of the nation and who "se proclama 'Président à vie' et bien qu'il ignora tout de l'art militaire, "Maréchal de la République de Darako" (proclaimed himself "President for life" and Marshal of the Nation, although he knew nothing of military art).

Few writers in Africa have been able to penetrate the minds of the illiterate masses as deeply as Diabaté. With him, the novel ceases to be a privileged medium whereby a disgruntled intellectual projects his own frustrations onto some traditional characters, if not puppets, designed by him; the novel becomes a direct echo of the traditional theater, the *Kotéba,* in which the masses mock the unnatural and the undesirable, such as the abusive husband, the mean-spirited daughter-in-law, the charlatan, and—why not—the heavy-handed ruler and the tyrant. If there is a writer who served the people of Mali, it is Massa Diabaté, and if there is a writer who was conscious of his social mission, it is Massa Diabaté. Diabaté's deep social and political consciousness is revealed in his statement regarding the role of the griot: "Etre griot, c'est participer à la mémoire sociale d'un peuple, en l'occurrence du peuple manding" (To be a griot is to participate in the social memory of a nation—in this case, the Mandenka nation).[14]

In conclusion, one can say that the life and work of Banzumana Sissoko, the Old Lion, and Massa Makan Diabaté lie at the heart of the problems of modern Mali. As griots, they struggled to define the country's potential in its effort to enter the modern era by holding on proudly to the moral patrimony of their ancestors. They proved through their lives that to be a true *jali,* you have to be willing to be a *sarafo,* a person who will sacrifice his life for the truth in which he believes, for an ideal, even if others in your family, your caste, and your country have betrayed it. In their work, Sissoko and Diabaté showed that in our modern world, where materialism has eroded the old distinctions between sexes, castes, and social roles, there is still value in honoring one's word. Just as there is a Malinke song called the Duga, which the griots sing only for those who have achieved great feats on the battlefield or in other areas of human endeavor, there is also a song called the Lamban, which the griots sing only to celebrate the memory of those members of their caste who have been faithful to the truth and to the great traditions of the Word. I would like to end this essay with a few lines from that song:

> Salam Aleikum, eminent griots
> Eminent griots of Manden, As-salam Aleikum
> You owe your distinction to *jaliya*
> *Jaliya* is hard to define, it is hard to know
> *Jaliya* is unequaled, *jaliya* is satisfying
> The little bird knows for which patron to sing

Illustrious griots, I salute you
Illustrious griots of the Manden, to you my salute.

Griots of Manden, I shall call on the dead
Those who have never disappointed us
I salute you, griots of Manden
I salute you, griots of Niagassola
I salute you also, griots of Kirina
O you griots of Kita, the beautiful land of Kita
To you my humblest salutations.

If we must remember those who have gone before us
Let's salute Morifindian Diabaté
He was a man of his word
Who else shall we remember
We shall remember *jali* Faceli Kanté
He honored his *jaliya*
What makes *jaliya* difficult
It is finding the worthy patron
And what makes *jaliya* pleasant
It is finding the right patron
Let us all remember *jali* Banzumana Sissoko
And *jali* Massa Makan Diabaté, the *jali*-with-a-pen
For they have honored us by honoring their *jaliya*
O people of Manden, let's respect *jaliya*
Because *jaliya* is difficult.

Sarafo (Banzumana Sissoko)

I ye sanu yo
Sanu fama deni
Sanu fama de do
Bugu den kè sarafo
Sanu ka baro kadi

I yo sanu yo
I ne cè lu ma kèñè
Sarafo ni cè si maa nkan
Bugu den kè Sarafo
Sanu ni cè si maa nkan

I yo sanu
I ka baro kadi ne ye
Sarafo ka baro kadi
Bugu den kè sarafo
Sanu ka baro kadi

I yo sanu yo
I na saa i tè malo
Sarafo na sa ati malo
Bugu den kè sarafo
na sa atè malo

I yo jaliw yo
A ye darapo naani ne ye
A ye darapo naani
Baro ro jaliw yo
Aw ka sarafo naani

I yo numuw yo
a ye darapo naani ne ye
A ye darapo naani
Baro ro numuw yo
Aw ka sarafo naani

I yo finew yo
Aw ye darapo naani
Aw ye darapo naani
Baro ro finew yo
Aw ka sarafo naani

Sokè diira ne jali nii ma
A ko kwa tè sokè fè
A ko ni sanu tè
Sanu fama denye
Bugu den kè sarafo
Sanu ka baro kadi

Jonkè dira ne jeli nii ma
A ko kwa tè jonkè fè

A ko ni sanu tè
Sanu fama denye
Bugu den kè sarafo
Sanu ka baro kadi

Misi dira ne jeli nii ma
A ko kwa tè misi fè
A ko ni sanu tè
Sanu fama denye
Bugu den kè sarafo
Sanu ka baro kadi

Nbèna ni julaw ye
U bi darapo wele ne ye
Nbèna ni kodiware jula baw ye
Jula bi sarafo wele

Nbèna ni julaw ye
U bi darapo wele ne ye
Nbèna ni wagadugu jula baw ye
Jula bi sarafo wele

Nbèna ni julaw ye
U bi darapo wele ne ye
Nbèna ni dakaro jula baw ye
Jula bi sarafo wele

Nbèna ni julaw ye
U bi darapo wele ne ye
Nbèna ne bamba niare jula baw ye
Jula bi sarafo wele

Nbèna ni julaw ye
U bi darapo wele ne ye
Nbèna ni fini ya ya jula baw ye
Jula bi sarafo wele

Nbèna ni julaw ye
U bi darapo wele ne ye
Nbèna ni woro ya ya jula baw ye
Jula bi sarafo wele

Saya mañi bana mañi
Malo bi horo de dwaya
Bugu den kè sanu yo
Sanu na sa ati malo.

Sarafo: The Bravest of the Brave

Sanu, I call you
Son of the lord of gold
Yes, the lord of gold

Bugu's hero son
I love to sing about Sanu.

Sanu, I am calling
You have no equal among men
Bravest of the brave, you have no equal
Bugu's hero son
Sanu has no peer among men.

Sanu, I invoke you
I love to celebrate you
I love to celebrate the best of the heroes
Bugu's hero son
I love to celebrate Sanu.

Sanu, I call on you
You can die but you will never know humiliation
The hero can die but will never be humiliated
Bugu's hero son
Sanu will die but never suffer humiliation.

Jali, I call on you
To bring the flag for me
Bring the flag
Eloquent *jali*, I ask you
To call on the bravest of the brave.

Blacksmiths, I call on you
To bring the flag
Bring the flag
Eloquent blacksmiths, I ask you
To call on the bravest of the brave.

Finè, I call on you
To bring the flag
Bring the flag
Eloquent *finè*, I ask you
To call on the bravest of the brave.

A *jali* was offered a horse
I do not want a horse, he said
Gold is what I prefer
Because I am the lord of gold
Bugu's hero son
I love to celebrate Sanu.

A *jali* was offered a slave
I do not want a slave, he said
Gold is what I prefer
Because I am the lord of gold
Bugu's hero son
I love to celebrate Sanu.

A *jali* was offered a cow
I do not want a cow, he said
Gold is what I prefer
Because I am the lord of gold
Bugu's hero son
I love to celebrate Sanu.

I will bring the merchants
They will raise the flag for me
I will bring the great merchants of the Ivory Coast
They will call on the bravest of the brave.

I will bring the merchants
They will raise the flag for me
I will bring the great merchants of Wagadugu
They will call on the bravest of the brave.

I will bring the merchants
They will raise the flag for me
I will bring the great merchants of Dakaro
They will call on the bravest of the brave.
I will bring the merchants
They will raise the flag for me
I will bring the great merchants of Bamba Niare
They will call on the bravest of the brave.

I will bring the merchants
They will raise the flag for me
I will bring the great textile traders
They will call on the bravest of the brave.

I will bring the merchants
They will raise the flag for me
I will bring the great kola traders
They will call on the bravest of the brave.

Death is cruel, illness is cruel
It is the *horon* that humiliation belittles
Sanu, the son of Bugu
Sanu will die but he will never be humiliated.

Notes

1. The French created the so-called freedom villages where the precolonial social distinctions were invalidated.
2. Diabaté (1984:119).
3. Meillassoux (1970:104–105).
4. Diabaté (1984:119).
5. Diabaté (1985:62–63).

    6. Diabaté (1984:119).
    7. Maïga (1979:55).
    8. "Sarafo" Le Vieux Lion II, Maxi KS 1787, side B.
    9. Maïga (1979:55).
    10. Charles Bird and Martha Kendall (1980) describe *fadenya,* literally translated as "father-childness," as the dynamic principle which motivates individuals to compete against each other for fame and reputation, both within the context of a family and in the society at large. Using the Malinke proverb which says "i fa y'i faden folo de ye" (your father is your first *faden* [rival]), they show that every individual has to compete with the reputation attained by his or her patrilineage.
    11. Diabaté (1984:118).
    12. Diabaté (1985).
    13. Diabaté (1984:117).
    14. Ibid., 115.

References

Bird, Charles S., and Martha B. Kendall. 1980. "The Mande Hero: Text and Context."
    In *Explorations in African Systems of Thought,* ed. Ivan Karp and Charles Bird.
    Bloomington: Indiana University Press.
Diabaté, Massa Makan. 1984. "Etre griot aujourd'hui: Entretien avec Massa Makan
    Diabaté." *Notre Librairie* 75–76:115–19.
———. 1985. *L'Assemblée des Djinns.* Paris: Présence Africaine.
Maïga, Mohammed. 1979. "Interview avec Mohammed Maïga." *Jeune Afrique* 985:55.
Meillassoux, Claude. 1970. "A Class Analysis of the Bureaucratic Process in Mali."
    Journal of Development Studies 6 (2):97–110.

CONTRIBUTORS

Charles S. Bird is a former Professor of Linguistics at Indiana University.

David C. Conrad is Associate Professor of History at the State University of New York at Oswego, and President of the Mande Studies Association. He has done field research in Mali, Guinea, Côte d'Ivoire, and the Gambia, and is the editor and cotranslator with Soumaila Diakité of *A State of Intrigue: The Epic of Bamana Segu According to Tayiru Banbera.*

Barbara E. Frank is an art historian on the faculty at the State University of New York at Stony Brook. Her research has focused on issues of identity, comparative technology, and the distribution of styles and types in the reconstruction of Mande artistic traditions. She has done fieldwork in Mali and Sierra Leone on Mande leatherworking traditions, and her most recent work has been with women potters in Mali.

Barbara G. Hoffman is a cultural and linguistic anthropologist at Cleveland State University. In addition to questions of social identity and language use, her research in Mali, Senegal, and Burkina Faso has focused on gender, literacy, higher education, cooperative development, and sustainable culture change.

Cheick Mahamadou Chérif Keita is a member of the Department of Romance Languages and the African and African-American Studies Program at Carleton College. His latest research focuses on post World War II political and cultural nationalism in Mali and on the relationship between orality and literature in the Mande world.

Martha B. Kendall is Professor of Anthropology at Indiana University.

Robert Launay is Associate Professor of Anthropology at Northwestern University. He has conducted extensive research among the Dyula of northern Côte d'Ivoire. He is the author of *Traders without Trade: Responses to Change in Two Dyula Communities* and *Beyond the Stream: Islam and Society in a West African Town.*

Adria LaViolette is an archaeologist in the Anthropology Department at the University of Virginia. In addition to the ethnoarchaeology of craft production in Jenne, Mali, she is conducting archaeological research on the Tanzanian coast, with a focus on Swahili settlements as evidence of site specialization and cultural exchange.

Patrick R. McNaughton is on the art history faculty of the Indiana University Hope School of Fine Arts. His publications focus on the roles of African art for institutions and individuals, the aesthetic, social, and spiritual qualification of artists, and the constitution of history in African artworks. He is currently doing research on the history of horizontal masks and the construction of meaning in the visual arts, and he is the author of *The Mande Blacksmiths: Knowledge, Power and Art in West Africa*.

Tal Tamari is a researcher at the Centre National de la Recherche Scientifique (France) and a lecturer in anthropology at the University of Paris X-Nanterre. Her doctoral dissertation was a comparative study of "castes" in West Africa, and she is now pursuing research on the relationships between Islam and traditional religion among the Bamana of the Segu and Beledugu regions of Mali.

Kalilou Tera has done research on linguistics and oral tradition in Mali and Côte d'Ivoire, with his most recent affiliation being at the Institut de Linguistique Appliquée in Abidjan, Côte d'Ivoire. Among his many publications in both French and Bamana are *Jeli Baba Sisoko: Lamidu Soma Nyakaté* and *Syllabaire dioula*.

INDEX